Adventure Guide to
Arizona

Eleanor Morris & Steve Cohen

HUNTER PUBLISHING

Hunter Publishing, Inc.
300 Raritan Center Parkway
Edison NJ 08818
(980) 225 1900 Fax (908) 417 0482

ISBN 1-55650-725-9

Cover Photo: Wyman Meinzer

Maps by Nikki Krider

Other titles in the **Adventure Guide Series** include:

NEW MEXICO (1-55650-727-5/$12.95/250pp)
COLORADO (1-55650-724-0/$12.95/220pp)
HIGH SOUTHWEST, 2nd Edition (1-55650-723-2/$15.95/400pp)
COSTA RICA, 3rd Edition (1-55650-722-4/$16.95/550pp)
GREAT SMOKY MOUNTAINS (1-55650-720-8/$13.95/340pp)
COASTAL ALASKA & THE INSIDE PASSAGE, 2nd Edition
(1-55650-731-3/$14.95/228pp)
BAHAMAS (1-55650-705-4/$12.95/176pp)
BERMUDA (1-55650-706-2/$12.95/176pp)
CATSKILLS & ADIRONDACKS (1-55650-681-3/$9.95/224pp)
OREGON & WASHINGTON (1-55650-709-7/$11.95/160pp)

Contents

Maps

Introduction

Once isolated, Arizona has become incredibly popular in the last few years. The name alone evokes visions of Indians and cowboys, snow-capped peaks and arid deserts, buttes and mesas, howling coyotes, cattle drives, wild rivers, and long sunsets. This is aside from the top-class resorts, golfing in the desert, and ultra-modern sunbelt cities that trade shamelessly on this fashionable, natural, cachet. Outside the bursting Phoenix-Tucson corridor, the treasured secret is that Arizona has always been in fashion to those in the know about wide open spaces beneath skies so clear they lend a brightness to the air.

The earliest nomads probably wandered down from Canada and the Bering Land Bridge, over time blending their culture with already-existing populations. Their descendants were the ancient and now extinct Anasazi Indians whose skillfully constructed, then mysteriously abandoned, communities are the source of many of today's ruins. Other descendants were the Hopi Indians, whose oldest inhabited dwellings are now tourist attractions.

The Spanish came to the southwestern United States in the 16th century to search for gold. They came upon Navajos and other modern tribes. It's really only in the last 150 years or so that the area has experienced modern civilization. First came gold, silver, or copper miners, then ranchers, cowboys, and business people who created small towns – many of which stayed small or have since become smaller.

Most of the mines are closed, but ranching and the cowboy arts are still widely practiced on vast, open rangelands. Despite areas of major development, the rugged contours of the land haven't changed much. Arizona still resists massive development though it cannot be denied that once-inhospitable places are today's pleasure spots. In the boonies, towns are still few and far between, but they do exist. Confronting modern realities, these towns have survived by cashing in hard land for tourism dollars.

The enormity of Arizona gives you space that cannot be found in urban areas. And even if you are accustomed to the outdoors, there are few places where you can find so many diverse geological, historical, cultural, and just plain drop-dead beautiful features. The possibilities are endless.

In today's Arizona the pickup truck is the vehicle of choice for ranchers. Horses continue to carry cowboys who really do wear pointy-toed boots, broad-brimmed hats or, increasingly, baseball caps advertising farm equipment. In the stereotypical cowboy style, dusty jeans and shirts with pearl snaps are a pervasive presence here. Except for ceremonial occasions, most of Arizona's native Americans wear clothing that looks a lot like cowboy duds.

The unlikely blending of three cultures – Indian, Hispanic, and Anglo – in this remote land has created a unique atmosphere exclusive to Arizona.

Accommodations range from campgrounds and dude ranches – where you can spend as much time on horseback as you can handle – to deluxe resorts.

Dining in the boonies is mostly unsophisticated – not the chi-chi grilled avocado and mango salsa one finds in Phoenix, but corn dogs and chili, sloppy joe's and salad bars. There are also several quality restaurants widely spaced over Arizona's many miles.

As for entertainment, you may be content to gaze at night skies filled with stars. But there are stomping cowboy bars with free two-step lessons or Indian dances to attend. Some of these are ceremonial and restricted to tribal members only, while others are open for all to enjoy.

There is no shortage of ever-popular Indian jewelry offered by roadside vendors, trading posts, and galleries. What you'll find on sale ranges from cheap trinkets to high-priced objects. Blankets, rugs, baskets, and pottery that were once offered as simple trade goods are pricey these days, reflecting their recent return to the halls of fashion.

Activities related to the terrain and the seasons draw the ski crowd in winter and bikers and river runners in spring. Campers and hikers arrive in summer, leaf peepers and hunters in fall, suggesting that Arizona has been claimed by a young, dynamic, fun-loving crowd. You will certainly see sun-tanned hikers and kayakers cruising along in expensive four-wheel-drives with bike or boat racks. Alongside will be cowboys and Indians riding the range on horseback or in battered pickups with gun racks.

Personal values aside, the land remains the dominant force here. Arid and expansive desertscapes characterize Arizona. Broad, arroyo-tracked flats stretch to the horizon, broken only by cacti, a rare mesquite tree, or prehistoric sea-bed rocks rising in wind- and water-carved majesty, seeming to defy gravity itself. Through the Grand Canyon, the earth reveals deep cracks, dropping precariously to distant rivers. Buttes and mesas are nearby, striped in iron-tinged red and orange colors, with mountains – usually snow-capped – looming beyond.

You can go a long way out here without seeing another human being but you probably won't get far without finding evidence of deer, elk, rattlers, coyotes, eagles, ravens, turkey vultures, or hawks. Less frequently spotted are black bears, mountain lions, pronghorn antelope, and bighorn sheep.

Arizona was created over the ages by the geological forces of volcanoes, wind, erosion, flowing water, and movements of geological plates inside the earth's crust. The result is sometimes phantasmagoric – improbably shaped sandstone towers, serpentine canyons, or brooding mountains crowned by massive thunderheads. Water, though sometimes scarce, is abundant where it flows from the snowmelt of high mountains. The streams it forms nourish forests and the giant Colorado River system, which drains the 130,000-square-mile Colorado Plateau. Even in the driest deserts a turbulent, impetuous downpour can fill thirsty stream beds in a frightening instant. Sudden flash floods can carry away homes, trees, and cars, then subside as rapidly as they appeared, leaving only a damp testimony to nature's dominance of the land.

Arizona has managed to attract a long line of explorers and settlers. Indians constructed primitive cities and cultures 1,000 to 2,000 years ago with a sharp eye to the vagaries of nature, yet even this devout respect could not protect them from its omnipotent energy. Deserted structures – once dwellings and now ruins – pepper the area and attest to ancient conflicts with drought, crop failures, and ensuing famine. Dusty trails may be all that remain of once-productive grassland that was thoughtlessly overgrazed and is now reclaimed by the desert. Crumbling mine structures recall expended mineral resources and dreams.

Humans are neophytes here in view of geologic eras that have created Arizona. Artifacts suggest prehistoric human habitation as far back as 10,000 years ago; the date would position these primitive peoples among the earliest known residents of North America. Modern researchers believe that these nomadic hunter-gatherers were predecessors of the Anasazi, presumed to be the area's first settlers 1,500 years ago – coinciding with the advent of agriculture and the farming of beans and corn (which became dietary staples). Around 500 years later another nomadic strain of Athabaskan Indians of Asian descent began its migration south through Canada. The earliest of these arrivals began filtering in 600 years ago – at just about the same time the Anasazi were abandoning their cities and disappearing into the sands of time. They are thought to be the ancestors of today's Navajos, Apaches, and several other tribes. The term *Anasazi* actually comes from the Navajo language. Various interpretations give the meaning as "the ancient enemies" or simply "the old ones." From these differing beginnings a variety of cultural conventions emerged, lending distinctive spice to today's Navajo, Hopi, and other Native American communities. In Northern Arizona there are popular Anasazi ruins in the Canyon de Chelly National Monument and Navajo National Monument.

In the mid-1500s Spanish conquistadors, flushed with success after the plundering of Mexico, moved north through Texas, Arizona, and New Mexico. Failing to find treasure, they still managed to sow the seeds of religious conversion, building fortified churches which grew into settlements. Ultimately they established administrative bureaucracies in concert with the Catholic church. These alliances continue to exert powerful cultural influences to this day.

The earliest Anglos were ambitious, mostly hunters or traders exploring the territory of Arizona after the Mexican War of Independence in 1825. A scant 23 years later the United States government purchased 530,000 acres of the Southwest from Mexico, including today's New Mexico, Arizona, Utah, and part of Colorado. About 620 years after the Civil War, Anglo migration began in earnest. News of gold, silver, and copper discoveries encouraged prospectors. Shopkeepers followed and word of the vast new region spread. By the 1880s, the railroads had begun to lay tracks, signaling the beginning of the end of centuries of isolation in Arizona and the southwest.

Once the US government recognized the value of this epic wilderness, Indian interests were ignored and violated, igniting conflicts that would be resolved after much strife and bloodshed. Eventually ancestral territories that belonged to the Indians in the first place were returned to various tribes in the form of reservations (or in some cases less desirable land substitutions). These enforced real estate selections cover a good deal of Arizona's geography.

Across northern Arizona, foliage becomes scarce as canyons deepen below desertscapes. Summer temperatures are fiercely hot all across the Navajo Nation and Hopiland to the Grand Canyon. They often top the century mark with brief respite in the high country around Flagstaff and Sedona's partly shaded Oak Creek Canyon. Famous for its red rocks, this canyon seems to hold a particular appeal to seekers of New-Age wisdom, crystal-gazers, vortex-hunters and the like.

Beyond Flagstaff the desert is more than a flat expanse of sand – it contains a variety of deep canyons, cliffs, and rock towers looming over 1,000 ft. high. The **Painted Desert** and **Petrified Forest National Park** are virtual laboratories of prehistory. This amazing part of the state includes six life zones, ranging from lower desert to arctic/alpine, from saguaro cactus flats to the world's largest ponderosa pine forest. It also includes the Grand Canyon, deservedly considered one of the wonders of the world.

The Grand Canyon is usually a primary destination when visiting Arizona. It draws more people than any other southwestern locale. Few are disappointed by the mile-deep abyss. The scale of this extreme geography is both humbling and challenging. The commercially developed South Rim is really a small city with airfields and fast food restaurants. It can be reached most directly from Flagstaff or Williams. Although it is only 10 miles as the crow flies across the canyon to the North Rim, driving is actually a 200-mile adventure. Travelers will generally find more privacy on the North Rim – far less developed and closed in winter. Below either rim there's plenty of solitude to be found, no matter where you start.

Other parts of Arizona have never really been fully explored. There are desert areas in southern Arizona that are as close to primal wilderness as you are likely to find in the lower 48 states. Turbulent whitewater rivers still churn from snowy peaks in early springtime. After an average winter with more than 300 inches of snow in the high country, the Colorado River may run 40 ft. above normal. Rafters float over rocks they would normally be floating under. Of course the river comes back down and hardens into blistered, parched lowlands under the unforgiving summer sun. Yes, there are towns and dammed rivers, roads, airports, convenience stores on the reservations, satellite dishes everywhere – some crowning home lots featuring Navajo hogans made of mud, sticks, and straw. You can even book a flight directly to the Grand Canyon.

The roads are better than they were in the mining days, but rugged mountains and parched desert areas continue to defy all but temporary development, as evidenced by abandoned mines and ghost towns. Wildlife, wildflowers, and man all benefit as much from what's not here as what is.

Regarding fashion, the vagaries of style that are in today and laughable tomorrow, Arizona may be experiencing its Warholian 15-minutes of fame right now. For those who come in search of adventure, the mountains, rivers, canyons and mesas are very much the same as they were before they were stylish. They change at a glacial pace. They will be here tomorrow.

A big part of the attraction of this state is finding yourself on the turf of cowboys, Indians, mountain men, and desert rats, amid historic geology that is testing and undeniably attractive. It's open to all comers but resists easy change. That is exactly what makes it so challenging.

Geography & History

The first people to inhabit Southern Arizona were Indians who introduced agriculture into the Southwest about 2000 BC. Maize, beans, cotton, and squash were being grown by about 300 BC, and by 700 AD a group known as the Hohokam were one of the most productive Indian groups north of Mexico.

Their ancestors are believed to have been archaic hunter-gatherers who lived in Arizona for several thousand years. They also drew from Mesoamerican civilization. They settled in the lower Salt and middle Gila River basins; a ruin of a four-story Hohokam structure can be seen today at Casa Grande Ruins National Monument near Phoenix.

The Hohokam abandoned their lands for unknown reasons. The Sinagua Indians arrived in the area sometime in the 14th century. The Apache and Navaho moved into eastern Arizona in the 16th and 17th centuries.

The first white person to enter Arizona is believed to have been Cabeza de Vaca, around 1536, followed by Franciscan Fray Marcos de Niza, both looking for the Seven Cities of Cibola, the fabled cities of gold. In 1540 came Coronado, who trekked across what is now the Coronado National Memorial, also in search of the cities.

Missions were founded by Jesuits in the late 1600s and early 1700s in Tucumacacori, the Santa Cruz Valley, and Quiburi in the San Pedro Valley. Warfare between the Spanish and the Indians and between Apaches and other Indians raged during the 18th century. Spanish soldiers established a *presidio* (fort) at Tubac, the first white settlement, in 1752. This was transferred to Tucson in 1776, during which time the Apaches and the whites began a truce lasting until the late 1820s.

The United States annexed the area of Arizona north of the Gila River as part of the spoils of victory from the Mexican War of 1846-48. It became part of the New Mexico Territory in 1850. The land south of the Gila River was acquired from Mexico through the Gadsden Purchase (1853).

Since settlers were mainly from the South, during the Civil War sentiment was predominantly for the Confederacy – there was even a battle at Picacho Pass, just south of Tucson, in April of 1862.

Arizona was created as a separate Union territory in 1863. The capital moved back and forth between Tucson and Phoenix for awhile, finally settling in Phoenix in 1889.

Agricultural settlements such as Gila Bend, Florence, and Phoenix were founded. In 1879 silver was discovered in the area that became Tombstone. Meanwhile, the names of Apache chiefs Cochise and Geronimo were becoming famous as the Indians kept on resisting the takeover of their land. Fort Bowie is the site of Cochise's surrender.

In the 1880s and '90s copper was discovered, and the remains of the huge mines – great gaping red holes in the earth – are something to see in Bisbee and Ajo, as well as the still-operating mine in Morenci, one of the largest man-made holes in the world.

In 1912 Arizona was admitted into the Union as the 48th state.

The Nature of Adventure

In the 1990s, adventure travel has come into its own. It is no longer considered the province only of daredevils seeking the hang-by-your-teeth type of adventure, although that sort of trip is surely available in abundance out here. You probably won't have to cheat death unless you choose to but, if you sample this book's suggested activities, you will certainly raise your chances for having a life-affirming experience, without necessarily having a life-threatening one. Adventure doesn't need to be a death-march expedition, but it does need to get the juices flowing. At the least it should provide attainable challenges that any reasonably fit and active participant with an open mind can enjoy.

Inside this book you'll find extensive information on a range of activities, many of which will provide challenges relating to climate, altitude, remoteness, and physical fitness. Others may be less physically stressful, while confronting your cultural perceptions. From easy-to-accomplish soft adventures, family and senior's trips, to daredevil exploits that will really get your adrenalin pumping, you can find them here. There are activities you can pursue for an hour, a day, a week, or a month. Whatever your inclination may be, the payoff is in the remarkable regenerative power of a classic river trip, a cattle drive, an Indian ceremony, or an archaeological dig. Arizona offers hundreds of miles of maintained trails for you to hike, bike, and ride on horseback. If you're a waterlover, river trips will lure you into canoes, kayaks, and even some whitewater rafts. There are evocative back roads for you to explore by jeep and mammoth vistas to gaze upon from the gondola of a hot-air balloon. You can visit historic and modern Indian and cowboy sites. You can climb cool mountains in summer, and explore canyons and deserts in fall, when mornings and evenings are cool, days warm, and changing leaves enhance the countryside with a special, multi-dimensional glow.

How to Use This Book

This book divides Arizona into regions: The Grand Canyon Area, The Navajo Nation & Hopiland, The High Country, The Old West, The West Coast, and The Valley of the Sun. The order of these chapters essentially describes two large circles, one of northern Arizona and the other the land south of the Mogollon Rim. It is unlikely that you will try to cover the entire state on one trip but just about anywhere in Arizona is going to offer high rewards.

Each chapter starts with an introduction to the region. This covers information on climate, history, and culture, along with the main sites and activities. It is followed by a short section called *Getting Around*, which outlines the main roads and transportation options as well as the general route the chapter will follow. Each region is then broken down into touring sections listed in the same order as they appear on the selected route. These sections provide information and useful contact numbers such as chambers of commerce, regional US Department of Agriculture Forest Service offices, Bureau of Land Management (BLM) offices, National Park Service offices, and airline and rental car services.

After the general touring sections, a separate section detailing specific adventures within each region follows. These include options for independent travelers or those seeking guided tours. There are many activities to choose from and many more limited only by your imagination. For example, you can generally

Arizona

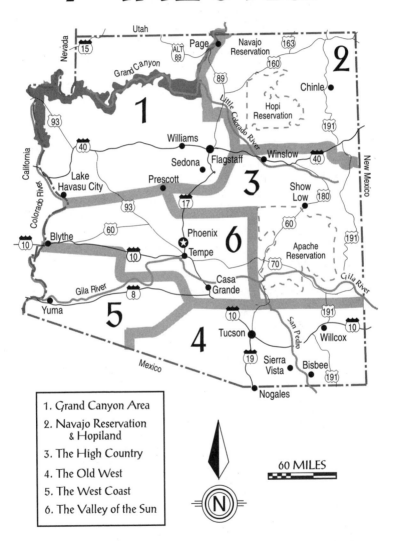

1. Grand Canyon Area
2. Navajo Reservation & Hopiland
3. The High Country
4. The Old West
5. The West Coast
6. The Valley of the Sun

60 MILES

experience an enjoyable hike on a listed bike trail, or bike on a jeep road.

Adventures

The following is a brief description of the range and nature of activities covered under *Adventures*.

ON FOOT

Hiking/Backpacking/Rock Climbing

Whether you want to do it on your own or with a guided tour, this category will show you where to go and how to do it. There are hundreds and hundreds of miles of hiking trails in Arizona. Some are strenuous, requiring specialized rock climbing skills and equipment; others are more like a walk in the park. It is impossible to list them all, but you will find a cross-section of the hikes for all levels of ability – short walks over easy trails to multi-day routes through national forests.

When hiking in backcountry, the more popular short trails are usually well worn and marked, but it's still remarkably easy to get lost. Don't head out into the wilds on your own without some preparation. Figure out where you want to go, then consult the Forest Service, BLM, or Park Service for up-to-date topographical maps and information. Discuss with them the difficulty of various trails and technical climbing skills or specialized equipment that may be required. Some adventures in this area can be accomplished easily alone, while others require special gear, permits, and expertise. If you're short on equipment or doubt your skills, seek help from professionals before attempting a demanding adventure. This is serious country, often short on absolution. If you question going it alone in Arizona then you probably should not. Even if you know what you're doing there's no substitute for direct contact with people whose business is understanding the areas and activities you're pursuing. Numerous local contacts are provided in this book. The USDA Forest Service suggests that all users of the backcountry remember the following:

- [ ] Take no chances. Assistance can take hours or days.
- [ ] Be aware of conditions. Varied terrain exposes you to hypothermia, dehydration, and lightning hazards on exposed ridges. There can be snow fields in early summer.
- [ ] Start hiking early in the day – mornings are generally clear. Later in the afternoon you may encounter storms of varying intensity. An early start gives you time to get to your destination and set up your camp in comfort, not having to fight the elements.
- [ ] Travel with a companion. File a hiking plan with someone who is staying behind and check in with revisions so you can be found if something goes wrong.
- [ ] Be in shape. Don't push past your limits. Allow time to acclimate to altitude.
- [ ] Always take fresh water with you, especially in the desert, where heat can be deceiving and water may not be available. A gallon of water per person, per day is recommended for summertime desert travel.
- [ ] Pack extra food just in case something goes wrong and you're out longer than you planned.

ON HORSEBACK

You want to get out there on your own two feet but you don't want to lug heavy gear. An alternative, if you prefer not to be burdened with packs but want to travel into some of the most improbable terrain imaginable, is hiking with pack animals. These trips are run with horses or mules to carry the gear. Without weight restrictions imposed by the strength of your own back, you can experience deep backcountry with a case of beer or a few bottles of wine, an extra pair of dry shoes, and other heavy and awkward items that will make your trip more enjoyable.

Harder on your bottom than your feet is the venerable primary mode of transportation – horseback riding. Horses are still common out here and trips on well-trained, tractable mounts or high-spirited animals are easily arranged for an hour, a day, or overnight.

If you want to be a cowhand, working ranches often accommodate guests who can participate in all ranch activities, such as herding and branding, or actual cattle drives, moving a herd from one place to another over several days or longer. Ten to 12 hours a day in the saddle, moving at a slow pace, is hard work, but it is, for some, the ultimate adventure.

ON WHEELS

Railroads/Jeeps/Stagecoaches/Wagons/Bicycles

There are one or two short train trips offered in Arizona on some of the most scenic, compelling, and historic rail lines in the world. We're not talking about subways here, nor even about Amtrak, though one of its trains does make several stops along the I-40 corridor.

A jeep or other four-wheel-drive may sometimes be the only motorized vehicle able to negotiate the hundreds of miles of remote, minimal roads that are among the most scenic and historical in the high southwest. Please stay on established roads and don't chew up the backcountry by carving your own route.

Mountain biking has really blossomed as a mainstream activity throughout Arizona. New high-tech bikes with 18, 21, or more speeds, make it possible for just about anyone who can ride to negotiate at least some of the terrain. Mountain bikers move faster than hikers, and knobby tires can transport you into certain regions where motorized vehicles cannot go.

Throughout the region, the topography for biking is testing but picturesque. The assortment of logging roads, jeep routes, and single-track trails on public lands is immense, offering something for everyone, from easy paved bikeways to world-class backcountry excursions.

Again, it's impossible to include all the great biking routes here. The selections offered in this book suit varying skills and abilities, along with information sources for further exploration. Guided bike tours suggested here will generally handle logistical arrangements an independent rider would have to manage alone. Most guided tours provide a sag-wagon in case you really can't make it those last few miles. On a tour or on your own, every rider needs to carry extra food and water, a head lamp, maps, and rain gear (a helmet is essential).

Local bike rental operators, repair shops, and tour resources are included throughout the text. Other valuable sources of information are the experts in local bike shops who know the terrain.

Although bike riding is generally supported in Arizona, continuing access to backcountry trails is partly dependent on the goodwill inspired by you and other outdoor folk. The International Mountain Biking Association has established rules of the trail to help preserve mountain bikers' trail rights:

- ☐ Ride on open trails only. Respect trail and road closures, private property, and requirements for permits and authorization. Federal and state wilderness areas are closed to cyclists and some park and forest trails are off-limits.
- ☐ Leave no trace. Don't ride on certain soils after a rain, when the ground will be marred. Never ride off the trail, skid your tires, or discard any object. Strive to pack out more than you pack in.
- ☐ Control your bicycle. Inattention for even a second can cause disaster. Excessive speed frightens and even injures people, gives mountain biking a bad name, and results in trail closures.
- ☐ Always yield. Make your approach known well in advance to others using the trail. A friendly greeting is considerate and appreciated. Show respect when passing by slowing to walking speed or even stopping, especially in the presence of horses. Anticipate that other trail users may be around corners or in blind spots.
- ☐ Never spook animals. Give them extra room and time to adjust to you. Running livestock and disturbing wild animals is a serious offense. Leave ranch and farm gates as you find them, or as marked.
- ☐ Plan ahead. Know your equipment, your ability, and the area in which you are riding and prepare accordingly. Be self-sufficient at all times, keep your bike in good condition, carry repair kits, and supplies for changes in weather. Keep trails open by setting an example of responsible cycling for all to see.

As for the terrain, even routes classified as easy by locals may be strenuous for a flat-lander. Most downhill routes will include some uphill stretches. Pay particular attention to your personal limits if you're on your own.

ON WATER

Whitewater Rafting/Canoeing/Kayaking/Boating/Fishing

From around mid-May to mid-June rivers rise dramatically and the flows are at their highest, fastest, and coldest. Sometimes by August things are pretty sluggish. It all depends on the winter's snowfall, spring rains, and summer thunderstorms.

In general, at high or low water levels, it takes an experienced hand to negotiate the rivers of Arizona. Unless you really know what you are doing, it is highly recommended that you consider a river tour, rather than an independent river trip. Tour operators also handle the permits that are necessary for certain popular stretches, permits that may only be offered through lottery drawings and are therefore hard to come by.

For any river trip, the smaller the vessel, the bigger the ride. Be sure to inquire about the size of a raft and how many people it holds. Ask if you'll need to paddle or simply ride along while guides do the work. Listings that mention paddle boats mean you will have to paddle. Oar boats mean a guide does the work. Kayaks accommodate one person who will obviously do all the paddling.

Lakes and reservoirs throughout Arizona offer boat ramps for your vessel. Larger bodies of water feature marinas offering boat rentals where you can secure a rowboat, a canoe, a motorboat, a windsurfer, and other equipment.

If you're seeking fishing waters rather than rapids, lakes and reservoirs are suitable for canoe and boat excursions. In addition, there are innumerable places to fish from the shores of streams and rivers. Many waters are well-stocked with a variety of fish, including several species of trout, large and smallmouth bass, crappie, bluegill, and channel catfish.

ON SNOW

Downhill & Cross-Country Skiing/Snowmobiling

You'll find good downhill skiing in the Flagstaff vicinity and the White Mountains along the Mogollon Rim. When the snow is good, which is typical, the skiing is fantastic. Temperatures are often 10 to 15° warmer than more northerly locales; hang up your ski jacket and enjoy the weather.

Cross-country skiing areas are generally more peaceful and less crowded than developed downhill areas but, unless you plan to stick to the easiest groomed trails, it is wise to know what you are doing. You can ski the backcountry for an hour or for days, but snow conditions are often unstable and avalanches are frequent in certain areas or under certain conditions. To help match your abilities with appropriate terrain, it is highly recommended that you consult with ski shop personnel or regional information sources before approaching the backcountry.

The listings in each chapter are some of the safest cross-country routes. Remember that conditions are completely unpredictable and depend entirely on weather conditions that can and do change rapidly. For current trail and wind conditions, on-the-spot research is essential before any backcountry ski trip. Dress warmly and carry high energy foods. Though less physically demanding, the same rules apply if you're snowmobiling or dog sledding.

IN AIR

Scenic Flights/Ballooning/Soaring

If you think Arizona looks impressive from the ground, then you might want to consider seeing it from the air on a scenic flight. A range of options are available, including fixed-wing aircraft, helicopters, gliders, and balloons.

Eco-travel & Cultural Excursions

This catch-all category includes trips that don't fit elsewhere. Another heading for this section might be "Arizona Adventures for the Mind."

Where to Stay & Eat

Although not expressly an adventure, finding good places to stay and eat in the Southwest can be a challenge.

In some remote areas, there may be only a campground with a fire grill, or a single, shabby motel for many miles. In other places you'll find a number of excellent establishments. All listings are subjective and are included for some good reason, whether for exceptional service, ambiance, great food, or good value. Rates range from inexpensive to deluxe. Because these services may change rapidly, local information sources may come in handy for updates.

Camping

Public campgrounds and information sources are included in this section. You will also find details regarding camping on Indian reservations and remote backcountry campsites.

Travel Strategies & Helpful Facts

Since Arizona is rather spread out, consider whether you will be travelling to one area, say for a week or a five-day pack trip, or whether you plan to sample several areas. If you've booked a multi-day outfitted trip the outfitter may be able to meet you at the closest airport. Otherwise you need a car. Rentals are available in many places.

Airlines offering service directly to Arizona are Continental Express, United Express-Mesa Airlines, and America West. Grand Canyon Airways flies from Phoenix to the South Rim in summer. Major airports in Phoenix and Tucson are served by many carriers with connections on the smaller feeder airlines to airports in Flagstaff, Arizona.

An increasingly important factor to consider when visiting Arizona is its exploding popularity. In many areas, visitations have doubled in the last five years and the effects on privacy and the wilderness environment have resulted in controls being placed on access to certain public lands at certain times. Consider travelling outside the traditional summer season or the peak winter months. It's uniformly busiest from the Fourth of July through Labor Day. If you're here for the skiing, you may want to schedule trips in December or March instead of January and February. Spring skiing is a particularly good idea; the snow is the deepest, the weather's warmest, and many skiers' thoughts are already turning to cycling and kayaking so there are fewer folks on the slopes.

Climate

The diverse topography here causes wide variations in climate. The season you visit will depend on what sort of activities you wish to pursue; be aware that summer is not necessarily the most comfortable time. Summer weather is considerably milder the higher you go into the mountains, and it is spectacular on an 80°, blue sky day in the mountains. Down below, in the flatlands and arid deserts, it can get dangerously hot, especially if you're hiking the Grand Canyon or biking around Ajo in July or August. Just the reverse is true in winter. There are always trade-offs. Certain outfitting or adventure tour businesses are only open during particular seasons; certain lodgings even close during the winter. The road to the North Rim of the Grand Canyon is closed in winter, while the South Rim is open year-round, but with curtailed services. Parts of Chiricahua National Forest are closed in winter, although that needn't prevent you from snowmobiling or cross-country skiing on unplowed, snow-covered park roads, with the few open ruins virtually to yourself (and the ghosts).

If you come in the spring to raft rivers, you need to be prepared to deal with mud in the lowlands, or dust storms in the deserts. Fall is considered by many to be the perfect season. The air is cooler, but not yet cold. Desert areas are once again tolerable after the scorching summer, while mountains boast colorful foliage and fewer crowds. Because of the great ranges in elevation, fall lasts several months (until September in the high mountains, to November in the deserts).

Count on daytime temperatures of well over 100° in the deserts by July and August. At the same time, temperatures are likely to be 70-80° in Flagstaff. A temperature drop of 30-40° after the sun goes down is common throughout Arizona. January through March may be cold in the northern regions.

Clothing & Gear

Arizona is a casual place. Shorts and t-shirts are fine for summer days but long pants and a sweater or jacket may be needed at night, particularly at higher elevations, where it has been known to snow in every month except July. Because conditions can change very quickly, layering your clothes is the best idea so you can remove or add clothing as it gets hotter or colder.

Sneakers may not be rugged enough footwear for backcountry hiking; heavier, lug-soled boots are recommended. A broken-in pair of cowboy boots may be a good idea for extended horse travel. Hiking boots with heels to catch in your stirrups will probably do for short trips of a few hours to a day.

Find out in advance everything you can about your destination, such as water supplies, restroom facilities, fireplace availability, and restrictions on camping, group size, fires, and wood cutting. Plan your gear accordingly – bring shovels, cook stoves, water jugs, or saws as needed.

Outfitters and tour operators can usually supply any special gear that may be required for specific activities. Check with them regarding rental equipment before buying expensive items.

Always carry extra food and water on any backcountry excursions. You never know when these things may come in handy.

Depending on the activities you wish to pursue, special clothing and gear may be needed. Rafting in spring may call for a wetsuit. In winter, if you're cross-country skiing hut-to-hut, special touring skis with metal edges are highly recommended. Cross-country skiing produces a lot of heat so you can easily work up a sweat, but when you stop moving you will feel how cold it really is out there. Again, layers are the answer. And, even in mid-summer, on a backcountry bike ride you might start out in 80° weather then run into a thunderstorm that drops the temperature dramatically. If you always plan for the most severe conditions, you will be able to weather these changes in fine form.

At any time of the year the sun can be quite strong. Wear a hat, sunscreen, and bring sunglasses which can prevent snow blindness in winter when the glare can be oppressive.

Insect repellent is a good idea in the summer, particularly at lower elevations.

Driving

To get out and really experience the deserts and mountains of Arizona you need a car, and some of the best places to go are not on main roads. Always inquire of locals about current road conditions. Some of these back roads may be marked for four-wheel-drive vehicles only. Do not test local wisdom or the warning signs in your low-slung sports car or the family's overloaded Chevy. You will be in deep trouble if you travel several miles down an ultimately impassable dirt road and discover you cannot turn around. After rain, dirt roads can become muddy tracks from which there is no easy escape. In the desert, sandy roads can swallow a car up to its hubcaps before you know what hit you. Snow frequently closes main highways (though generally for short periods) and unmaintained back roads may disappear until spring.

Those cowboys in their pickups know what they're doing. A truck or a four-wheel-drive with high ground clearance are clearly the vehicles of choice but, with or without one, precautions are de rigueur. The farther out you plan to go, the more important it is to carry spare fuel and water for your radiator. Top up the gas tank wherever you can. The next gas station may be 100 miles away. Smart backcountry winter travel means good snow tires, windshield wipers that work, a couple of blankets, and a shovel in your car.

Local people understand the conditions and will probably help you out if you have trouble, but there may be nobody around for many miles. A cellular phone or CB radio could make a big difference in getting help. And don't forget to travel with the most up-to-date maps. Reliable maps are available from offices of the Forest Service or BLM. Outdoors stores are also good sources. Excellent driving maps are published by the Automobile Club of America and are available for sale or free to AAA members.

WEATHER & ROAD CONDITIONS

Always check with local offices of the state patrol and the National Weather Service for current information. Don't be lazy about this. Just because it looks okay where you're standing does not mean it's going to be that way where you're going. Conditions can change fast. Anticipation is the key to success on any wilderness trip.

Special Concerns

The areas covered in this book are here for all to enjoy and special care should always be taken to insure their continued existence. Some remote spots are designated wilderness areas, with seriously enforced rules of etiquette, including restricted access limited to those on foot or with pack animals only. Throughout Arizona, fishing and hunting are subject to state or tribal law.

Certain areas have restrictions on camp fires and, even where fires are allowed, dry weather may lead to prohibitions on open fires. It's always safest to cook on a camp stove. If you need to make a fire, do not cut standing trees – burn dead wood only. And do not be tempted to pocket an arrowhead or a pottery shard you may find on your travels. Think of the next person who'll be coming along, and remember that artifacts are protected by strictly enforced laws.

It's a sound policy to take only photographs and leave only footprints. Before leaving a camp site, replace rocks and scatter leaves and twigs to restore the area to a near-natural condition. Pack out all your garbage and any other trash you may find. Take care with human waste; it should be buried 100 ft. or more from any water source and not near possible campsites. Use only biodegradable soap and, whenever possible, wash from a bucket of water far from running sources.

Do not travel into a fenced area as the Forest Service or BLM may be protecting it for re-vegetation or protecting you from dangerous conditions, such as extremely wet roads. Private landowners do not need a reason to keep you out; respect private property. Cross streams only at designated crossings.

Watch out for lightning. Especially avoid exposed areas above the treeline during thunderstorms. If you are in a thunderstorm, don't hide under a tree or in your tent. Get back into your car, if you can, or look for a cave or a deep protected overhang. If none of these are possible, crouch down as low as you can and hope for the best. Avoid narrow canyons during rainy weather; check weather reports for thunderstorm predictions. Disastrous flash flooding is a real danger.

Drinking water in lakes, rivers, and streams is not exactly the same wilderness treat it once was. Now it's more likely to contain *giardia lamblia*, a tiny protozoan that can cause big problems. Animal waste found in many water sources can give you diarrhea and violent stomach cramps, symptoms which may require medical attention that could be far away. To avoid problems, make sure you always have adequate fresh water. On longer trips this usually means boiling all lake and stream water for 20 minutes or carrying effective water purification paraphernalia, which can be purchased from area sporting goods stores.

The water is fine for swimming, but relying on it as your primary water source without adequate treatment may be dangerous.

Information Sources

The Bureau of Land Management (BLM) administers millions of acres of public lands in the Southwest. Because the lands are enormously diverse, these extensive holdings are divided into various regions. Regional headquarters will refer you to local offices, which are listed throughout the book, or check the index for specific offices.

Many of these information sources are included in the chapters that follow, but these general sources can be a big help in getting you started before you make up your mind about exactly what you want to do. Most provide free information.

INFORMATION

Arizona Office Of Tourism, 1100 West Washington Street, Phoenix AZ 85007. ☎ 602/542-8687.

Arizona State Parks, 800 West Washington Street, Phoenix AZ 85007. ☎ 602/542-4174.

Arizona Game & Fish Commission, 2222 West Washington Street, Suite 415, Phoenix AZ 85007. ☎ 602/542-4174.

Flagstaff Chamber of Commerce Visitor Center, 101 West Santa Fe Avenue, Flagstaff AZ 86001. ☎ 520/774-9541.

Havasupai Tourist Enterprises, Supai AZ 86435. ☎ 520/448-2121.

Hopi Tribal Headquarters, PO Box 123, Kykotsmovi AZ 86039. ☎ 520/734-2415.

Navajo Cultural Resources Department, PO Box 308, Window Rock AZ 86515. ☎ 520/871-4941.

Sedona Ranger District (National Forest Service), Box 300, Sedona AZ 86336. ☎ 520/282-4119.

Sedona-Oak Creek Chamber of Commerce, Box 478, Sedona AZ 86336. ☎ 520/282-7722 or 800/288-7336.

Grand Canyon Area

The predominant feature in this area is, of course, the **Grand Canyon National Park**. It is more than impressive; it is one of the seven wonders of the world and the term "Grand" scarcely does it justice. Two billion years in the making, it is the largest hole in the earth – 277 miles long, averaging a mile deep and 10 miles wide. Hundreds of smaller canyons, creeks and trails lie within its boundaries.

There's no place else on earth where you can see so much of the earth's physical history on display. In the rock layers exposed over eons you can literally see into the beginning of time. The Grand Canyon's staggering depths and immense spaces contain extensive opportunities for adventures.

Ride the definitive North American river trip floating the Grand Canyon's main architectural force – the **Colorado River**. Roll the wheels of your bike or jeep up to the Canyon's edge. Hike down into its unimaginable depths or simply stand there on the lip of eternity, looking down at a 5,000-ft.-deep universe carved over thousands of millennia.

The route starts near the **North Rim**, only 10 miles across from the far more popular and heavily used South Rim, but 214 circuitous miles by road. Only one in 10 visitors to the Grand Canyon ever visits the North Rim. This is not a small number, around 400,000 yearly, but with all visitor services clustered around the relatively compact North Rim facilities, there's a lot of space for adventurous types.

The **South Rim** provides its own rationale, with a far larger commercial area, including the greatest concentration of visitor activities. Despite the relative congestion around the South Rim's Grand Canyon Village – particularly during the summer – you can still find plenty of space to get away from it all. You just have to venture a little farther from the best-known, well-worn paths of the South Rim.

From the South Rim, it's a short distance to explore the **Williams** and **Flagstaff** areas – a mountainous, cool region containing the world's largest stand of ponderosa pines and Arizona's tallest mountains, the **San Francisco Peaks**.

From Flagstaff (7,000 ft.), the 30-mile descent through diverse forests and famed red rock scenery in **Oak Creek Canyon** to nearby

Sedona (4,500 ft.) is captivating. The area has always been an attraction for artists and creative types and is now enjoying an influx of visitors drawn to its supposedly commanding spiritual locale.

Is Sedona the locus of powerful forces of cosmic energy? No one has ever proven the presence of these so-called energy vortices, but that does not deter the four million yearly visitors, including hikers, art buyers, crystal gazers, and vortex seekers. Perhaps Sedona's magical power resides in its colorful geology and characters.

Geography & History

Where else can you find a stark, scenic, largely undeveloped piece of US real estate the size of Vermont, New Hampshire and Massachusetts combined, with a culturally distinctive population and maybe 1,000 hotel rooms?

The contrasts awaiting discovery in other areas of Northern Arizona range from the high, pine-shaded, 9,000-ft. plateaus of the Grand Canyon's North Rim, to the lingering pastel expanses of the Painted Desert. Elevations range from 3,000 to more than 12,000 ft.

You can hike over red rocks and among cacti in the morning, then ski the San Francisco Peaks in the afternoon. Humphries Peak, northwest of Flagstaff, is Arizona's highest point – 12,633 ft. at its summit.

The Grand Canyon has been likened to an upside down mountain, and any hike into it is considered strenuous. What goes down must come up in this case, and hiking out of the canyon takes at least twice as long as hiking in.

There are easier ways to go than hiking. Some choose to make the descent on the back of a large, well-trained and sure-footed animal making its way along the narrow, precipitous trails, although many people prefer sore feet to a sore bottom.

As for rafting the Colorado River, it flows in all its modern-day, dam-regulated glory through the Grand Canyon, still offering what many consider to be the premier whitewater experience in the United States, if not the world. You can spend a day floating through here.

For those who prefer sinking a fishing line to boating through rapids, there's trophy fishing to the south of the Glen Canyon Dam and in numerous lakes throughout Arizona's high country.

The mountains and deserts surrounding Flagstaff make the area a year-round recreational wonderland. The terrain for hiking, biking, and jeeping is superb from spring to fall. Cool mountain summers and warm desert winters are fine for outdoor activities. When the snow flies, the mountains become a winter sports mecca.

There are also upscale resorts and restaurants in this part of the state, mainly around Sedona, providing a stylistic counterpoint to accommodations and dining options found in certain other areas. There's even a steam train to the Grand Canyon from Williams. You can leave the driving to someone else and simply soak in the sunny ambiance of Northern Arizona.

Getting Around

The suggested route through this area starts in **Page, Arizona**, on the shores of **Lake Powell**. From there it's on to the Grand Canyon's **North Rim** and the **Arizona Strip**, the undeveloped northwestern corner of the state between the North Rim and the Utah border.

The **North Rim**'s accommodations and services are only open from mid-May until the first snow, usually around mid-October. Accommodations are available outside the North Rim year-round and the area is accessible for winter sports, though without in-park services. For Arizona road and weather reports, ☎ 520/638-7888.

From the North Rim it's necessary to backtrack to US 89 and head south along the western edge of the Navajo Nation to **Cameron**, where there is an evocative, old-time trading post not far from the east entrance to the Grand Canyon's South Rim.

The **South Rim**, open year-round, is the state's most visited attraction. There is snowfall on the South Rim too, but usually not enough to close trails into the canyon.

There are quite a few choices of South Rim accommodations and restaurants, though nowhere near enough to handle the flow of tourists in peak season. Make your plans as early as possible; reservations are accepted as far as 23 months in advance. The South Rim is also the center for all sorts of tours, including mule trips, scenic flights, and rafting excursions.

The **Grand Canyon** has already been forced into compromises in order to accommodate dramatic increases in visitors while protecting the scenery everyone is coming to see. Vehicle restrictions are enforced on parts of the South Rim in the summer. Even so, on a typical day 6,000 cars still try to squeeze into 1,500 parking places. Further restrictions will be instituted for the South Rim and a permit system is being considered for the North Rim.

After touring the South Rim, it's a short trip south to Williams, the terminal for the Grand Canyon Railway, a restored turn-of-the-century steam train. Then continue east to **Flagstaff**, a center for area-wide excursions. These include visits to three National Monuments: **Wupatki**, site of 800 Indian ruins dating to the 11th century; **Sunset Crater**, a 900-year old volcano; and **Walnut Canyon**, containing 300 cliff dwellings built by Sinagua Indians 1,000 years ago.

Grand Canyon Area

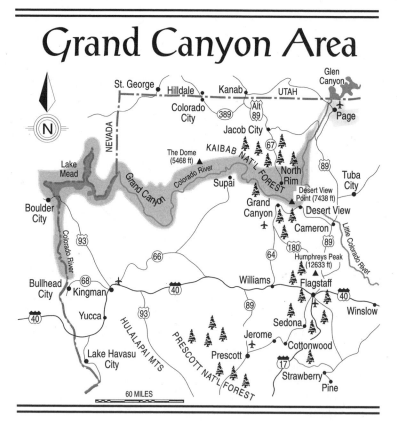

From Flagstaff the route heads south to **Sedona** and **Oak Creek Canyon**, a landscape of natural pools and rapids winding through 16 miles of sheer red rock cliffs. There's even a natural waterslide at **Red Rock State Park**, between Flagstaff and Sedona.

After passing these refreshing waters, the route turns eastward to the sandy deserts of **Petrified Forest National Park**, site of the largest concentration of mineralized wood in the world. The **Painted Desert**, north of the National Park, is the last stop before the Navajo and Hopi Tribal Lands.

There are airports and rental cars for use in Flagstaff and at the Grand Canyon. Again, you really need to drive to make your way through the whole area covered in this chapter.

Time is of a special essence in Arizona, which does not acknowledge daylight savings time. Mountain standard time is observed year-round. The exception is the Navajo Reservation, which sets its clocks ahead one hour in May, then back one hour in October. To confuse this issue, the Hopi Reservation, which is completely surrounded by the Navajo Reservation, does not change its clocks for daylight savings time.

It may help to think of it this way: in summertime, most of Arizona is on the same time as California; in winter, its on the same time as Colorado, New Mexico, and Utah; the Navajo Reservation is on the same time as Colorado, New Mexico, and Utah year-round.

TOURS

Fred **Harvey Transportation Company, ☎** 520/638-2525, offers taxi service and airport transfers, plus narrated sightseeing tours based at the South Rim. Half-day Grand Canyon tours to the West or East Rim or a Yaki Point sunset tour are available. Tours leave from El Tovar, Maswik, Yavapai, and Bright Angel lodges. Full-day tours are offered outside the park. These include itineraries covering the East Rim Drive, Wupatki, Sunset Crater and Walnut Canyon National Monuments, Flagstaff's Museum of Northern Arizona, Monument Valley, or a rafting tour to Marble Canyon. Reservations can be made through the transportation desks at Bright Angel, Maswik or Yavapai Lodges.

Nava-Hopi Tours, PO Box 339, Flagstaff AZ 86002, ☎ 520/774-5003 or 800/892-8687, fax 520/774-7715, runs daily buses to the Grand Canyon from Phoenix, Flagstaff, and Williams and offers guided sightseeing bus tours.

BUS & RAIL

Amtrak, ☎ 800/USA-RAIL, serves Flagstaff, with bus service to the Grand Canyon provided by Nava-Hopi tours (see above). The historic Grand Canyon Railway, ☎ 800/843-8724, makes daily runs between Williams and the South Rim. Transportation between the rims of the Grand Canyon is offered from May to November by **Trans Canyon Shuttle**, Box 348, Grand Canyon AZ 86023, ☎ 520/638-2820.

Several bus lines, as well as **Amtrak,** ☎ 800/872-7245, offer service through Flagstaff. Amtrak's service connects Chicago, Albuquerque, Flagstaff, and Los Angeles.

FLIGHTS

There is a small airport a few miles southwest of Sedona on Airport Road off US 89A. Daily service to Phoenix is provided by **Air Sedona**, ☎ 520/282-7935 or 800/228-7654.

Phoenix is only a few hours by car south of Sedona, and it is a gateway worth considering. The city offers some of the best air connections in all of Arizona, with service on **America West Airlines**, ☎ 800/235-9292; **American Airlines**, ☎ 800/433-7300; **Continental Airlines**, ☎ 800/525-0280; **Delta Airlines**, ☎ 800/221-1212; **Southwest Airlines**, ☎ 800/435-9792.

Scheduled Grand Canyon air service operates out of **Grand Canyon Airport** in Tusayan, six miles south of the park on AZ 64/US 180.

Air Nevada Airlines, 5700 South Haven, Las Vegas NV 89119, ☎ 702/736-8900 or 800/634-6377, runs daily flights between the Grand Canyon and Las Vegas.

Grand Canyon Airlines, 6005 Las Vegas Boulevard South, Las Vegas NV 89119, ☎ 702/798-6666 or 800/634-6616, runs flights between the Grand Canyon and Las Vegas or Los Angeles.

Scenic Airlines, 241 Reno Avenue, Las Vegas NV 89119, ☎ 702/739-1900 or 800/634-6801, runs scheduled service between the Grand Canyon and Las Vegas.

Arizona Air, ☎ 602/991-8252 or 800/445-8738, and **Arizona Pacific Airlines,** ☎ 602/242-3629 or 800/221-7904 in Arizona and 800/974-4280 out of Arizona, also offer daily service to and from the Grand Canyon.

Limited air service is offered from **Flagstaff Municipal Airport,** five miles south of town. **America West,** ☎ 520/525-1346 or 800/247-9292, provides daily service to the Grand Canyon, Phoenix, and Las Vegas. **Skywest Delta Connection,** ☎ 520/774-4830 or 800/453-9417, offers daily service to Phoenix or Page.

RENTALS

All the major and many minor rental car companies are also represented in Phoenix, with most offering airport locations or transfers.

Car rentals are available from **Budget,** ☎ 520/282-5602. There are numerous taxi services in town and there is bus service to Phoenix, Flagstaff, and other Arizona locations several times each day.

RV rentals and leasing can be arranged in Phoenix. **Adventure Werks,** ☎ 800/736-8897, specializes in renting outfitted Volkswagen camper vans that can sleep up to four passengers. Camping packages and mountain bike rentals are also available. **Cruise America,** 11 West Hampton Avenue, Mesa AZ 85210, ☎ 602/464-7300 or 800/327-7799, is the largest American company in the RV rental business and rents throughout North America. Also: Motorcycle rentals (touring, sport, and street bikes) are available to qualified riders. Company headquarters is in Mesa.

Rental cars at the airport are available from **Dollar,** ☎ 520/638-2625, or **Budget,** PO Box 758, 100 North Humphreys Street, Flagstaff AZ 86002, ☎ 520/638-9360.

Rental cars are available at the airport from **Avis,** ☎ 520/774-8421, **Budget,** ☎ 520/779-0306, or **Hertz,** ☎ 520/774-4452. Motorhome rentals are available from **Cruise America,** 824 West Route 66, Flagstaff AZ 86001, ☎ 520/774-4797.

INFORMATION

Arizona Office of Tourism, 110 West Washington, Phoenix AZ 85007. ☎ 602/542-8687 or 800/842-8257.

Arizona Game and Fish Department, 2222 West Greenway Road, Phoenix AZ 85023. ☎ 602/942-3000, fax 602/789-3924.

Arizona State Parks, 800 West Washington, Phoenix AZ 85007. ☎ 602/542-4174, fax 602/542-4180.

Bureau of Land Management, 3707 North 7th St., Phoenix AZ 85011. ☎ 602/640-5501, fax 602/640-2398.

For those who overdo it on the back of a mule or hiking around, **Grand Canyon Massage Therapy**, 385 Park Circle, ☎ 520/638-9468, is inside the park and offers half- and one-hour massages, sport massage, and acupressure.

If massage doesn't work, **Grand Canyon Health Center,** ☎ 520/638-2551 (after hours 520/638-2477), offers 24-hour emergency service and a pharmacy, ☎ 520/638-2460.

Phoenix & Valley of the Sun Convention & Visitors Bureau, One Arizona Center, 400 East Van Buren Street, Suite 600, Phoenix AZ 85004-2290, ☎ 602/254-6500, fax 602/252-5588, provides traveller information for the Phoenix area, as well as the whole state.

Nava-Hopi Tours, PO Box 339, Flagstaff AZ 86002, ☎ 520/774-5003 or 800/892-8687, provides daily motorcoach service from Phoenix's Sky Harbor Airport to Flagstaff.

Grand Canyon National Park, PO Box 129, Grand Canyon AZ 86023, 520/638-7888. The phone number will give you a recorded message on how to reach appropriate park divisions or receive an informative Trip Planner. For tour information, same-day accommodation reservations, emergency vehicle towing, or night-time taxi services, ☎ 520/638-2631. For advance accommodation reservations ☎ 520/638-2401. For daytime taxi service phone ☎ 520/638-2822.

Grand Canyon Chamber of Commerce, PO Box 3007, Grand Canyon AZ 86023.

South Rim Travel, PO Box 3651, Grand Canyon AZ 86023, ☎ 520/638-2748 or 800/682-4393, provides central hotel reservations, air and ground tours, plus air and car rental reservations.

Grand Canyon Natural History Association, ☎ 520/638-2481, provides a substantial number of books, videos, and maps focusing on the Grand Canyon.

Tusayan Ranger Station, PO Box 3088, Grand Canyon AZ 86023, ☎ 520/638-2443, administers the area of the Kaibab National Forest just south of the South Rim. The office is south of the park, near Moqui Lodge, and can provide information on camping, hiking, and other recreational activities.

Flagstaff Chamber of Commerce Visitor Center, 101 West Santa Fe Avenue, Flagstaff AZ 86001, ☎ 520/774-9451 or 800/842-7293, provides free information on area attractions and services, including a self-guided historic downtown walking tour.

Flagstaff Current Events Hotline, ☎ 520/779-3733.

Coconino National Forest Supervisor, 2323 East Greenlaw Lane, Flagstaff AZ 86004, ☎ 520/556-7400, administers areas north and south of Flagstaff.

Peaks Ranger Station, 5075 North US 89, Flagstaff AZ 86004, ☎ 520/526-0866, deals specifically with areas north of Flagstaff.

Mormon Lake Ranger District, 4825 Lake Mary Road, Flagstaff AZ 86001, ☎ 520/556-7474, operates the southern district.

Road conditions: ☎ 520/779-2711.

Weather conditions: ☎ 520/774-3301.

Sedona-Oak Creek Chamber of Commerce, PO Box 478, Sedona AZ 86336, ☎ 520/282-7722 or 800/288-7336.
Sedona Ranger District, 250 Brewer Road, PO Box 300, Sedona AZ 86336, ☎ 520/282-4119, provides maps, hiking trail guides, plus camping and back road information.

Touring

Page/Lake Powell

On US 89 is Page, Arizona, the largest town on the shore of Lake Powell. It developed in 1957 as the construction base for the 710-ft.-high Glen Canyon Dam, which created the 250-square-mile lake, most of which is in Utah. The dam was completed in 1964. Page has since grown as a major service town, offering motels, campgrounds, RV parks, restaurants, gas stations, and shops. Boat rentals are available at Wahweap Marina, a few miles north of town.

Most people don't spend a lot of time in Page, but passing through here there are a few interesting attractions. These include the free tour of Glen Canyon Dam, ☎ 520/645-2511.

INFORMATION

The **Carl Hayden Visitor Center,** ☎ 520/608-6404, features a movie about Lake Powell, exhibits on the construction of the dam, and a Navajo rug display.
The **National Park Service,** PO Box 1507, Page AZ 86040, operates an information booth in the visitor center adjacent to the dam. This is where you can get details on camping, hiking, and boating activities within Glen Canyon National Recreation Area.
Page/Lake Powell Chamber of Commerce, 716 Rim View Drive, PO Box 727, Page AZ, ☎ 520/645-2741, offers information on town and lake activities. It also makes tour reservations.
Sky West/Delta Connection, ☎ 520/645-9200 or 800/453-9417, offers scheduled service connecting Page with Salt Lake City, Flagstaff, Phoenix and Las Vegas.

Avis, ☎ 520/645-2024, rents cars at the airport. **Budget,** ☎ 520/645-3977, has an office in town.

The **John Wesley Powell Memorial Museum**, at Lake Powell Boulevard and North Navajo Drive, ☎ 520/645-9496, displays historical exhibits on the Colorado River and the people who have run it over the years. Other displays tell the movie-making story of the area, as well as more distant geological and social history.

Lake Powell's nearly 2,000 miles of shoreline extend throughout hundreds of branching fingers of sheer-walled canyons that range in color from pale tan to flaming orange. Networks of waterways intertwine through the canyons, offering ever-changing waters for a variety of watersports. Scuba diving to submerged Indian ruins in the lake is just one option. Part of the adventure that lures three million travellers each year is the varying water level; you can never be sure to see the same coves, caves, or inlets again. You can travel in your own boat or rent one at a marina. Stepping ashore you can find hiking trails into remote backcountry, including the Escalante River Canyon, Dark Canyon or the Grand Gulch Primitive Area.

Wahweap Lodge and Marina, Box 1597, Page AZ 86040, ☎ 520/645-2433, is six miles north of Page and includes the Rainbow Room restaurant and an RV park.

Guided tours available include half-day or full-day boat excursions to **Rainbow Bridge National Monument**. For information, see below under *Lake Powell Boating*. Also offered are dinner and sunset tours on Wahweap Bay aboard the **Canyon King,** a stern-wheel paddleboat. All manner of boat and water accessory services can be found here: houseboats in various sizes, motor boats, jet skis, waterskis, and fishing gear. You can stock up on provisions for your houseboat or picnic at the nearby campground operated by the Park Service.

Wahweap operates a free bus service for guests from mid-May through mid-October, between the lodge and selected Page destinations, including the airport, the shopping center, river float tour offices, the John Wesley Powell Museum and the Carl Hayden Visitor Center at Glen Canyon Dam.

Dangling Rope Marina, ☎ 520/645-2969, is situated 40 miles uplake from Wahweap and is accessible only by water. Facilities include a ranger station, grocery store, and marine gas station.

Marble Canyon/Lees Ferry/AZ Strip

The **North Rim** offers what some might consider to be the best views of the Grand Canyon. Don't get the wrong idea; the South Rim is mighty nice too, but it's a lot more crowded and sees 10 times the number of visitors as the North Rim. For some, this makes all the difference in the world.

To reach the **North Rim** from Page you drive southwest for 25 miles on US 89 to **Bitter Springs**, then north for 14 miles on US 89A to the **Navajo Bridge**, 616 ft. long and 467 ft. high. On the west side of the bridge is **Marble Canyon**, five miles south of **Lees Ferry**, the put-in point for many Grand Canyon river trips.

Marble Canyon doesn't have a lot of services to offer but the scenery is fine, with the river coursing through an 800-ft.-deep gorge. Fishing is excellent in the trophy waters of the Colorado below the Glen Canyon Dam. There are places to stay in this vicinity: The **Cliff Dwellers Lodge & Trading Company**, eight miles west of Marble Canyon; **Lee's Ferry Lodge**, three miles west; and **Marble Canyon Lodge**. You can also get gas and groceries, and there are camping areas here.

Lees Ferry was the original site of a ferry operated by a man named Lee, who was hiding out from the law because of his part in the 1857 Mountain Meadows Massacre in Utah. It took 20 years to catch him but he was eventually returned to the spot of the massacre north of Cedar City and executed by a firing squad.

For years, until the completion of the bridge in 1929, the ferry was the only way to get across the dangerous Colorado River. The bridge was, however, a little too late for the last ferry passengers. Three people drowned on the final crossing of the ferry in 1928. The ferry sank in the turbulent, uncontrolled river. That was in the days before the dam, when the waters were less predictable.

There are old structures and equipment in the Lees Ferry area, including a log cabin, a ranch house and some orchards at **Lonely Dell Ranch Historic District**, a mile northwest of Lees Ferry, on the Paria River. Several old mine buildings, an old post office, a wrecked steamboat, and **Lees Ferry Fort**, close to the actual ferry crossing, are within the **Lees Ferry Historic District**.

There's a strenuous, steep, unmaintained hiking trail that starts near the remains of the steamboat and leads a mile and a half to an overlook 1,500 ft. above Marble Canyon.

The greatest usage of the Lees Ferry area is for launching river trips into the Grand Canyon. A boat ramp is also used for trips up-river to the Glen Canyon Dam. The 15 miles to the dam are popular for fishing. For information, a ranger station is near the Lees Ferry Campground.

From Marble Canyon US 89A heads west across the **Vermillion Cliffs** for 40 miles to **Jacob Lake** and the junction with AZ 67, the only paved road leading to the North Rim of the Grand Canyon. US 89A continues northwest for 30 miles from this junction to Fredonia.

It meets US 89 seven miles north of Fredonia in Kanab, Utah. AZ 389 heads west from Fredonia to wilderness areas of the **Arizona Strip**, the remote area between the North Rim and southern Utah, which is accessed off AZ 389 or UT 59. It's the same road, but the designation changes at the border between **Colorado City**, Arizona and **Hilldale**, Utah, two unusual small towns that have achieved minor notoriety as the residences of modern-day Mormon polygamists. Colorado City, you may recall, was in the news in the early 1990s for expelling an elementary school student who had the audacity to wear a Batman t-shirt to school.

UT 59 continues on to Hurricane Utah in 23 miles from Hilldale, or there is a dirt road turn-off seven miles northwest of Hilldale at Big Plain Junction, Utah, offering a 10-mile back way to UT 9 and **Zion National Park**.

If you can't wait to see the North Rim, or at least the part of lower Marble Canyon that leads to it, the graded dirt House Rock Buffalo Ranch Road starts south 24 miles west of Marble Canyon, or 16 miles east of Jacob Lake, and leads 25 miles from US 89A to several viewpoints in the vicinity of **House Rock Valley**, where a rare herd of wild bison roams freely. The main road and spur roads to overlooks should be passable in a passenger car if the weather is dry.

At the end of House Rock Road you are only 15 miles east of AZ 67, near **Kaibab Lodge**. A rugged series of jeep trails connects these areas but travellers in a passenger car will need to retrace the route back to US 89A.

There's good hiking and backcountry camping near the end of House Rock Road, in the vicinity of **Saddle Canyon** and nearby **Saddle Mountain**.

Another dirt road, Forest Road 610 swings east from AZ 67, south of Kaibab Lodge, 18 miles north of **Bright Angel Point**, to these areas, linking up with rougher jeep trails that eventually lead to House Rock Valley. See below for information on contacting the Kaibab Forest office in Fredonia or the ranger station at Jacob Lake for maps and detailed road information.

Although a certain amount of North Rim traffic comes from Page and Lake Powell, the Arizona Strip and the North Rim are primarily and much more directly accessed through Southern Utah, on US 89 south from Kanab to Fredonia, or on various dirt roads branching off from AZ 389-UT 59. The main dirt roads that eventually lead through the isolated backcountry of the Arizona Strip to the most secluded parts of the North Rim are rugged and long. They should not be taken lightly. These back roads are covered below, under *Arizona Strip/Grand Canyon National Park North Rim Jeeping.*

Jacob Lake is primarily a service area for North Rim travellers from May to October. Facilities include a motel, restaurant, grocery store, and gas station. There are also seasonal campgrounds open from May to October, for tents or RVs.

In the winter AZ 67, from south of Jacob Lake to the Grand Canyon, is closed by snow. Then Jacob Lake becomes a center for cross-country ski trips. There are many gravel and dirt back roads, bicycle and hiking trails, and primitive camping areas throughout the **Kaibab National Forest**, south of Jacob Lake.

A **Kaibab Forest Information Center**, ☎ 520/643-7295, south of Jacob Lake Lodge, can provide information. If no one's around, the **North Kaibab Ranger District** office is located at 430 South Main Street, Box 248, Fredonia AZ 86022, ☎ 520/643-7395.

Fredonia, 32 miles northeast of Jacob Lake on US 89A, boasts a population of around 1,400, which makes it the metropolis of the Arizona Strip. There are a few modest motels and restaurants, as well as the Kaibab Forest office.

About 15 miles west of Fredonia on AZ 389 is **Pipe Spring National Monument**, ☎ 520/643-7105. It was set aside by the federal government in 1923 to memorialize pioneer life at a one-time Mormon ranch. The original ranch buildings are collectively called **Winsor Castle** and, during the summer, costumed National Park Service interpreters offer recreations of frontier life, including blacksmithing, baking, and weaving demonstrations. There are also maintained orchards and gardens offering produce at harvest times, plus a Visitor Center and book shop. A snack bar is operated by the Paiute Tribe, which also runs a campground just north of the Visitor Center.

If you do venture off the main paved roads of the Arizona Strip into the spacious backcountry, it is possible to visit no fewer than nine isolated wilderness areas.

Two areas are accessible off of I-15, 20 miles south of St. George, Utah. These are the 20,000-acre **Beaver Dams Wilderness** north of the interstate and notable for the presence of rare Joshua trees, and the 85,000-acre **Paiute Wilderness** south of the interstate.

There are no hiking trails in the Beaver Dams area but you can wander freely through the desert. Paiute Wilderness contains rugged hiking trails ranging from 2,000-ft.-high desert terrain through 8,000-ft.-high evergreen forests.

These areas are managed by the BLM out of their **Arizona Strip** District Office, 390 North 3050 East, St. George UT 84770, ☎ 801/673-2545. The office can provide maps and other information about the areas.

The same Arizona Strip BLM office administers **Cottonwood Point Wilderness**, a 6,000-acre tract containing tall cliffs and plunging canyons, plus **Cottonwood Point**, where unexpectedly verdant flora is surrounded by desert. The area lies east of Colorado City off AZ 389 and south of Hilldale, Utah on dirt roads.

Several other wilderness areas administered by this office are accessed off the dirt roads south from St. George, Colorado City and Pipe Springs Monument, which lead to the North Rim. These include the virtually inaccessible **Grand Wash Cliff Wilderness Area**, due south of the Paiute Wilderness and 30 miles south of I-15. It contains 36,000 acres of isolated canyons along the western border of the Colorado Plateau. The only roads that access the area are rough, unpaved, and unmaintained. **Mount Logan Wilderness** and **Mount Trumbull Wilderness** may be reached by any of the main dirt roads from the north. The areas lie just north of the National Park boundary, close to the North Rim's **Toroweap Point**. Together the two areas encompass 22,000 forested acres laced with rugged hiking trails, including trails to the top of 7,866-ft. **Mount Logan** and 8,028-ft. **Mount Trumbull**.

Along with miles of remote backcountry there are several little-visited Anasazi sites in the Arizona Strip, including **Little Black Mountain Petroglyph Interpretive Site**. It is eight miles southeast of St. George at the base of a 500-ft. sandstone mesa covered by a lava flow. It contains a wide variety of designs in 500 individual petroglyphs or elements carved into boulders and cliffs stretching for 800 yards. Although it's not far from St. George, gravel and dirt back roads to the site are rough. Four-wheel-drive is recommended.

Information is available from the **Shivwits Resource Area**, 225 North Bluff, St. George UT 84770, ☎ 801/628-4491.

Farther south, in the vicinity of Mount Trumbull, a site called **Nampaweap**, meaning "Foot Canyon" in Paiute, also contains hundreds of petroglyphs on boulders beneath a lava wall. The site is also known as **Billy Goat Canyon**. It is administered by the BLM's Vermillion Resource Area, at the same address and phone as the Shivwits office (above).

The southwestern portion of the 77,000-acre **Kanab Creek Wilderness**, which contains the largest canyon network near the North Rim, is also administered by the BLM offices in St. George. The rest of the area is administered by the North Kaibab Ranger District office in Fredonia.

Within the Kanab Creek Wilderness are numerous backcountry trails, including one providing a multi-day hike along **Kanab Creek** to **Kanab Point** overlooking the Colorado River. The area is accessed west of AZ 67 by a network of back roads through the **Kaibab National Forest**.

Also administered by the North Kaibab office is the 40,000-acre **Saddle Mountain Wilderness**, east of AZ 67 and just north of the Grand Canyon on the **Kaibab Plateau**. There's good fishing and plenty of trails for hiking and horseback riding here.

The **Paria Canyon-Vermillion Cliffs Wilderness** encompasses 110,000 acres north of US 89A between Jacob Lake and Lees Ferry, extending into southern Utah.

Grand Canyon National Park

NORTH RIM

Travelling south on AZ 67 from Jacob Lake toward the North Rim, you gain elevation through the northern portion of the Kaibab National Forest.

The road is also known as the **Kaibab Plateau-North Rim Parkway**. The pine and spruce forests surrounding mountain wildflower meadows are full of wildlife such as mule deer and elk. This road is usually closed in the winter which means, most years, driving access is limited to a May-through-October season.

It's 45 miles south from Jacob Lake to the end of the paved road at North Rim's **Bright Angel Point**, which is adjacent to the classic, cut-stone **Grand Canyon Lodge**. There are, however, unpaved back roads along the way leading to even more isolated North Rim viewpoints.

Twelve miles south of Jacob Lake you can turn west and follow signs through the Kaibab Forest for 26 miles to **Crazy Jug Vista**. To return to AZ 67 and the main North Rim service area, you can backtrack for 16 miles. Instead of continuing east and following the road you came in on, turn south along **Lookout Canyon**, at the first dirt road junction, and follow the road for 17 miles back to the pavement, just south of **Kaibab Lodge.**

The lodge offers the closest accommodations and dining outside the North Rim and offers mountain bike and cross-country ski rental. The full list of services is detailed under *North Rim Accommodations & Restaurants* and various *Adventures* categories below.

Another viewpoint is reached by a turn-off to the east onto Forest Road 611, a mile south of Kaibab Lodge, off AZ 67. The gravel road is usually accessible to passenger cars and there are signs showing the way in only five miles to the **East Rim Vista.**

Since the area is outside the park boundaries, you can camp in the Kaibab Forest backcountry without a permit. It might be handy to remember this if you don't have reservations for the camping space on the North Rim in high season.

From Kaibab Lodge it's 18 miles on AZ 67 to the end of the road at the North Rim which, on average, is 1,200 ft. higher than the South Rim. It's a quarter-mile walk on a paved trail from the parking lot at the end of the road to Bright Angel Point.

Because of the colder, wetter weather at the higher elevation, there are many more trees, and larger ones, than at the South Rim, adding a touch of liveliness to the scenery that the rocky faces of the South Rim lack.

The big difference is really the shortage of crowds at the North Rim, allowing for a more intimate experience of the Grand Canyon, which looks absolutely incredible and humbling from wherever you stand. You'd have to be numb not to sense the power of the place.

The **Grand Canyon Lodge** is an imposing stone and log structure where all visitor services are located, including information on hiking trails and tours, mule trips into the depths, and rafting excursions. Camping supplies and gas are also available here. There is a restaurant as well as various accommodations in lodge rooms, cabins, or a campground. The 1½-mile **Transept Trail** heads along the North Rim from the lodge to the campground.

A ranger station, where backcountry information is available, is located a quarter-mile north of the campground. It is generally open from mid-May through October.

A list of scheduled ranger-led activities is posted at the Grand Canyon Lodge. During the summer season these include campfire talks on geology, nature and history, ranger-guided hikes, and special children's programs.

Although the Grand Canyon Lodge, ranger station, and roads are closed in winter, visitors are still permitted to hike (best accomplished with snowshoes) or ski in the area of the North Rim.

There is only one paved road leading to canyon overlooks on the North Rim. It starts three miles north of the Grand Canyon Lodge and heads northeast for eight miles to **Point Imperial**, elevation 8,800 ft., affording the highest rim views of the park. Alternatively, you can turn south at the Point Imperial turn-off and drive 15 miles to **Cape Royal**. You reach Cape Royal by walking a half-mile from the parking lot at the end of the road. There are several other viewpoints on the way to Cape Royal, including **Vista Encantadora** and **Walhalla Overlook**.

The only other road in this area of the North Rim is a 17-mile four-wheel-drive road west of Grand Canyon Lodge to **Point Sublime**. It starts 2½ miles north of the lodge.

There are a number of trails from the North Rim leading down into the Grand Canyon. These are detailed below under *North Rim Hiking*.

SOUTH RIM

To reach the South Rim by car from the North Rim you have to backtrack all the way to Marble Canyon and south to Bitter Springs on US 89A – a distance of 95 miles. Continue south on US 89 through the western edge of the Navajo Nation for 59 miles to **Cameron Trading P**ost, Box 339, Cameron AZ 86020, ☎ 520/679-2231 or 800/338-7385. Here accommodations, a restaurant, a campground which accepts RVs, a grocery store, and a gas station are located. Cameron has been an operating trading post since 1916 and offers a large range of goods. **Cameron Collector's Gallery**, next door to the main trading post, is where they keep the good stuff.

The quickest way to the South Rim is to turn west, a mile south of the Cameron Trading Post, onto AZ 64, which leads 32 miles to the **East Entrance Station** of the National Park. There's an overlook of the Little Colorado River 15 miles west of Cameron.

The first stop past the entrance station on the East Rim Drive is **Desert View**, the highest point on the South Rim, elevation 7,500 ft. You can see the bend in the Colorado River as it flows out of Marble Canyon into the Grand Canyon. Here is the **Desert View Watchtower**, which was built in 1932. It's 70 ft. tall and you can climb to the top for a better view of the river and the Painted Desert.

There is also a ranger station, a gas station, a snack bar, a grocery store, and a campground.

Lipan Point, two miles west of Desert View, offers one of the better viewpoints for assessing the incredible scope of the geological history contained in the park.

Tusayan Ruin is a mile west of Lipan Point and contains a small Anasazi ruin. There is also a small museum focusing on the Anasazi and more modern Indian tribes.

Other viewpoints and several picnic areas are along the 26 miles between Desert View and Grand Canyon Village. These include **Moran Point, Grandview Point**, and **Yaki Point**, the closest to the South Rim Visitor Center.

Grandview Point, close to the mid-point of the East Rim Drive and 14 miles west of Desert View, offers one of the best rim overlook views of any site you can drive to in the park.

A number of trails start at the various East Rim overlooks.

Most visitor facilities are in the vicinity of Grand Canyon Village, 26 miles west of Desert View, at the western end of the East Rim Drive.

Coming from the East Rim Drive you first pass **Mather Point**, a popular view site, then the **Yavapai Museum**. There are big windows in the museum overlooking the canyon and visible sites are named, so you know what you're looking at. Displays include rocks from the various geologic layers, billion-year-old fossils, and a geologic clock that ticks off 11-million-year segments of geological activity. There are also scientific exhibits and displays revealing Indian legends about how the Grand Canyon was formed.

A mile west of the museum is the **South Rim Visitor Center**, featuring an outdoor display of various water craft that have been used to ply the waters of the Colorado River and indoor displays relating to natural and human history of the Grand Canyon. Exhibits recount the lives of ancient Indians, early explorers, miners, and the annals of tourism in the area. Other displays recommend ways to explore the park. A listing of ranger-led activities is posted. Books, maps, and information are available here and a ranger is on duty.

Clustered around the visitor center are a number of services including the **Backcountry Reservation Office, Mather Center**, a grocery store, bank and post office, an RV dump station, a gas station, **Yavapai Lodge**, and **Mather Campground and Trailer Village**, with hook-ups for RVs, showers and laundry facilities.

A mile west of the visitor center are additional visitor services at Grand Canyon Village, including **El Tovar Hotel, Maswik Lodge**,

Kachina Lodge, Thunderbird Lodge, a ranger station, movie theaters, several souvenir shops, and the railway station where the steam train from Williams arrives and departs.

Over the Edge! Theater, PO Box 600, Grand Canyon, ☎ 520/5382229, a block east of Maswik Lodge in Grand Canyon Village, shows a 30-minute multi-media slide presentation on the history and geology of the Grand Canyon.

A free shuttle loops through Grand Canyon Village during the busy summer season.

West Rim Drive starts just west of the **Bright Angel Lodge** and is closed to automobile traffic in the summer. You can, however, ride a bike or a free shuttle bus along the drive. The West Rim shuttle starts at Bright Angel Lodge and stops at all the West Rim viewpoints, including **Powell Memorial, Hopi Point, Mohave Point,** and **Pima Point.** You can get on and off as often as you like. The drive covers eight miles to **Hermit's Rest** where there are bathrooms and a snack shop.

Sightseeing bus tours that are not free depart from El Tovar, Maswik Lodge, Yavapai Lodge and Bright Angel Lodge. Options include tours to Hermit's Rest and Desert View (or both). A short sunset tour is also offered. For information contact **Bright Angel Lodge Transportation Desk,** Grand Canyon National Park Lodges, PO Box 699, Grand Canyon AZ 86023, ☎ 520/638-2631, extension 6577.

The more challenging hiking trails from the South Rim are detailed below, under *South Rim Hiking.*

Among the easier rim-top trails, the popular **South Rim Nature Trail** is an option for those who want to stay atop the South Rim. A short half-mile unpaved section leads east from Yavapai Museum to Mather Point. It's paved for 3½ miles from Yavapai Museum to **Maricopa Point,** on the West Rim Drive, then continues for five unpaved miles to Hermit's Rest. You can get off the trail and onto the free shuttle bus every half-mile or so along the West Rim Drive.

Many additional services and facilities are a few miles south of the park entrance on AZ 64 in Tusayan. These include motels and restaurants, which are listed below, RV parks, **Grand Canyon Airport,** gas stations, stores and shops, miniature golf and bowling. There's a McDonald's and a movie theater showing popular Grand Canyon-related fare.

Tusayan-Grand Canyon Shuttle, ☎ 520/638-2475, operates bus service between Grand Canyon Village and Tusayan and includes stops at the airport.

Grand Canyon IMAX Theater AZ 64/US 180, PO Box 1397, Grand Canyon AZ 86023, ☎ 520/638-2203, fax 520/638-2807, shows a feature called *Grand Canyon: The Hidden Secrets* on a seven-story-high screen with six-track Dolby sound.

There's a Taco Bell at the theater complex and an **Arizona Tourist Information & Visitor Center,** where you can book scenic flights and other tours.

Havasupai & Hualapai Reservations

It's 35 air miles from Grand Canyon Village to Havasu Canyon but a lot longer ride by car. The most common route from the South Rim is to drive 56 miles south on AZ 64/US 180 to Williams. Then drive 43 miles west on I-40 to **Seligman.** Here you can cruise a short motel strip, perhaps eat a meal, and definitely fill the tank with gas; it's likely to be the last chance for fuel on the 180-mile trip to Havasu Canyon and back.

For information contact **Seligman Chamber of Commerce,** East Chino Avenue, PO Box 65, Seligman AZ 86337, ☎ 520/422-3352.

From Seligman it's 30 miles northwest on AZ 66, and 61 miles northeast on Indian Route 18 to **Hualapai Hilltop.** You'll pass **Grand Canyon Caverns,** ☎ 520/422-3223, on AZ 66, 25 miles northwest of Seligman, 13 miles east of Peach Spring, or seven miles east of Tribal Road 18 to Hualapai Hilltop. The vaulted limestone caverns lie 21 stories underground. You can take an elevator down to the cave for a 45-minute tour. There's a year-round motel, campground, and restaurant.

There are dirt road shortcuts west from Tusayan and points farther south off AZ 64 that shave the distance to Tribal Route 18 and Hualapai Hilltop by two-thirds. You'll save miles, but the trip will probably take just as long on these bad roads with poor or non-existent signs. These back routes are recommended for map-reading four-wheel-drivers only.

The Havasupai Tribe, who have lived in this area from long before there was a National Park, don't want an easier or shorter road from Grand Canyon Village. The tribe's 200,000-acre reservation includes the area around Hualapai Hilltop. This is where most visitors park and prepare to hike or ride a horse or mule down 2,000 ft. in eight miles to the main village of **Supai,** on the bank of **Havasu Creek.**

To get into the village you must pay a fee. There is a small grocery store in Supai and a café. If you want to stay in Supai at the

Havasupai Lodge or campground, which are the only places available, you need a reservation. The only way you will have time to see the waterfalls and canyon scenery the tribe has protected for hundreds of years is to stay overnight.

For campground information contact **Havasupai Tourist Enterprises**, Supai AZ 86435, ☎ 520/448-2121. This is the same office that handles the reservations needed to secure transportation from Hualapai Hilltop to Supai by horse or mule, or a seat on a mule or horse's back for a scenic tour from Supai to the waterfalls. You may bring your own horse if you prefer.

For Supai Lodge information contact **Havasupai Lodges**, Supai AZ 86435, ☎ 520/448-2111.

The great scenery starts a mile down the rushing waters of Havasu Creek from Supai. Three impressive waterfalls are clustered in a space of only two miles. **Navajo Falls** is 75 ft. high. Nearby, **Havasu Falls** plunges 100 ft. into a rock-rimmed pool of turquoise water that has graced many postcard views of the Grand Canyon. You can swim in the pool. **Mooney Falls** is the farthest of these three waterfalls from Supai. It's also the tallest, dropping 196 feet into another pretty blue pool. It's harder to get to this pool, though. You have to hike a narrow trail through two tunnels, then grab onto chain handholds and metal stakes to lower yourself to the swimming hole.

Two miles farther down Havasu Creek is **Beaver Falls**. It's four miles from there to the Colorado River. Remember that the only permissible camping is at the campground near Mooney Falls. If you decide to go to the river this way, make sure you are fully prepared to make it back the same day.

The **Hualapai Indian Reservation** covers almost a million acres, including areas of the South Rim. Any travelling on reservation land requires a permit which may be obtained in **Peach Springs**, on AZ 66, 55 miles north of Kingman, or seven miles west of Tribal Route 18 on AZ 66.

There are two things that most people want to do here. One is to drive the **Diamond Creek Road**, the only road to the Colorado River within the Grand Canyon. The second is to ride the tribal-run motorized rafts through the Lower Grand Canyon into Lake Mead. For information about the raft trips see below, under *Grand Canyon River Trips*.

Diamond Creek Road covers 21 gravel miles from Peach Springs to Diamond Creek on the Colorado River. Four-wheel-drive is only necessary in wet weather. There are picnic tables and outhouses at the end of the road. To drive it you must first obtain a backcountry permit from the Hualapai River Runners office (see below, under *Grand Canyon River Trips*).

Williams/Flagstaff

There are three highway routes to Flagstaff from the South Rim:

❒ Drive 51 miles out the East Rim Drive to Cameron, then south on US 89 for 45 miles into town.

❒ Drive south for 56 miles from Grand Canyon Village on AZ 64/US 180 to Williams, then east on I-40 for 32 miles to Flagstaff.

❒ Twenty-eight miles south of the South Rim on AZ 64/US 180, the third route to Flagstaff splits off in a southeasterly direction at Valle, home of **Bedrock City**, ☎ 520/635-2600. Bedrock City features camping areas for tents or RVs and has the added allure of models of Flintstones' characters wired for sound in a little cement theme park. AZ 64 continues south to Williams at I-40 while US 180 cuts southeast through the **San Francisco Peaks** for 52 miles from Valle to Flagstaff. Many mountain activities based in this area are covered below under *Adventures*.

Williams is the closest town to the Grand Canyon on the interstate, so plenty of traffic passes through here on the way to somewhere else. The town is unimpressive but it's geared for tourism and there are gas stations and restaurants. It's also easier to reserve a room in one of Williams' 30 or so motels than at the Grand Canyon and rates are lower than the South Rim.

The National Park is only 2½ hours north on the **Grand Canyon Railway.** The train offers a practical, stress-reducing alternative to automobile and bus traffic at the South Rim. For information see below, under *Rail Trips*.

The forested areas around Williams, elevation 6,780 ft., offer opportunities for hiking, camping, fishing, and other activities, including winter sports.

The **Sycamore Canyon Wilderness Area,** southeast of Williams, might be thought of as the back side of Sedona's Oak Creek Canyon, a scant 15 miles east as the crow flies, though many more miles by road. The forested red rock terrain is essentially the same, the main difference being that Sedona attracts millions of visitors yearly and undeveloped Sycamore Canyon sees a lot more wildlife and only a small fraction of those people.

The only nearby access road to the wilderness area, which is otherwise accessible only to hikers or horseback riders, is 23 miles southeast of Williams at **Sycamore Canyon Point,** where a panoramic view site overlooks the west rim of the 21-mile-long, five- to seven-mile-wide canyon. To reach the overlook drive eight miles south of Williams on Fourth Street, then 15 miles east on Forest Road 110.

Sycamore Canyon can also be approached from the south, on a dirt road north from **Tuzigoot National Monument,** 15 miles southwest of Sedona off US 89A, or from Forest Road 525C, northwest from US 89A on the edge of West Sedona.

Another scenic drive near Williams is the road to the top of **Bill Williams Mountain,** which is probably best enjoyed in a four-wheel-drive. It starts five miles south of Williams on Fourth Street. From there it's seven miles west to the 9,255-ft. peak.

For Kaibab National Forest information regarding the areas south of Williams, contact **Williams Ranger District,** Route 1, PO Box 142, Williams AZ 86046, ☎ 520/635-2633. For areas east of Williams, contact **Chalender Ranger District,** 501 West Bill Williams Avenue, Williams AZ 86046, ☎ 520/635-2676.

For general information about Williams and the Grand Canyon contact **Williams-Grand Canyon Chamber of Commerce,** 820 West Bill Williams Avenue, PO Box 235, Williams AZ 86046, ☎ 520/635-4061.

Flagstaff is 32 miles east of Williams on I-40 or 45 miles south of Cameron on US 89. There's a worthwhile detour 20 miles south of Cameron at **Wupatki National Monument.** It adds only 20 miles to your trip if you follow a scenic 35-mile road loop east through Indian ruins at Wupatki, then turning south. After 15 miles it leads to a volcanic cinder cone at **Sunset Crater National Monument.** The loop returns to US 89 three miles west of Sunset Crater and 15 miles north of Flagstaff.

Wupatki National Monument, Box 444A, Flagstaff AZ 86001, ☎ 520/527-7040, contains primitive masonry ruins built by Indians who lived and farmed here from 1100-1300 AD. Only a few sites, out of an estimated 2,000, have been excavated and much of the reserve is protected by restricted access. Overnight hiking is prohibited, except for special ranger-led hikes offered in April and October.

Entering Wupatki from the north means the visitor center, 14 miles east of US 89, is one of the last places you'll reach on a drive through here. There are small exhibits of ancient Indian artifacts and other historical displays, as well as information pamphlets, maps, and activity schedules. You don't really need the visitor center brochures to find the several ruins sites that can be driven to on the well-signed park road. From the north these are **Lomaki Ruin, Citadel Ruin, Wukoki Ruin** and, the largest site, **Wupatki Ruin,** near the visitor center, containing 100 rooms. Short trails to each site provide views of other scattered ruins.

Directly south of Wupatki is the **Strawberry Crater Wilderness Area,** containing 10,000 acres of sparsely vegetated volcanic lava fields, and **Sunset Crater National Monument,** Route 3, Box 49, Flagstaff AZ 86004, ☎ 520/527-7042, 11 miles south of the Wupatki Visitor Center.

Sunset Crater is a black, volcanic cinder cone 1,000 ft. high. Not much has grown near the crater in the 700 years since the last eruption, so the area is a good one to observe the effects of a volcano.

You can hike the short **Lava Flow Trail,** around the base of the crater, but hiking up the crater is prohibited.

Nearby, **Lenox Crater** is open to hikers. A quarter-mile west of the Sunset Crater Visitor Center is a turn-off for Forest Road 545A, which goes north for five steep miles to the 8,965-ft. summit of **O'Leary Peak.** From the peak you can look down into Sunset Crater.

Sunset Crater Visitor Center is near the southwestern entrance to the park, 3½ miles east of US 89. Displays deal mainly with the forces of volcanism. Ranger-led activities schedules are posted. A campground is situated nearby and is open May through October.

Flagstaff is 12 miles south of Sunset Crater on US 89. Its population of 46,000 surpasses any other city in this book by far and, if you're just passing through on the main roads, you will see undeniable evidence that Flagstaff does have more gas stations, motels, and restaurants than any other place this book covers. It's the biggest city between Albuquerque and Los Angeles on I-40, which runs coast to coast.

Flagstaff is well situated, amid cooling pine forests at 7,000 ft., to provide central access to the many adventurous things to do in the area. This includes hiking or biking in Arizona's highest mountains, the San Francisco Peaks, just northwest of the city, skiing there in winter, or fishing on numerous lakes. There are Indian ruins, volcanoes, and wilderness areas nearby, as well as a historic downtown district, museums, an observatory where astronomers first spotted Pluto, a university community that contributes nearly 20% of the city's population, and numerous galleries.

Northern Arizona University is situated on 700 acres, just seven blocks south of downtown. Free shuttle buses travel across the large campus.

A lot of things are generally going on here, including changing shows at **NAU Art Gallery, ☎ 520/523-3471**, sporting events, plus theatrical and musical performances. For the school's information desk, ☎ 520/523-2391.

A few blocks south of the University, **Riordan State Historic Park**, 1300 Riordan Ranch Road, Flagstaff, ☎ 520/779-4395, offers guided tours of Flagstaff's largest home, circa 1904. The log and volcanic rock structure contains original interior furnishings.

Lowell Observatory, 1400 West Mars Hill, Flagstaff, ☎ 520/774-3358, is where the planet Pluto was discovered in 1930. It's still a functioning space research facility and is just a mile west of downtown Flagstaff. A visitor center offers exhibits and a slide show about the observatory. You can also see the observatory's original 1896 telescope.

You can see stars for yourself through a modern telescope, not the 24-inch antique, several nights a week during the summer, once monthly the rest of the year. Call for schedules. You can also look through a telescope one night a week at **NAU Campus Observatory, ☎ 520/523-7170**.

You may see stars of a different nature at the **Museum Club**, 3404 East Santa Fe Avenue, Flagstaff, ☎ 520/526-9434, a genuine Western nightclub, complete with mounted trophy animals on display in a cavernous log cabin structure. The dance floor straddles five tree trunks. Check the schedule; big names have appeared.

Pioneer Historical Museum, 2340 North Fort Valley Road, Flagstaff, ☎ 520/774-6272, is two miles northwest of downtown on US 180. Displays focus on Flagstaff's pioneer history and include an 1880s pioneer cabin. An exhibit on Lowell Observatory's founder Percival Lowell includes a mechanical computer he built in the early 1900s. Other exhibits display the work of early local photographers, farm equipment and machinery, ranching and logging paraphernalia, old wagons, cars, and a stuffed bear.

Coconino Center for the Arts, 2300 North Fort Valley Road, Flagstaff, ☎ 520/779-6921, is a block north of the Pioneer Museum. It offers regional folk art exhibits, musical, dance and theatrical performances and workshops. The primary focus of the museum is on western and Indian arts and each year the center hosts a summer-long **Festival of Native American Arts**. From late June through early August, Indians from the Four Corners lead craft workshops and demonstrations as part of a special series of displays, dances, lectures, concerts, and theatrical performances related to the Indian cultures of the Southwest. For information contact **Festival of Native American Arts,** PO Box 296, Flagstaff AZ 86002, ☎ 520/779-6921.

Art Barn, 2320 North Fort Valley Road, Flagstaff, ☎ 520/774-0822, is next door to the Coconino Center and offers gallery sales of paintings, photographs, pottery, rugs, jewelry, and other regional creations.

Museum of Northern Arizona, 301 North Fort Valley Road, Flagstaff, ☎ 520/774-5211, is a mile northwest of the Coconino Center on US 180 and features a highly-regarded collection. Exhibits on archaeology, ethnology, biology, geology, Indian and Western fine arts, and modern Indian folk arts are displayed. One exhibit includes a replica kiva. There's also a well-stocked Southwestern bookstore and a large Southwestern research library.

An annual, 10-day **Hopi Artists Exhibition** has been a tradition for the last 60 years over the 4th of July weekend. Three weeks later, a **Navajo Artists' Exhibition** has been a successful annual event for the last 40 years.

A half-mile northwest of the Museum of Northern Arizona, **Shultz Pass Road** turns to the northeast for 12 scenic, unpaved miles, skirting the southeastern border of the San Francisco Peaks and the **Kachina Peaks Wilderness Area,** and passing to the west of **Mount Elden.** All are popular areas for outdoor recreation. It's a scenic, short drive that can usually be achieved in fair weather by passenger cars. It returns to the paved US 89 near Sunset Crater National Monument. From the end of the dirt road it's 11 miles south on US 89 to Flagstaff.

Oak Creek Canyon/Sedona

Sedona is 28 miles south of Flagstaff on US 89A. The two towns are separated by another remarkable piece of scenic geography called Oak Creek Canyon. The road descends 2,600 ft. on the trip. Coming down off the forested rim into Oak Creek Canyon, you pass through eight major plant communities, surrounded by vertical, monolithic red rocks and mazes of leafy subordinate canyons at 4,400 ft. elevation in Sedona. It's less than 30 miles south but the elevation change means Sedona is usually 15 to 20° warmer than Flagstaff, though still considerably milder than the scorching deserts and cities to the south.

The terrain includes the extremely popular Oak Creek area, **Slide Rock State Park,** eight miles north of Sedona on US 89A, and many other camping, fishing, horseback riding, biking and hiking spots. Four-wheel-drive tours are a booming industry here. It's all set amid dramatic canyons and rocks, borderland forests, stark mesas and buttes giving way from the cool alpine and evergreen slopes near Flagstaff, to the hot, deserts of southern Arizona.

Wildlife is apparently attracted to these climes; the area contains more than 50 species of mammals, approximately 175 species of birds, several dozen species of reptiles, and 20 species of fish living along Oak Creek amid more than 500 varieties of flowering plants.

For a small town of around 15,000 residents, Sedona's cachet as a world-class resort owes its foundations to the incredible scenery. Mountain-sized, smooth-faced, bare red rocks sprout through wreaths of low-lying, broad-leaf foliage, a fringe of greenery tracing the flow of Oak Creek. Sedona lies in a basin at the lower end of Oak Creek Canyon. The picturesque locale has attracted visitors, artists, and film makers to the area since the 1920s.

Sedona has had a long time to become a sophisticated tourist town, so inevitably commercial and public interests have made certain inroads on the natural environment. There are a lot of places to stay, including deluxe golf resorts and B&Bs, and there are excellent restaurants. There are around 40 art galleries and many, many shops, from unusual ones offering one-of-a-kind items, to factory outlets in the village of **Oak Creek,** south of Sedona on AZ 179.

An entire sub-culture of New Age believers in crystals, vortices, power centers, UFOs, and paranormal phenomena has also made a visible impact on Sedona. Several bookstores specialize in New Age materials. Racks throughout town offer brochures touting jeep tours, balloon flights, motels, restaurants, tarot-card readers, crystal and cosmic energy experts, fortune tellers, and spiritual healers.

Many claim, from one perspective or another, that the distinctive red rocks glowing through a palette of crimson shades according to the angle of the sun, the interplay of clouds and shadow, radiates extraordinary cosmic power. Enthusiasts postulate that, among other things, the vigorous energy emitted by **Bell Rock** stimulates activity while, in contrast, the soothing strength of **Cathedral Rock** reduces stress. It all has to do with so-called vortices, the places where powerful lines of energy that cross the earth intersect. Some people think that Sedona's supposed to be a magical place because it has as many as a dozen of these uncommon junctions nearby. To others, the vortex conception remains theoretical.

It is well-known that the iron-tinged red sandstone terrain provides a colorful landscape for extraordinary adventures, ranging from numerous guided tour options, including some to otherwise inaccessible areas, to roughing it on your own in the backcountry, to channeling the vibes – if that's the wavelength on which you're broadcasting.

Travelling south from Flagstaff on US 89A, you enter narrow **Oak Creek Canyon** nine miles south of Flagstaff. This is the preferred direction to travel for maximum scenic impact. You can get pretty good views of the canyon from a car but, if you want to look more closely, there are many turn-offs and parking areas with short walks to scenic view sites.

At the head of the canyon the rim drops away at **Oak Creek Overlook,** providing a view of 1,200-ft. canyon walls and the road dropping down through 15 twisting miles to Sedona, where the canyon walls are twice this size. Driving down the steep, narrow road, vegetation changes around each lowering switchback. At differing elevations each turn reveals a new perspective of the red, yellow, and white cliffs and rock forms that rise out of the mile-wide canyon. It's stunning anytime but be prepared for especially slow-going due to heavy traffic on a summer weekend, or in September and October, during Arizona's most colorful autumn display, as aspens, oaks, and maples shed their leaves. A good thing about fall travel is that, although the main roads are crowded, the backcountry is not.

Sterling Springs Fish Hatchery sits near the bottom of the switchbacks, at the head of Oak Creek. The rainbow and brown trout found in Oak Creek come from here.

About a mile farther south, adjacent to **Pine Flat Campground**, is a short but steep half-mile hike on **Cookstove Trail** to the East Rim.

Several miles farther south is **Slide Rock State Park**, PO Box 10358, Sedona AZ 86336, ☎ 602/282-3034, which was created to further environmental education. Its 286 acres include stunning red rocks, short and long hiking trails, orchards and a primal water theme park along Oak Creek, terraced rock pools and natural waterslides created over thousands of years.

There is, of course, the famous **Slide Rock**, a slippery but not-so-smooth chute (wear long pants and shoes) plunging into Oak Creek. Other wading or swimming areas in smaller pools stretch along the creek and broad tiers of horizontal red rocks beckon swimmers to dry out beneath the Arizona sun or just work on a tan. Many people do exactly these things – too many people for some tastes on a summer weekend. Picnic sites, a natural trail, a snack bar and restrooms are available. There is no camping permitted, although the park is open for day-use year-round.

Sedona has its surrounding scenery and well-honed tourism infrastructure offering abundant services to recommend it. Remarkable sites in town are mostly unique stores, resorts, or good restaurants. If you enjoy shopping or just browsing, and perhaps a round of tennis or golf followed by an excellent meal, you can find these things here.

Sedona Arts Center, at the north end of town on US 89A at Art Barn Road, ☎ 602/282-3809, is a good place to get a handle on the southwestern sensibilities favored by local artists. Local talent is featured in art exhibitions. Concert, dance, and theater performances are regularly scheduled here.

A popular site is the **Tlaqupaque Arts & Crafts Village,** a recreated Mexican village and market featuring restaurants, gift shops, and art galleries in a vine-draped, adobe-walled, tree-shaped courtyard complex. It's a quarter-mile south of US 89A, of AZ 179.

Three miles south of town on AZ 179, then a mile east on Chapel Road is the **Chapel of the Holy Cross,** set dramatically on a hilltop, nestled among the looming red rocks.

Shrine of the Red Rocks, two miles west of Sedona on US 89A, on **Table Top Mountain,** features a very large wooden cross and views looking down on the red rocks.

As for the most popular vortex sites, common interpretations credit Sedona's enchanted appeal to the sites' invisible powers of magnetism or electricity, their perfect Oriental balance of grace and harmony, or ancient mysteries contained here in hidden well springs of Indian shamanic wisdom – sometimes all of the above at once.

Regardless of the explanation, believers ascribe enhanced creativity, psychic talents, and sensations of passion to particular rocks.

Bell Rock Vortex, five miles south of US 89A, on the east side of AZ 179, between Sedona and the village of Oak Creek, is sometimes called the Electric Vortex. It is thought by some to be a preferred landing zone for extraterrestrial space travellers. **Cathedral Rock Vortex** is in West Sedona, situated 4½ miles west of AZ 179 on US 89A to Red Rock Loop Road. Turn south two miles to a "Slow" sign and follow signs for another 1½ miles on dirt roads to a parking area. Although quite solid in stature, some feel that this large rock radiates a tender tranquility. Its magnetic effects are said to project 500 yards from the rock, which is plenty of room for an idyllic picnic in its shadow.

Another vortex site is **Boynton Canyon Vortex,** the largest of the vortices and considered to radiate electromagnetism. Its effects are supposed to radiate several miles, but if you want to visit the actual spot northwest of Sedona go three miles west of AZ 179 on US 89A to Dry Creek Road, then north five miles on a well-signed route to a parking area and several hiking trailheads. It's a mile hike to reach the rock.

Other hiking trails wind among red hills, cliffs, and dry washes dropping from narrow canyons topped in pinyon and juniper.

Airport Mesa Vortex, another electric vortex, is a mile west of AZ 179 on US 89A to Airport Road, then south a few blocks to a parking area beside the road. The vortex is on the east side of the road and several short trails lead up a hill to a cliff overlooking the valley. The electrical energy can supposedly be felt over a field of 100 yards from the hilltop.

Capital Butte, Chimney Rock, and **Lizard Head** are other famous rock formations around town.

A site that has appeared in thousands of photographs illustrating Sedona is called **Red Rock Crossing.** It's four miles west of AZ 179 on US 89A, then south on paved Red Rock Upper Loop Road/Forest Road 216. Bear left after two miles onto Forest Road 216A for a half-mile to Red Rock Crossing. It's designated a day-use area by the Forest Service. There are picnic sites and areas where you can wade in Lower Oak Creek.

Schnebly Hill Scenic Drive starts east off AZ 179, a half-mile south of US 89A, and covers 12 partly paved miles, through red rocks and possibly the best scenic views of the area, to I-17, 20 miles south of Flagstaff. The road should be accessible to passenger cars.

South of Sedona

Cottonwood is 19 miles southwest of Sedona on US 89A. The town has motels and restaurants, plus an old western false front street in **Historic Old Town Cottonwood.**

Just north of town is **Tuzigoot National Monument,** PO Box 219, Cottonwood AZ 86326, ☎ 520/634-5564, site of excavated Sinagua Indian ruins 600 to 900 years old. A visitor center contains displays of artifacts retrieved from the ruins and exhibits pertaining to the Sinagua culture. A short trail leads from the visitor center to the ruins.

Dead Horse Ranch State Park, ☎ 520/634-5283, is located on the north end of Cottonwood, east of Tuzigoot, and offers fishing for bass, catfish and trout, hiking along the Verde River, and camping.

Little Clarkdale has some old buildings and it is the terminal for the **Verde River Canyon Rail Trip,** detailed below under *Rail Trips.* Clarkdale is two miles northwest of Cottonwood. For additional information contact **Verde Valley Chamber of Commerce,** 1010 South Main Street, Cottonwood AZ 86326, ☎ 520/634-7593.

Jerome, atop a hill overlooking Verde Valley, six miles west of Cottonwood on US 89A, is an old, partly restored copper mining boom town, now taken over by galleries, shops, bars, and cafés. Among sites of interest are the following:

❒ **Jerome State Historic Park,** ☎ 520/634-5381, is a museum of mining and local history situated in a 1917 mansion at the lower end of town.

❒ **Jerome Historical Society Mine Museum,** ☎ 520/634-5477, contains more mining era memorabilia on the corner of US 89A and Jerome Avenue.

❒ **Gold King Mine Museum,** ☎ 520/634-0053, has lots of big, old pieces of mining equipment on display and a petting zoo. Location is just a mile northwest of Jerome on Perkinsville Road.

For information contact **Jerome Chamber of Commerce,** 317 Main Street, Jerome AZ 86331, ☎ 520/634-5716.

To cover another interesting nearby area, drive east on AZ 260 from Cottonwood, or 15 miles south from Sedona on AZ 179 to I-17 at **Camp Verde.** AZ 260 continues east to **Clints Well** and ultimately northeast to **Winslow,** on I-40, midway between Flagstaff and the Petrified Forest. There's good hiking, biking, fishing, and camping through these areas, plus several interesting historic sites.

Three miles north of AZ 260 on I-17 is **Montezuma Castle National Monument,** PO Box 219, Camp Verde AZ 86332, ☎ 520/567-3322. It contains a five-story structure that you can see but not enter, built under a protective cliff by Sinagua Indians in the 1300s. The monument also has a campground and a visitor center featuring exhibits describing primitive but effective irrigation and farming techniques and clearly durable building techniques employed by Sinagua Indians and earlier Hohokam Indians.

Ten miles northeast of the castle is **Montezuma's Well**, a water-filled sinkhole measuring nearly 500 ft. across. This is also the site of other Indian ruins.

Two miles east of I-17 on AZ 260 is **Fort Verde State Historic Park**, Lane Street, Camp Verde AZ 86332, ☎ 520/567-3275. In the 1870s the US Army cavalry headquarters located here all but terminated local Indian disturbances. There are exhibits in four restored adobe structures, an administration building, commanding officer's quarters, doctor's office and bachelor's quarters. Displays cover frontier life, with illustrations pertaining to Indians, soldiers and their families, Indian scouts employed by the Army to root-out other Indians, and settlers.

Modern Indians have established the **Cliff Castle Casino**, I-17 and Middle Verde Road (Exit 289), PO Box 4677, Camp Verde AZ 86332, ☎ 520/567-9469.

For area information contact **Camp Verde Chamber of Commerce**, PO Box 1665, Camp Verde AZ 86332, ☎ 520/567-9294.

The **Yavapai-Apache Visitor Center,** ☎ 520/567-5276, sits beside I-17 at the Montezuma Castle/Camp Verde exit. Displays describe area attractions and travel information is available.

For details about public lands west and south of Camp Verde contact **Verde Ranger District**, Main Street, PO Box 670, Camp Verde AZ 86332, ☎ 520/4567-4121.

These include the 20,000-acre **Pine Mountain Wilderness**, 15 miles south of Camp Verde on I-17, then 20 miles east on a Forest Service Road. In addition, river rafters and kayakers can receive information from this office on running the Verde River south from Camp Verde as far as 60 miles to Horseshoe Lake. The best time of year for this trip is the desert spring, February and March. There are commercial river trips offered on the Verde River in late spring. See below, under *River Trips,* or contact the Chamber of Commerce for information.

For information about areas east and north of Camp Verde contact **Beaver Creek Ranger District**, Box 240, Rimrock AZ 86335, ☎ 520/567-4501. These regions include two exceptionally rugged wilderness areas where you are likely to discover solitude, wildlife, and swimming holes.

West Clear Creek Wilderness can be driven to 12 miles east of Camp Verde. It contains 13,000 acres of virtually pristine canyon country.

Wet Beaver Creek Wilderness is accessed 12 miles north of Camp Verde and east of I-17, adjacent to the Beaver Creek Ranger office.

In addition, the Beaver Creek office can supply information on the **General Crook National Recreation Trail,** a restored 135-mile section of a 200-mile-long military supply route initiated in the 1870s. It runs right through Camp Verde and starts 115 miles east, near **Show Low.** The western end of the trail is 20 miles west of Camp Verde.

For information about forests in the vicinity of Clints Well contact the **Blue Ridge Ranger Station,** Box 300, Happy Jack AZ 86024, ☎ 520/477-2255.

Petrified Forest/Painted Desert

From Sedona the quickest way to reach **Petrified Forest National Park** is to return to I-17 North and take I-40 east for 120 miles.

The shortest and most scenic route to the interstate is travelling east out of Sedona on **Schnebly Hill Scenic Drive** to I-17, 20 miles south of Flagstaff. Otherwise, you can drive north on US 89A, back through Oak Creek Canyon, or south on AZ 179 for 15 miles to I-17, 40 miles south of Flagstaff.

Seven miles east of Flagstaff on I-40, then three miles south on a well-signed paved road, is **Walnut Canyon National Monument,** Walnut Canyon Road, Flagstaff AZ 86004, ☎ 520/526-3367. The site was occupied by Sinagua Indians for 100 years in the 1100s. A visitor center displays ancient Indian tools and household items, along with descriptions of Sinagua life.

Two short trails start near the visitor center. **Island Trail** covers a paved mile and a descent from the visitor center of 185 ft. It leads to more than 20 ruins built into cliff walls. The half-mile **Rim Trail** is not as steep. It leads to several view sites and stabilized ruins.

Forty miles east of Flagstaff, 20 miles west of Winslow and south five miles on I-40, is **Meteor Crater,** a privately owned, enormous cavity created 50,000 years ago when a meteor hurtling through space crashed on this spot. Although the space rock was only 100 ft. in diameter, it made a hole nearly 600 ft. deep and more than 4,000 ft. wide.

A visitor center contains exhibits relating to meteorites and US lunar astronauts, who trained here during the Apollo program. Unlike the astronauts, you cannot go down into the crater but you may walk a 3½-mile rim trail encircling the world's first proven and best preserved meteorite impact crater.

Winslow is a convenient but unexciting city on I-40, 50 miles west of the Petrified Forest. Noted mainly for the profusion of motels and restaurants that dot the interstate through this community of 9,000, Winslow also has interesting natural areas.

McHood Park, ☎ 520/289-3082, five miles southeast of town, is operated by the city and offers fishing for catfish, trout and bass, boating, and a campground.

Two miles northwest of Winslow is **Homolovi Ruins State Park,** 523 West Second Street, Winslow AZ 86947, ☎ 520/289-4106, possibly one of the last areas occupied by Anasazi Indians. The park includes a half-dozen large and small pueblos among 300 archaeological sites. Nine miles of paved roads lead to various sites that include ancient Indian rock art panels and a cluster of 1,400-year-old pit houses. There is a visitor center with a small museum. A mile-long hiking trail leads to two main ruins sites.

Little Painted Desert County Park, ☎ 520/524-6161, 15 miles north of Winslow off AZ 87, contains 900 acres of Painted Desert scenery at 5,500 ft. There's a two-mile scenic drive and a mile-long hiking trail down into the eroded gullies at the bottom of 300-ft. hills, all shaded in differing muted, earthy colors that take on a spectral glow early or late in the day.

For area information contact Winslow Chamber of Commerce, 300 W. North Road, Box 600, Winslow AZ 86047, ☎ 520/289-2434. Winslow is served by major bus lines and **Amtrak,** ☎ 800/872-7245.

Holbrook, population 6,000, is 32 miles east of Winslow and 18 miles west of Petrified Forest National Park, on US 180. It provides the nearest accommodations, dining and picnic supplies to the National Park but mainly it's just an interstate pit-stop, replete with modest motels, restaurants and shops offering petrified wood specimens for sale. Stock up here. You're not allowed to pocket samples from the National Park. The oldest shops in town are **Sun West Trading Co.,** 905 West Hopi Drive, and **J &J Trading Post,** 104 Navajo Boulevard.

Navajo County Museum, 100 East Navajo Street, Holbrook AZ 86025, ☎ 520/524-6558 contains historic exhibits in a restored 1898 court house ranging from the prehistoric Indian era, through Wild West shoot-em-up days, up to contemporary scenes.

For area information, the **Holbrook Chamber of Commerce,** ☎ 520/524-6558, is in the same building and shares the same address with the museum.

The 93,533-acre **Petrified Forest National Park** can be reached either from the north by travelling 26 miles east on I-40 from Holbrook or, from the south, by travelling 18 miles east on US 180, which you pick up a mile south of Holbrook off AZ 77. The two routes lead you to opposite ends of a 28-mile scenic drive through the park.

This is the final stop before heading north to the **Navajo Reservation and Hopiland.** The suggested route through the park starts at the southern end of the drive and ends at I-40. You can make the drive from either direction.

The attractions of the Petrified Forest are more subtle than many of the other overwhelming sites in the Southwest but the austere, pastel-shaded hills contain more than 200 million years of fossils, including the world's largest concentration of petrified wood. These are ancient trees felled by primeval rivers then turned to stone by the interaction of minerals present in the water. The multi-colored, crystalline wood turned to stone looks like stained glass. When specimens catch the light they glimmer through a range of jeweled hues amid cacti and desert wildflowers.

Outside the park, just north of US 180, the **Petrified Forest Museum and Trading Post,** offering the last gas station and campground before entering the park, is across the road from **Crystal Forest Museum and Gift Shop.** These privately-owned shops sell rocks and exhibit some impressive specimens of petrified wood. Since the penalty for pocketing petrified wood from the park is jail time and a fine, these places offer a preferable alternative.

At Petrified Forest Trading Post you can actually pay a fee to gather samples from the 6,000-acre grounds. Rock hounds are given a map to the best sites. Hammer and chisel rentals are available.

Petrified Forest National Park, PO Box 2217, Petrified Forest National Park AZ 86028, ☎ 520/524-6228, has a year-round visitor center, food services, and ranger facilities at both ends of the scenic drive. There are no services in between for 25 miles. There are no camping facilities or other accommodations inside the park.

Backcountry permits are required for overnight camping in designated wilderness areas. These are available from the ranger stations along with backcountry maps and other information.

Rainbow Forest Museum and visitor center is two miles north of the south park entrance on the scenic drive. Exhibits portray ancient reptiles, sea creatures who lived here millions of years ago, and other ancestral area residents, including much more recent Anasazi Indians, who may have lived in the vicinity for nearly 1,000 years. There's a snack bar and a souvenir shop across the road and a picnic area nearby.

Behind the visitor center is a half-mile walking loop, **Giant Logs Trail**, lined with glittering fallen petrified logs, some five to six ft. in diameter.

Every few miles along the scenic drive are turn-offs for parking areas and short trails displaying more petrified wood. Among the more interesting stops are the following:

- ☐ A quarter-mile past the visitor center is a turn-off to **Agate House**, an unusual reconstructed Indian ruin. Seven hundred years ago it contained seven rooms made of bejeweled blocks of petrified wood. Park rangers rebuilt two rooms in the 1930s.
- ☐ Agate House is just off the main **Long Logs Trail** which covers a half-mile through the greatest convergence of petrified wood in the park, including numerous petrified tree specimens more than 100 ft. in length.
- ☐ Seven-and-a-half miles north of the visitor center is **Agate Bridge**, a large petrified tree. It's 111 ft. long, with its ends encased in sandstone, and stretches horizontally across an eroded ravine 40 ft. wide.
- ☐ Three miles north of Agate Bridge and three miles east on a side road, midway through the park, is **Blue Mesa**. A mile-long trail provides good, close-up views of badlands. It descends to the low, orange, red, white, and blue striped hills, sloping steeply above scattered samples of petrified logs.
- ☐ Three-and-a-half miles north of Blue Mesa, at **Newspaper Rock**, you can look through a telescope to see Indian petroglyphs carved into a big rock down below. A number of petroglyph sites in the park appear to be connected with solar cycles and primitive astronomy.
- ☐ A mile farther north are **Puerco Ruins**. They contain petroglyphs, a kiva and foundations of a 76-room pueblo that was abandoned 600 years ago.
- ☐ Six miles north of Puerco Ruins, a mile after you cross over I-40 into the northern section of the park, is the first of five **Painted Desert overlooks** of the epic expanses to the north and west.
- ☐ A sixth overlook, **Kachina Point**, nine miles north of Puerco Ruins, is also the trailhead for the backcountry at the north end of the park. It's adjacent to the **Painted Desert Inn Museum**, originally a Route 66 roadside inn in the 1920s, now a historic adobe structure with displays relating to the natural and human history of the

area. Two rooms contain murals by a famous Hopi artist and there is a good Southwestern bookstore in the basement.

❑ As you loop south toward I-40 from the northernmost point on the scenic drive there are two more overlooks of the Painted Desert. They show the most expansive and colorful part of the park, best appreciated in the early morning or late evening when the low angle of the sun casts long shadows. From the overlooks you can see the undulating layers of mineralized desert mauves, purples, reds, pinks, and oranges to the best advantage.

❑ A half-mile before returning to I-40 is the **Painted Desert Visitor Center,** featuring a film about the park, fossil displays, a ranger station for permits or information, a cafeteria dining room, a gift shop, and a gas station.

Adventures

Adventures in isolated backcountry can provide enlivening challenges, excitement, and fun. This may be one of the most hauntingly beautiful places you'll ever see, but it is still quite rugged. Lack of preparation can swiftly turn an outing into a disaster. A topographic map is a must for backcountry excursions. Always carry sufficient water for everyone (a gallon daily, per person), and it is highly recommended that you consult with Forest Service or BLM offices for updates on conditions and predicted weather changes. Roads and trails that are passable when dry may not be when wet. Canyon bottoms and washes may flood in sudden thunderstorms. River conditions change all the time. Extremely hot and dry weather can compromise your enjoyment in the shadeless backcountry. For state-wide weather reports call the **National Weather Service, ☎** 801/524-5133. For road conditions, ☎ 801/964-6000 or 800/492-2400.

For those preferring to engage the demands of the backcountry with a skilled guide, a number of reputable outfitters are included below. For additional information contact **Utah Guides & Outfitters,** 153 East 7200 South, Midvale UT 84047, ☎ 801/566-2662.

On Foot

LAKE POWELL RECREATION AREA

Nobody says much about hiking around Lake Powell. Most of the hiking near the lake is rugged and over difficult, unmarked trails. It is also spectacularly remote and uncompromised in the backcountry where you can find numerous arches, hidden canyons, and prehistoric sites. Areas to consider are near Rainbow Bridge National Monument, which is equally far from any of the major marinas, or the Escalante River Canyons, Grand Gulch Primitive Area, and Dark Canyon Wilderness, which are most easily accessed through the northern marinas at Hite, Hall's Crossing, or Bullfrog. Contact park rangers at Lake Powell marinas for information, or phone the National Park Service at ☎ 520/645-2511.

Of course, you can hike just about anywhere from a boat, but there are a couple of decent hikes accessible by car, too.

Wiregrass Canyon offers a three-mile backcountry hike to the lake, not far from the Glen Canyon Dam. Drive 10 miles north of the dam on US 89 to Big Water, then east on UT 277 to UT 12. It's 4½ miles south on Warm Creek Road to a sign that says *Wiregrass Canyon Backcountry*. You can park here. About a mile from the parking lot is a little stone arch.

The **Lower Escalante Canyons** are accessible around mid-lake on the north side, providing both easy and challenging terrain, from stream beds you can walk through, to slickrock configurations you must negotiate otherwise. Drive here through Escalante and Hole-in-the-Rock Road, or come by boat. No permit is required for day hikes, but overnight trips require a free backcountry permit available from the ranger station in Escalante, ☎ 801/826-5499 or 801/826-4315.

Flint Trail heads north from Hite Marina into the Orange Cliffs area. Numerous slickrock hiking options are possible, as well as backcountry camping overlooking Canyonlands National Park. This is also a popular mountain biking area.

A popular and relatively easy seven-mile hike is to **Rainbow Lodge Ruins**. The trail starts a mile past Rainbow Bridge National Monument on the San Juan Arm of Lake Powell, and leads southeast through **Horse Canyon** to the site of a once fashionable lodge that counts John Wayne and Teddy Roosevelt among its guests. Several other trails veer off to nearby arches and rock formations. From the same spot, east of Rainbow Bridge, you can hike 13 miles northeast to Navajo Mountain.

These hikes are on Navajo land. Hikers need permission from **Navajo Nation Recreational Resource Department,** Box 308, Window Rock AZ 86515.

Destiny Adventures, 52 6th Avenue, Page AZ 86040, ☎ 520/645-9496, operates daily hiking tours in the vicinity of Lake Powell, and rock climbing tours. You can register at the sports shop (outdoor gear, clothing and gifts) on 6th Avenue, or at the John Wesley Powell Museum.

ARIZONA STRIP

There are nine wilderness areas in the Arizona Strip plus portions of the Kaibab National Forest (see above, under *Touring*), all offering hiking possibilities for a few hours or days on end. Among these are the following:

Beaver Dam Wilderness, 20 miles south of St. George, Utah, accessed from an I-15 rest area, offers no trails but easy terrain leading through a Joshua tree forest.

In the **Mount Trumbull Wilderness Area,** 55 miles south of Fredonia, on the way to Toroweap Point, you can hike to the top of Mount Trumbull and back in a few hours. It's only a three-mile round-trip with an elevation change of 1,500 ft.

GRAND CANYON NATIONAL PARK

Any hiking into the Grand Canyon is arduous. It's frequently over 100° in the summer. At night, even in the summer, you will require some warm clothes. It's always cooler at the North Rim than the South Rim.

There are a few places on certain trails to stop for water but, for the most part, independent hikers need to plan on being self-sufficient and prepared for extreme conditions.

You don't need a permit for day-hiking. Reservations for accommodations at **Phantom Ranch** in the canyon bottom should be made, unless you plan on camping. A backcountry permit is required for overnight travel in the Grand Canyon. These permits are available by mail or in person from the **Backcountry Reservations Office,** Box 129, Grand Canyon AZ 86023, ☎ 520/638-2474.

The office is located on the South Rim, just south of the visitor center. Permits are also available from the **North Rim Ranger Station**, a quarter-mile north of the campground, and from the **Tuweep Ranger Station**, near Toroweap Point, west of Bright Angel Point. These sources are also good ones for backcountry hiking information.

The number of permits available in a given area at a given time is limited by park rangers. It's a good idea to plan as far ahead as possible. Reservations are accepted at any time for the rest of the year, and after October 1 for the following year.

There are a lot of interconnecting trails that can be hiked, though some are unmaintained. Experienced hikers with proper equipment, including ropes, can find many completely remote, off-trail areas to spend time. Depending on the time of year and conditions, it's a good idea to consult with park rangers for possible routes. Pick up a Grand Canyon hiking guide from the visitor center on the South Rim or at the Grand Canyon Lodge on the North Rim.

Unless you are in exceedingly good shape and ready for a major challenge, it's probably not wise to try to hike down to the Colorado River and back up in a single day. Even a very strong hiker would probably need at least 12 hours for the most direct round-trip. Most people plan on taking at least two days for the round-trip hike.

You need to carry water and food and generally be well-prepared for hot weather and no shade in summer. You need to have reservations for **Phantom Ranch** or established camping areas at **Indian Gardens, Bright Angel** or **Cottonwood;** no other camping is permitted on maintained park trails. Unmaintained trails are a different story; you still need a permit. Route-finding and map reading skills are essential to reach remote areas in the park where primitive backcountry camping is allowed.

It is possible to hire a mule to carry your gear to or from Phantom Ranch. For information see below, under *Grand Canyon, On Horseback*. If you decide to hike from one rim to the other and need a ride back, contact **Trans Canyon Shuttle, ☎** 520/638-2820.

If the logistics of self-sufficiency seem overwhelming, you don't have to go it alone into the Grand Canyon. A number of outfitters offer guided hiking trips, among them the following:

The busiest hiking concessionaire is probably **Grand Canyon Trail Guides,** Box 735, Grand Canyon AZ 86023, ☎ 520/638-2391, or **c/o Canyoneers/North Rim Hikes & Tours**, Box 2997, Flagstaff AZ 86003, ☎ 520/526-0924 or 800/525-0924. Their Grand Canyon office is adjacent to the Backcountry Reservation Office on the South Rim and is open April to October. They offer a number of standard guided hiking trips or customized trips year-round, plus equipment rental (hiking boots, backpacks, sleeping bags, tents, cook stoves, water purification kits, mountain bike rentals for guided tours only), and repair service. Among North Rim options are half-day to two-day guided hikes in the Kaibab National Forest from May to October. These trips leave from the Kaibab Lodge, on the Kaibab Plateau-North Rim Parkway, five miles from the North Rim entrance to the national park. For information on North Rim hikes from May 15-November 15 contact **Kaibab Lodge,** Box 30, Fredonia AZ 86022, ☎ 520/638-2389.

Museum of Northern Arizona Ventures, Route 4, Box 720, Flagstaff AZ 86001, ☎ 520/774-5211, runs a variety of guided hiking trips. Some involve extended hiking while others call only for short excursions from a car or motel. Trips are led by naturalists, biologists, geologists, and historians.

Expeditions, Inc., RR 4, Box 755, Flagstaff AZ 86001, ☎ 520/774-8176 or 520/779-3769, operates guided backpacking trips in the Grand Canyon. They also run a complete backpacking and river running store at 625 North Beaver Street, Flagstaff, ☎ 520/779-3769.

The Open Road, 1622 East Gardenia, Phoenix AZ 85020, ☎ 602/997-6474 or 800/766-7117, operates a variety of wilderness hiking and backpacking trips, with departures from Phoenix. These focus primarily on the Grand Canyon area but include a range of locales throughout the area. Grand Canyon trips are scheduled from January through November and include the following:

- ❏ A five-day backpacking trip in January, March or November, from the South Rim to the Havasupai Reservation.
- ❏ A four-day January backpacking trip from Grand Canyon Village to Bright Angel Campground.
- ❏ Day hikes to Angel Falls and Phantom Canyon.
- ❏ A five-day backpacking trip offered in March, April, and October from the South Rim, on the Hermit Trail, across the Tonto Trail to Indian Gardens and out on the Bright Angel Trail, including camping at Hermits Camp, Monument Creek, and Horn Creek or Indian Gardens.
- ❏ Five days hiking and camping in June on the North Rim of the Grand Canyon and Zion National Park.
- ❏ Nine days hiking and mountain biking in August on the North Rim of the Grand Canyon, Bryce and Zion National Parks.
- ❏ Other trips are also available.

Willard's Adventure Club, Box 10, Barrie Ontario, L4M 4S9 Canada, ☎ 705/737-1881 or 705/728-4787, offers guided eight- to 10-day expeditions into the Grand Canyon in April and May.

On an eight-day, late-April **Arizona Grand Canyon Base Camp Trip,** the tour meets in Las Vegas and travels to the South Rim. Five days of hiking are based out of dormitory accommodations at Phantom Ranch. The hikes vary from strenuous to easy and include hiking the Inner Canyon trails to Ribbon Falls, Clear Creek, and Indian Gardens.

A nine-day **Arizona Grand Canyon Expedition** in early May includes seven nights camping and six days hiking on a backpacking expedition exploring the North and South rims. It starts in Las Vegas and includes five nights at wilderness campsites within the Grand Canyon, with two nights of camping on the South Rim.

All Adventure Travel, 5589 Arapahoe Road, Suite 208, Boulder CO 80303, ☎ 800/537-4025, fax 303/440-4160, offers a Grand Canyon Hiker tour in May and October. It lasts six days and heads to the South Rim, including hiking Bright Angel Trail and to the Havasupai Reservation. An Indians of the Grand Canyon itinerary, offered the same months, is a six-day tour focusing on Indian culture and includes a scenic flight to the Havasupai Reservation and day hikes.

NORTH RIM

There are some easy trails on the North Rim. The following trails stay on the rim and lead to canyon overlooks.

Widforss Trail starts a quarter-mile south of the turn-off for Cape Royal, heading west off the North Rim road. It doesn't go down into the canyon but winds over milder terrain along the forested rim for five miles to Widforss Point, which affords views of Haunted Canyon and the South Rim. The 10-mile round-trip can usually be accomplished in six hours.

Ken Patrick Trail is another 10-mile rim trail that starts at Point Imperial and descends only 560 ft. to the North Kaibab Trailhead, which is two miles north of the Grand Canyon Lodge. You can hike three- or seven-mile portions of the trail. The entire hike should take six hours.

Another rim trail is the **Uncle Jim Trail,** which starts on the Ken Patrick Trail at the North Kaibab Trailhead, then veers southeast to

Uncle Jim Point for stunning rim views. The round-trip hike is five miles. This trail is also used for mule rides.

Then there are harder North Rim trails that descend into the Grand Canyon:

The most popular North Rim trail is probably the **North Kaibab Trail.** It starts just north of the ranger station, at the head of Roaring Springs Canyon, and covers 14 miles one-way, with a descent of 5,840 ft. to Phantom Ranch. In five miles, after a 3,100-ft. descent past vertical rock faces that shed water in rivulets after a storm, there is a picnic area with water available at Roaring Springs (at the head of Bright Angel Creek). There are also some swimming holes nearby and this is as far as most day-trippers go. It's another two miles along the creek to Cottonwood Campground, where there isa ranger station and water available in summer. You need reservations for the campground. In another mile and a half you can take a side-trip to verdant Ribbon Falls, before the trail bottoms out at Phantom Ranch and Bright Angel Campground.

From there you can hike back to the North Rim or cross a suspension bridge to continue up to the South Rim by the Bright Angel Trail or South Kaibab Trail. This is the only North Rim trail into the canyon with drinking water available along the way

Clear Creek Trail starts off the North Kaibab Trail, a quarter-mile north of Phantom Ranch, and covers nine miles along the bottom of the Grand Canyon to Clear Creek. There's additional rugged hiking in side canyons feathering off Clear Creek or you can hike up the creek to Chevaya Falls.

The only other North Rim trail in the vicinity of Bright Angel Point is **Nankoweap Trail** and it is definitely not for those who are afraid of heights, nor for those who don't know how to read a topographic map. Don't even think about this trail if you don't know what you're doing. It's a narrow and steep unmaintained trail that starts 2½ miles northeast of Point Imperial. The closest driving access to the trailhead is by Forest Road 610 or House Rock Buffalo Ranch Road, which are detailed above under *Touring, Arizona Strip.* From the end of either road it's a three-mile hike to the trailhead, then 14 miles to the river.

Several other difficult trails descend below the North Rim from points farther west that are accessible by back roads through the Kaibab Forest. They include the short but treacherous trail from the Toroweap area to Lava Falls.

To reach the trailhead you drive west on a jeep road midway between the ranger station and the campground. The trail starts where the road ends and descends a vertiginous 2,500 ft. in only two miles. Despite its brevity, the strenuous round-trip hike takes the better part of a day. As always, before tackling extreme backcountry, consult with park rangers for helpful hints and details on conditions.

SOUTH RIM

There are maintained and unmaintained trails all along the South Rim leading into the Grand Canyon.

One unmaintained trail, the 92-mile **Tonto Trail,** threads through the inner canyon, staying 1,200 ft. above the river, from mid-way on the East Rim Drive to far west of Hermit's Rest. It also links with many other rim trails. There are specified backcountry campsites along part of the Tonto Trail.

There are enough linked trails from the South Rim so that you can hike down one trail and back up a different one. The most popular South Rim trails are **Bright Angel Trail** and **South Kaibab Trail,** which are also used for mule-back trips.

Bright Angel Trail starts on the west side of Bright Angel Lodge and descends in the most easily managed steps to the Colorado River in eight miles. The steps include rest stops equipped with emergency phones and drinking water at 1½ miles and three miles from the rim.

It's 4½ miles from the rim to Indian Gardens Campground, and a bit over three miles from there to the river. Day hikers usually go as far as Indian Gardens. The more ambitious push on another 1½ miles past the campground to Plateau Point, a wedge of land protruding 1,300 ft. straight above the Colorado River and offering unobstructed views of the inner canyon in all directions.

River Trail connects a distance of 1½ miles from the bottom of the Bright Angel Trail to the bottom of South Kaibab Trail. It is bisected by two suspension bridges across the river to Bright Angel Creek and the North Kaibab Trail.

South Kaibab Trail starts from a trailhead 4½ miles east of Grand Canyon Village, near Yaki Point, and descends 4,800 ft. in the 6½ miles leading to the river. It's shorter and steeper than the Bright Angel Trail. The only emergency phone is 4½ miles below the rim at the Tonto Trail, which connects in four miles with Indian Gardens on the Bright Angel Trail.

Hermit Trail starts near Hermit's Rest at the end of the West Rim Drive and descends 4,300 ft. in 8½ miles to the river. A mile and a half from the rim it connects with a 1½-mile section of **Dripping Springs Trail,** for a good day-hike.

You can also connect with **Boucher Trail** from the Dripping Springs Trail and descend 3,500 ft. to the Tonto Trail, where there are signs to Boucher Creek, which leads 1½ miles to the river. Many hikers on multi-day trips then hike east on the Tonto Trail, back to Hermit Trail. Others make a multi-day loop by hiking the Hermit Trail to the Tonto Trail, then heading east along the Tonto Plateau to Bright Angel Trail.

There are hiking trails into the western end of the Grand Canyon's South Rim through the Havasupai Reservation. These require special permits from the tribe (see above, *Touring*).

Other trails are found along the South Rim's East Rim Drive.

Grandview Trail, from Grandview Point on the East Rim Drive, descends 2,600 ft. in three miles to Horseshoe Mesa, making an attainable round-trip day hike. If you want to continue, there are several trails that lead from the mesa to the Tonto Trail.

Farther east, along the East Rim Drive, **New Hance Trail** starts from a trailhead between Grandview Point and Moran Point. It descends 4,400 ft. in eight miles to the river at Hance Rapids, which is also the eastern end of the Tonto Trail. Rock cairns mark the faint **Escalante Trail** that extends for 15 miles upriver from Hance Rapids to Tanner Canyon Rapids.

Tanner Trail starts farther east, near Lipan Point on the East Rim Drive, and covers a 4,700-ft. descent in 10 miles to the river at Tanner Canyon Rapids.

Beamer Trail starts at Tanner Canyon Rapids and runs alongside the river for four miles to Palisades Creek. Another five miles takes you to the confluence of the Little Colorado River.

WILLIAMS/FLAGSTAFF

West of Flagstaff, near Williams, are a number of hiking areas that haven't yet seen the overcrowding that sometimes plagues areas such as Sedona's Oak Creek Canyon.

There are several easy trails at Dogtown Lake, seven miles southeast of Williams, including a two-mile loop around the lake and a short nature trail.

White Horse Lake, 19 miles southeast of Williams, is a year-round recreation area, providing nearby access to **Sycamore Falls Trail**, which is two miles north of White Horse Lake Resort on Forest Road 109. Two waterfalls are a short distance on the trail but they run only in rainy weather or during spring run-off.

Sycamore Trail covers 11 miles in Upper Sycamore Canyon and can be hiked for short or longer stretches with access through Sycamore Falls and several other trailheads.

Two trails to the top of Bill Williams Mountain are open June through September. **Bill Williams Trail** covers a seven-mile round-trip up the north side of the 9,255-ft. mountain. It starts from the Williams Ranger Station, 1½ miles west of Williams on the I-40 frontage road. **Benham Trail** covers a six-mile round-trip up the south side of the mountain. To reach the trailhead go three miles south of Williams on Fourth Street, then a half-mile west on Benham Ranch Road.

Information on Williams area trails is available from the Williams or Chalender Forest Service offices listed above, under *Touring, Williams/Flagstaff.* The same offices can provide information on the two following hiking areas:

An unusual trail is 33 miles northeast of Flagstaff, off US 180, 18 miles southeast of Valle. **Red Mountain Trail** is a short, easy hike through a cleft in the side of a volcanic cone leading directly into the crater. You don't have to climb up the 1,000-ft.-high volcano to get inside it, although you can reach the top by hiking or driving a rough dirt road. This is probably the most easily accessed volcanic crater in the Southwest.

Access to the small **Kendrick Peak Wilderness Area** is west of US 180, 15 miles south of the Red Mountain turn-off, 18 miles northwest of Flagstaff. Kendrick Peak, elevation 10,418 ft., is lower than the famous San Francisco Peaks to the east. A gravel forest road crosses the southern border of the wilderness area and several signed hiking trails lead north in six- to 12-mile round-trips to the peak. Trails are generally open June through September.

Flagstaff's great variety of trails, many within a short distance of the city, climb to the highest peaks in the state, wind through wilderness areas restricted to hiking or horseback access, and pass by Indian ruins and volcanic fields.

Many trails start right in Flagstaff from the Peaks Ranger Station on Santa Fe Avenue/US 89. The office is the main information source for trail guides and conditions.

Mount Elden Lookout Trail ascends steeply from the ranger station, climbing 2,400 ft. up the east slope in just three miles, for a 9,299-ft. view of Flagstaff, the area around Sunset Crater, and vistas far beyond in all directions.

Several other trails lead to the top of Mount Elden, including the five-mile-long **Oldham Trail**, which is not as steep as the Lookout Trail. It starts at the north end of town, off Cedar Avenue at **Buffalo Park Trail,** and ascends around 2,300 ft.

An easy day-hike to sample the scenery might cover a mile up the Oldham Trail from the Buffalo Park Trail, or a half-mile up the Elden Lookout Trail, then follow the level three-mile **Pipeline Trail** that connects the two trails around the base of Mount Elden.

Other popular hiking areas close to Flagstaff start from many trailheads along Shultz Pass Road or Mount Elden Road, both accessed three miles northwest of town, off US 180. Shultz Pass Road links US 180 with US 89 near Sunset Crater. Mount Elden Road climbs to the top of Mount Elden.

Rocky Ridge Trail starts at Schultz Creek Trail, 1½ miles north of US 180 off Shultz Pass Road, and connects with the Oldham Trail in two fairly level miles.

Sunset Trail starts four miles north of US 180 on Shultz Pass Road, at Shultz Pass Trail, and climbs 1,300 ft. in four miles to the top of Mount Elden.

Schultz Creek Trail covers three easy miles, linking the trailheads for the Rocky Ridge and Sunset Trails.

The Peaks Ranger Station also administers the Kachina Peaks Wilderness Area, encompassing 18,200 acres of the San Francisco Peaks, including Humphrey's Peak, Arizona's highest mountain at 12,633 ft., plus other impressive but slightly smaller mountains that are accessible only to hikers or horseback riders.

Two main trails into the Kachina Peaks area are accessible on the north side of Shultz Pass Road, across from the parking area at Schultz Pass Trail – the Weatherford Trail and the Kachina Trail.

Weatherford Trail was once an automobile road into the Kachina Peaks. Today, only hikers or horseback riders can use it to reach Humphrey's Peak in 10 miles.

Kachina Trail covers six miles, linking the main road and trails through the Mount Elden area with the main road and other trails through the Kachina Peaks Wilderness. It starts at either of two places – off Schultz Pass Road at 8,000 ft. or at the 9,300-ft. Snowbowl Ski Area. You could conceivably hike Kachina Trail to Sunset Trail and on to the top of Mount Elden.

The most direct access to Humphrey's Peak is from the ski area, seven miles northwest on US 180 to the Snowbowl Road, then north. On the way there's a short, easy trail five miles up the road from US 180. It starts beside a small parking area for the **Lamar Haines Memorial Wildlife Area**. The trail's a mile long and leads to a peaceful spring-fed pond.

At the end of the Snowbowl Road, seven miles north of US 180 at the ski area, **Humphrey's Peak Trail** covers a nine-mile round-trip to the 12,633-ft. summit of Arizona's tallest mountain. The trail starts in evergreen and aspen forests and emerges around

12,000 ft. into alpine tundra. It's usually free of snow June through September but the weather can change dramatically year-round so it's a good idea to pack foul-weather gear. No camping or fires are allowed above 11,400 ft. so most hikers make this a day-trip.

Humphrey's Peak Trail joins the Weatherford Trail 1½ miles from Humphrey's Peak, at around 11,800 ft. It's eight miles on the Weatherford Trail from there to Schultz Pass Road, or around three miles to the ski area on Humphrey's Peak Trail.

The **Inner Basin** day-use area on the north side of the San Francisco Peaks offers additional hiking trails ranging from 8,500 ft. to more than 11,000 ft. No overnight camping is permitted here. The turn-off to Forest Road 552 is a mile north of Sunset Crater off US 89. It reaches Lockett Meadow, site of several trailheads, in five miles. Parking and camping are permitted in the vicinity of Lockett Meadow.

Southeast of Flagstaff the terrain becomes less vertical, leveling into high, forested plateaus marked by lakes for fishing, boating, and camping.

There are some short hiking trails around Mormon Lake, and more extensive and challenging trails in the **West Clear Creek Wilderness Area**, between Happy Jack and Clints Well. Sometimes the only trail through the West Clear Creek Wilderness Area is the creek itself and hikers should be prepared to get wet. Floating gear on a small inflatable raft usually is a good way to keep it dry.

INFORMATION

Mormon Lake Ranger District Office, 4825 Lake Mary Road, Flagstaff AZ 86001, ☎ 520/556-7474.

Happy Jack Ranger Station, PO Box 68, Happy Jack AZ 86024, ☎ 520/527-7371. The office is on Lake Mary Road, 12 miles south of Mormon Lake.

Blue Ridge Ranger Station, Box 300, Happy Jack AZ 86024, ☎ 520/477-2255. The office is eight miles northeast of Clints Well, on AZ 87.

SEDONA

Despite the overcrowded conditions that sometimes compromise the allure of Sedona, hiking trails around Sedona and Oak Creek Canyon do eventually lead to out-of-the-way places, including narrow canyons stretching vertically hundreds of feet and wilderness areas where even four-wheel-drive vehicles cannot travel.

You can hike for an hour or week and the season runs year-round. It's hot in mid-summer and some areas get a fair bit of snow in winter. The following are a sampling of interesting, readily accessible trails out of the many the region offers.

Pumphouse Wash is not really a trail but you can trek over rocks and through the stream flowing in this side canyon for 3½ miles one-way. The lower trailhead is at the bottom of the switchbacks, next to the Pumphouse Wash Bridge, 13½ miles north of Sedona on the east side of US 89A. It's 800 ft. lower than the upper trailhead, which is 16½ miles north of Sedona on the east side of US 89A. There are good swimming spots along this route.

The popular **West Fork Trail** begins 10 miles north of Sedona, on the west side of US 89A in Oak Creek Canyon, 1¼ miles south of Cave Springs Campground. It covers 14 mostly level miles but you'll be getting your feet wet crossing the tributary of Oak Creek repeatedly. The first six miles of the trail contain dramatic vertical canyon faces and the flowing waters feed brimming foliage. Unique vegetation found here prompted designation of this portion of the trail as part of the Oak Creek Research Natural Area in the 1930s, long before it was incorporated into the Red Rock-Secret Mountain Wilderness Area. No camping or fires are allowed in this portion of the canyon.

Part of the reason day-hikes are popular along segments of this route is because the middle miles of the trail entail rock scrambling and possibly swimming, which tends to discourage all but the most intent backpackers. Towards the end of the trail at Woody Mountain Road/Forest Road 231, where you may want to have a car shuttle waiting, the trail gets faint.

At 1½ miles south of West Fork Trail, on the west side of US 89A across from Bootlegger Campground, is the start of the **East Pocket Trail**. It covers a strenuous two miles one-way, up more than 30 switchbacks and gaining 2,000 ft. in elevation to reach the East Pocket Fire Lookout, which provides 360° views of the canyon and surrounding landscape.

Red rock buttes and spires begin to appear prominently as you pass Slide Rock State Park. A mile north of the Encinoso Picnic Area, and 5½ miles north of Sedona, is **North Wilson Mountain Trail**. It covers 2½ miles one-way, gaining 1,700 ft. in elevation, to the top of Wilson Mountain. Another way to reach the same place is to drive south to Midgely Bridge, spanning Wilson Canyon, two miles north of Sedona. Wilson Mountain lies to the north and **South**

Wilson Mountain Trail offers a more gradual, but longer ascent of 2,300 ft. to the summit. It meets and merges with North Wilson Trail a little past half-way on the 5½-mile one-way hike.

Four miles west of AZ 179 on US 89A, in West Sedona, Dry Creek Road goes north for two miles to Sterling Canyon Road and Forest Service-maintained trailheads for Devil's Bridge Trail, Brins Mesa Trail, Secret Canyon, and **Vultee Arch Trail.**

Devil's Bridge Trail is a mile northeast of Dry Creek Road off Sterling Canyon Road. The short trail gains 400 ft. elevation in just under a mile, ending at the base of Devil's Bridge, a graceful natural arch. A side trail leads to the crown of the arch.

The trailhead for **Vultee Arch** is three miles farther on Sterling Canyon Road from the Devil's Bridge Trailhead. It gains 400 ft. in elevation covering 1½ miles one-way to a small natural bridge named after a pilot who crashed nearby in the 1930s.

Boynton Canyon, of vortex fame, is considered by many to be the strongest local power spot of all. It's also the site of the 2½-mile one-way **Boynton Canyon Trail** that gains 440 ft. in elevation, through the wooded red rock canyon filled with Indian ruins.

To reach the trailhead, follow directions to the north off US 89A in West Sedona onto Dry Creek Road. Beyond the turn-off for Sterling Canyon Road, Dry Creek becomes Boynton Pass Road. Watch for trailhead signs.

At the south end of the village of Oak Creek, south of Sedona on AZ 179, Jack's Canyon Road/Forest Road 793, goes east three miles to Jack's Canyon Trail. The 6½-mile trail climbs 2,000 ft., providing the main route into the 18,000-acre **Munds Mountain Wilderness Area.**

Jack's Canyon Trail ends in a saddle between Munds Mountain and Schnebly Hill. **Munds Mountain Trail** leads 2½ miles from the saddle, and another 450 ft. higher to the mountain top, which offers excellent views of the red rock scenery.

Complete trail and back road information is available from the Forest Service office in Sedona.

PETRIFIED FOREST NATIONAL PARK

Park rangers estimate that only one in a thousand visitors to the Petrified Forest ever hikes through the backcountry. There aren't even really trails out there; it's pretty much open desert terrain that you can wander through at will.

There are two designated wilderness areas in the park – **Rainbow Forest Wilderness**, filled with petrified wood, in the south, and **Painted Desert Wilderness** – a pastel-shaded barrens of low hills and badlands, in the north. Overnight camping is permitted in these areas; a backcountry permit is required and these are available at no charge from the visitor centers at the north or south park entrance.

The 7,400-acre Rainbow Forest Wilderness is accessed from the **Flattops Trail**, five miles north of US 180 off the scenic drive. The area contains a lot of petrified wood among eroded badlands and desert spiked by scrub grass. The trailhead, though, is only that; there are no proper trails in the wilderness area.

The 43,000-acre Painted Desert area is accessed a mile north of I-40, off the scenic drive, at **Kachina Point.** It contains the majority of ancient Indian sites found in the park, hidden ruins, and rock art amid gnomish badlands, with horizontally striated mesas and buttes extending to a distant horizon. The highest point in the park, 6,235-ft.-high Pilot Rock, is six miles from the trailhead. The trail, such as it is, descends only a short distance from Kachina Point. Then you're on your own to pick out an overland route.

On Horseback

There are a number of specific hiking guides published on trails in Northern Arizona and the Grand Canyon. Usually a selection of these are available at gift shops or bookstores in the area. Among the better ones are: *The Hiker's Guide to Arizona,* by Stewart Aitchison and Bruce Grubbs (Falcon Press, 1987); *Hiking the Southwest,* by Dave Ganci (Sierra Club Totebook, 1983); *A Naturalist's Guide to Hiking the Grand Canyon,* by Stewart Aitchison (Prentice Hall, 1985), which includes route maps for 30 Grand Canyon trails.

GRAND CANYON NATIONAL PARK

The famous mule trips into the Grand Canyon generally require reservations far in advance, although occasional cancellations do occur.

A variety of trips are offered year-round from the South Rim, but only in summer from the North Rim. These range from an hour to overnight. Even though you will be sitting, the trips are formidable and it does take some energy to hang on. If heights are bothersome to you, be aware that the mules step very close to the edge of the narrow trail and it's a long way down. In addition, there are restrictions applied to the mule trips: Riders must speak English, stand over 4'7" and weigh less than 200 pounds fully clothed. If you don't qualify or decide you'd prefer to hike, a mule can be hired to carry your gear.

North Rim mule trips are offered when the Grand Canyon Lodge is open, usually mid-May to late-October. For information contact the lodge or **Bryce-Zion-Grand Canyon Trail Rides, Inc.,** Box 128, Tropic UT 84776, ☎ 520/638-2292 or 801/679-8665 (off-season), which runs one-hour to full-day trail rides at the North Rim.

South Rim mule trips are run under the auspices of **Grand Canyon National Park Lodges,** PO Box 699, Grand Canyon AZ 86023, ☎ 520/638-2401. They offer popular one- or two-day mule rides into the canyon on the Bright Angel Trail. Day-trips go as far as Plateau Point. Overnight trips cross the river and include accommodations at Phantom Ranch. The return to the South Rim the following day is accomplished on the South Kaibab Trail.

From mid-November through mid-March, three-day, two-night mule trips to Phantom Ranch are available, allowing an extra day to explore the river and the bottom of the canyon.

Make reservations as far in advance as possible. Booking space a year ahead of time is common. Information and reservations are also available from the **Bright Angel Transportation Desk,** ☎ 520/638-2631.

Apache Stables, PO Box 158, Grand Canyon AZ 86023, ☎ 520/638-2891 or 520/638-2424, is at Moqui Lodge, a quarter-mile south of the park's south entrance. The stables offer one- or two-hour trail rides, a half-day East Rim ride, and a campfire wagon and trail ride.

Wild & Scenic, Inc., Box 460, Flagstaff AZ 86002, ☎ 520/774-7343 or 800/231-1963, runs five-day horseback trips to the Grand Canyon, Zion, and Bryce Canyon National Parks.

Havasupai Tourist Enterprises, Supai AZ 86435, ☎ 520/448-2121, operates overnight mule trips to Havasupai Canyon.

FLAGSTAFF

Hartman Outfitters, 448 Lake Mary Road, Flagstaff AZ 86001, ☎ 520/774-7131, runs horseback rides daily (May to September) from the Hitchin' Post Stables into Walnut Canyon, the ancient home of cliff-dwelling Sinagua Indians. The canyon is said to be five miles and 100 years from town. The choice of trips include breakfast rides, steak rides, one- or two-hour rides, half-day, full-day or multi-day rides, all offering opportunities to see pictographs, explore caves or hiking trails from the ranch campsite where meals are provided and overnight camps are made. Also, horse-drawn wagon rides are available.

Hitchin' Post Stables of Flagstaff, 448 Lake Mary Road, Flagstaff AZ 86001, ☎ 520/774-1719, offers a variety of trail rides.

Ski Lift Lodge Stables, US 180 and Snowbowl Road, Flagstaff AZ 86001 ☎ 520/774-0729, runs trail rides in the San Francisco Peaks.

SEDONA

Kachina Stables, Lower Red Rock Loop Road, PO Box 3616, West Sedona AZ 86340, ☎ 520/282-7252 or 800/SADDLEUP, offers year-round trail rides among the red rocks to supposedly sacred Indian ceremonial sites. Scheduled rides are offered for one or two hours, or a full day. Customized overnight pack trips are also available.

El Rojo Grande Ranch, PO Box 4143, Sedona AZ 86340, ☎ 520/282-1898, offers horseback trips and trail rides.

Blazing Trails, PO Box 3430, Camp Verde AZ 86322, ☎ 520-567-6611, operates horseback trips and trail rides southeast of Sedona.

On Wheels

PAGE & LAKE POWELL

Most people come to Lake Powell for the water, not the jeeping possibilities, which are limited by the fact that the area east of Page is largely Navajo land and is not generally open to unsupervised visitation. The best bet is to take a guided jeep tour with **Lake Powell Jeep Tours**, 108 Lake Powell Boulevard, Page AZ 86040, ☎ 602/645-5501.

ARIZONA STRIP/GRAND CANYON (NORTH RIM)

Jeeping/Four-Wheel-Drive Trips

There's a network of back roads through the Arizona Strip leading to the North Rim of the Grand Canyon. These are not the best roads although the Forest Service does consider them passable in ordinary cars in good weather. Four-wheel-drive is a much better idea; make sure you start with a full tank of gas plus extra water and food. Tools and spare parts are not a bad idea. There should be signs along the way but these could be missing at certain points, so be sure to have a good map along.

The roads from **St. George** and **Pipe Springs** are maintained to some extent, but it's a long drive to the North Rim on any of these roads and you're unlikely to find help in an emergency. The road to the North Rim from **Colorado City** is the shortest but also in the worst condition. The last few miles to Toroweap Point are very poor. Remember: No water, gas, food, or any other supplies are available anywhere along these routes, and no services are available once you reach these remote areas of the North Rim.

The best road of the lot heads south off AZ 389, six miles east of Pipe Springs National Monument, and runs through deserted backcountry for 40 miles until it joins another dirt road, heading south from AZ 389, near Colorado City. This second dirt road covers 45 miles from AZ 389 to the wilderness junction. From there, it is another 20 miles south to **Toroweap Point** (sometimes called Tuweep) on the North Rim.

There is a year-round Tuweep Ranger Station a few miles north of a primitive campground at Toroweap. From the Point, you have the opportunity to experience the Grand Canyon at its narrowest, barely a mile across. The Colorado River flows through 3,000 ft. below and the voices of river rafters float up the tight canyon walls.

Mountain Biking

You can't ride a bike on park trails, but you can ride one on specified park roads on the North and South Rims. Better biking may be found outside the park in areas of the Arizona Strip, such as **Antelope Valley, Mount Trumbull** and **Mount Logan**, and **Kaibab National Forest**. The dirt roads through the Arizona Strip to Toroweap Point or other remote viewpoints make challenging bike trips. For details see above, under *Touring* and *Jeeping*, or contact the ranger station south of Jacob Lake for maps and information.

The rough jeep road to **Cape Solitude** from the East Rim Drive is a difficult, 30-mile, multi-day bike trip. You need a backcountry permit to camp.

AZ 67, from Jacob Lake to the North Rim, has been called one of the prettiest roads in America. There's not as much traffic as along roads leading to the South Rim, but there is traffic, so bikers beware of large travel trailers and the like.

On the South Rim heavy vehicle traffic takes some of the fun out of biking, but the **West Rim Drive**, though closed to cars in summer, is open to bicyclists. The **East Rim Drive** can make for good biking in low season, but not when contending with summertime traffic.

There are no bicycle rental facilities close to or in the park so you must bring your own from elsewhere. The Kaibab Lodge (see above, under *Hiking*), near the North Rim, rents bikes for guided tours only.

There are extensive back roads between Grand Canyon Village and the Havasupai Reservation, west of AZ 64/US 180, as well as east of the highway in the Kaibab National Forest, south of the East Rim Drive.

If you plan to camp here you will need a backcountry reservation, available at the ranger station. For other ways to obtain the permit, see below, under *Camping*.

Other dirt roads eventually leading to Toroweap Point start south from **Hurricane** and **St. George**, in Utah. Of these, the one from St. George is probably the better.

Also in this area are several fascinating BLM-maintained petroglyph sites. Little Black Mountain Petroglyph Site, and Nampaweap/Billy Goat Canyon are detailed above, under *Touring, Arizona Strip*.

Museum of Northern Arizona Ventures, Route 4, Box 720, Flagstaff AZ 86001, ☎ 520/774-5211, runs four-wheel-drive tours on the Colorado Plateau, offering an alternative to ranging through this area on your own.

Another possibility for touring this area is to check with operators based out of Kanab, Utah.

GRAND CANYON NATIONAL PARK (SOUTH RIM)

Jeeping/Four-Wheel-Drive Trips

A rough dirt road starts north from **Desert View** on the East Rim Drive and covers 15 miles to Cape Solitude, overlooking the confluence of the Colorado and Little Colorado rivers. Other rugged and remote roads branch off to more backcountry. Consult with park rangers for reports on road and weather conditions.

Several gravel and dirt roads head west from AZ 64/US 180 in the vicinity of Tusayan, more or less paralleling the South Rim all the way to Tribal Route 18, south of Hualapai Hilltop on the Havasupai Reservation. Take good maps.

WILLIAMS/FLAGSTAFF

Jeeping/Four-Wheel-Drive Trips

The only road access to the **Sycamore Canyon Wilderness Area** is 23 miles southeast of Williams at **Sycamore Canyon Point.** A panoramic view site overlooks the west rim of the 21-mile-long, six-mile-wide canyon. To reach the overlook, drive eight miles south of Williams on Fourth Street, then 15 miles east on Forest Road 110.

The seasonal road to the top of **Bill Williams Mountain** is probably more enjoyable in a four-wheel-drive. It starts five miles south of Williams on Fourth Street, then heads west for seven miles to reach the 9,255-ft. peak. The road is open May to October.

Flagstaff's back roads are plentiful. A popular jeep route is **Mount Elden Road** to the top of 9,299-ft. Mount Elden, just north of town. The road starts three miles north of downtown, a little north of the Museum of Northern Arizona. Continue driving straight (east) when Shultz Pass turns left to the north. Numerous hiking and biking trails cross the road before it reaches the mountain top. The view encompasses Flagstaff, Oak Creek Canyon, the Painted Desert, volcano fields, including Sunset Crater, and mountains.

North of Sunset Crater and west of US 89, a network of jeep roads leads to remote hiking trails of the Inner Basin of the San Francisco Peaks. These north slope trails are open only to hikers and horseback riders. You can drive to the lower trailheads, west to US

180, in 14 miles. From there it's 20 miles southeast on US 180 to Flagstaff.

The area southeast of Flagstaff is laced with four-wheel-drive roads, many leading to good fishing lakes. For details see below, under *Fishing*.

Mountain Biking

There's good biking in the forests around Williams. The curlicue road to the top of **Bill Williams Mountain,** 4½ miles south of town, is a challenging seven-mile ride to the 9,255-ft. summit. Three miles south of that turn-off are several gravel roads leading to White Horse Lake and Sycamore Canyon Point.

There are hundreds of miles of bike routes surrounding Flagstaff on all sides. Right in town is the **Urban Trails System & Bikeways System.** It connects the university area with downtown. Contact the visitor center or university for information.

A major network of bike trails traverses the Mount Elden area on the north end of Flagstaff.

The longest trail to the top of Mount Elden starts in North Flagstaff, at the Buffalo Park Trailhead, off Cedar Avenue. **Oldham Trail** climbs 2,300 ft. of the west side of Mount Elden in five miles.

Other major trail access is off Schultz Pass Road or Mount Elden Road, three miles northwest of downtown Flagstaff, and north off US 180.

Shultz Pass Road edges the San Francisco Peaks and the Kachina Peaks Wilderness northwest of Flagstaff for 12 miles to US 89. You can bike back to Flagstaff in 10 miles along US 89.

Sunset Trail starts four miles north of US 180 on Shultz Pass Road, at Shultz Pass Trail, and climbs 1,300 ft. in four miles to the top of Mount Elden.

Mount Elden Road is a longer but more gradual ascent of six miles on a rugged jeep road that starts where the Shultz Pass Road turns north, a mile north of US 180.

An easy 4½-mile ride, on mostly level ground, starts on the Oldham Trail but turns east after one mile onto the **Pipeline Trail.** The trail follows the base of Mount Elden to the **Elden Lookout Trail,** a half-mile from the Peaks Ranger Station. Elden Lookout Trail goes to the top of Mount Elden from there in 2½ miles. It's a steep climb of 2,400 ft. and suitable only for strong and fearless bike riders.

The forest office, on North Santa Fe Avenue/US 89 at the Elden Trail, can provide current information on the entire Mount Elden trail network.

Four miles northwest of Shultz Pass Road on US 180, the seven-mile **Snowbowl Road** offers a steep, 2,000-ft. ascent to the ski area. The fun part of this is the descent.

Flagstaff Nordic Center, ☎ 520/774-6216, 15 miles northwest of Flagstaff on US 180, offers bike and equipment rentals. It opens its cross-country ski trail network to bike riders from May through September.

A moderate road is the bike route through **Wupatki** and **Sunset Crater National Monuments** off US 89, north of Flagstaff. It covers 35 miles one-way so you might consider a vehicle shuttle.

There's a network of jeep roads good for biking four miles north of Sunset Crater on US 89, then west across the northern boundary of the Kachina Peaks Wilderness and the San Francisco Peaks. You can't ride a bike in the wilderness area, but you might ride on rough forest roads from US 89 to US 180 in 14 miles. From there it would be 20 road miles on US 180 southeast to Flagstaff.

Information on area biking routes is also available from the following Flagstaff bike shops. They provide sales, service, and rentals.

- ☐ **Absolute Bikes**, 18 North San Francisco Street, ☎ 520/779-5969.
- ☐ **Cosmic Cycles**, 113 South San Francisco Street, ☎ 520/779-1092.
- ☐ **Mountain Sports**, 1800 South Milton Road, ☎ 520/779-5156.
- ☐ **Southwest Cycle Expeditions**, PO Box 30731, ☎ 520/526-4882, rents bikes and related equipment, and offers guided bike tours throughout the Four Corners, including Verde Valley, Oak Creek, Sedona, and the Grand Canyon.

Rail Trips

Grand Canyon Railway, 123 North San Francisco Street, Flagstaff AZ 86001, ☎ 520/773-1976 or 800/843-8724, runs a train, powered by a turn-of-the-century steam locomotive. Trips run to the South Rim of the Grand Canyon from I-40 in Williams. Passengers ride in authentically restored 1920s Harriman Coach cars and there is on-board entertainment that includes a fake train robbery, as well as complimentary refreshments.

Since there are free shuttles available at the South Rim and traffic is a problem, this is certainly a legitimate alternative mode of transportation that helps ease overcrowding and allows you to sit back and enjoy the scenery. Round-trip service is available daily and if you're planning to stay at the Grand Canyon you can arrange to take the train back when you need.

SEDONA

Jeeping/Four-Wheel-Drive Trips

Some of Sedona's back roads are challenging while others are threatening. It's helpful to know the difference. A large number of visitors opt for guided jeep tours rather than independent journeys, and a considerable number of operators fill that need.

Guided jeep tours to vortex and ceremonial sites, isolated backcountry, overnight camping trips, or jeeping and hiking combination tours are offered by numerous companies. Friendly competition runs high among the most popular guides, who are known for their humorous routines. Most jeep tours operate year-round.

Pink Jeep Tours, 204 North US 89A, Box 1447, Sedona AZ 86339, ☎ 520/282-5000 or 800/283-3328, runs some of the most popular one- to three-hour, scenic, vortex and historic jeep tours in the backcountry around Sedona, including some over rugged terrain.

Sedona Red Rock Jeep Tours, 270 North US 89A, PO Box 10305, Sedona AZ 86339, ☎ 520/282-6826 or 800/848-7728, competes with Pink Jeep Tours for exciting trips and the funniest guides. Their Cowboy West Tour explores Sedona's western history on Soldiers Pass Trail, an old cavalry route from the 1870s, and Sedona's Indian history, including how Indians lived off the land and why the red rocks were sacred to them.

Another tour follows the Old Bear Wallow Stage Route and emphasizes opportunities to photograph wildlife such as elk, deer, great blue herons, wild turkeys, and red foxes. Also: customized photography tours can be arranged to suit a photographer's specifications.

The same company operates **Sacred Earth Tours,** 260 North US 89A, Sedona AZ 86339, ☎ 520/282-6826 or 800/848-7728, offering what they claim to be Sedona's original authentic vortex tour, visiting the sacred spots of concentrated energy.

In addition, full-day ancestral Hopi Mesa tours are offered, including stops at three Hopi villages on First Mesa and craft demonstrations.

Time Expeditions, 276 North US 89A, PO Box 2936, Sedona AZ 86339, ☎ 520/282-2137 or 800/999-2137, offers a variety of scheduled trips that consider the vortices scientifically. The specialty of the company is its historic Indian ruins tours. Customized tours are also available.

Sedona Adventures, 273 North US 89A, Suite C, PO Box 1476, Sedona AZ 86339, ☎ 520/282-3500 or 800/888-9494, offers two-hour jeeping and hiking tours, vortex tours, and overnight tours.

Earth Wisdom Tours, 293 North US 89A, Sedona AZ 86336, ☎ 520/282-4714 or 800/482-4714, specializes in vortex trips with an unabashed New Age-slant; driver-guides are versed in the domain of crystals, auras, healing plants, and Indian symbolism.

INFORMATION

Tours

Dorian Tours-Spirit Steps, PO Box 3151, Sedona AZ 86340, ☎ 520/282-4562 or 800/728-4562.

Kiva Serenity Tours, 135 Kiva Drive, Sedona AZ 86336, ☎ 520/282-5696, specializes in archaeology and geology tours.

Roadrunner Tours, 841 AZ 179, PO Box 498, Sedona AZ 86339, ☎ 520/282-4696.

Sedona Nature Excursions/Mystic Tours, 10 Traumeri Lane, Sedona AZ 86336, ☎ 520/282-6735.

Sedona Photo Tours, 252 North US 89A, Sedona AZ 86336, ☎ 520/282-4320 or 800/973-3662.

Tuzigoot International Tours, PO Box 2052, Cottonwood AZ 86326, ☎ 520/639-2844.

Four-Wheel-Drive Rentals

Arizona Jeep Rentals, Sedona Airport, PO Box 902, Sedona AZ 86336, ☎ 520/282-2227.

Canyon Jeep Rentals, 4548 North US 89A, Sedona AZ 86336, ☎ 520/282-6061 or 800/224-2229.

Desert Jeep Rentals, 6626 AZ 179, Sedona AZ 86351, ☎ 520/284-1099.

For back roads information and maps contact **Sedona's Chamber of Commerce** (☎ 520/282-7722 or 800/288-7336) or the local Forest Service office.

Rail Trips

Verde River Canyon Excursion Train, PO Box 103, Clarkdale AZ 86324, ☎ 520/639-1630 or 800/293-RAIL, fax 520/639-1653, is based out of Clarkdale, 30 minutes southwest of Sedona by car. The two-hour train ride winds through Coconino and Prescott National Forests and has been compared to the Durango-Silverton train for scenic splendor with a southwestern flair. It follows the Verde River through red rock scenery to Perkinsville, a small ranch site, and is the only way, aside from travel on foot, to view the riparian habitat of numerous bird and wildlife species, including many bald eagles, as well as Indian ruins, in this federal wilderness area that has no roads.

Passengers travel in pullman-style coach seats or first class cars that are more like living rooms, with access to open-air gondola cars for sightseeing and photography. The train operates year-round, Wednesday through Sunday, with extra Monday departures and two departures daily in April, May, October, and November. There is food and beverage service on board. Moonlight rides are offered in June, July, and August. Room, ride and meal packages may be purchased. They include overnight accommodations at the Railroad Inn in Sedona (see below under *Accommodations*).

Mountain Biking

Just about anywhere you bike around Sedona is going to be scenic. Roads in the immediate vicinity of Oak Creek Canyon and Sedona are bound to be heavily trafficked, but back roads and trails are still a good bet for getting away from it all.

The 28-mile ride down **Oak Creek Canyon** from Flagstaff on US 89A to Sedona is a nice downhill road trip if there's not too much traffic. Try starting early in the morning and avoid weekends.

Red Rock Loop Road, south of US 89A in West Sedona, to Red Rock Crossing is a short, easy ride to a beautiful spot.

Schnebly Hill Scenic Drive, from Sedona to I-17, includes a steep ascent of Schnebly Hill on the 11-mile ride. A lot of bike riders turn around midway and enjoy the easy coast back into town.

Bicycle rentals and information on area biking trails are available from the following Sedona bike shops:

- **Mountain Bike Heaven**, 1695 West US 89A, Sedona AZ 86336, ☎ 520/282-1312.
- **Sedona Sports**, 245 North US 89A, Sedona AZ 86336, ☎ 520/282-6956.

On Water

LAKE POWELL

You could spend a lifetime boating in the secluded coves and bays of Lake Powell and never see it all. Swimming is great at numerous Lake Powell beaches, with big rocks to leap from into the turquoise waters. Activities abound – jet skiing, houseboatins, waterskiing, people picnicking along the shore, or floating in the shallows in an inner tube, dragging a fishing pole. Summer is by far the busiest season at Lake Powell, but it gets hot, with daytime temperatures routinely topping 100°. You can rent or buy virtually any equipment you might need out here at the marinas, but be sure to make houseboat rental reservations far in advance. There are currently around 300 houseboats and 250 powerboats available for rent, as well as all kinds of personal watercraft, but these are snatched up quickly on the 4th of July or any summer weekend. Fall is a much quieter time to visit. The water is still warm and great for swimming, but the air temperatures are much lower.

Year-round marinas at **Hite Crossing, Bullfrog Basin, Halls Crossing**, and **Wahweap** are operated by **ARA Leisure Services**, PO Box 56909, Phoenix AZ 85079, ☎ 602/278-8888 or 800/528- 6154, or fax 602/331-5258. All offer boat rentals for fishing, waterskiing, or houseboating on the enormous lake, as well as tours to Rainbow Bridge and other sites.

A floating marina at **Dangling Rope**, ☎ 520/645-2969, a quarter of the way up the 186-mile-long lake, can only be reached by boat. There is a ranger station, a store, and gas. Addresses and phone numbers for the ARA-operated marinas are listed above, under *Touring*. Additional information regarding marinas, boat tours and rentals, plus accommodations and restaurants, may be obtained from ARA Leisure Services. The following are a variety of Explorer Packages available through ARA.

☐ **The Rainbow Explorer** trip combines a full- or half-day 100-mile guided tour from Wahweap or Bullfrog to Rainbow Bridge, side trips to several major canyons, lunch, and two nights' lodging.

☐ **Colorado Combo Explorer** includes a half-day Colorado River float trip from Glen Canyon Dam to Lee's Ferry, a day-tour to Rainbow Bridge and three nights' accommodations at Wahweap Lodge.

☐ **A Famous Monuments Explorer** offers three nights accommodations at Wahweap Lodge, a full-day guided cruise to Rainbow Bridge, a half-day tour of Monument Valley, plus a scenic flight over both sites.

☐ **Houseboat-Lodging Explorer** packages combine a one-night houseboat rental with one night's lodging or two nights' RV space at any of the ARA marinas.

ARA's houseboat rentals are particularly popular for navigating the scenic miles of Lake Powell. The lake offers astounding red rock side canyons, some displaying Indian rock art or ruins, while others are blissfully quiet spots to fish, calm waters beneath scenic buttes, spires and multi-colored striated cliffs that may be explored on foot. If you prefer, just kick back with a cocktail on the deck. Self-sufficient houseboats, which are similar to floating motor homes, range in size from 36 ft. to 50 ft., and are available for rent year-round. The lowest rental prices are from November to March. Boating instructions are included with rentals. You can also rent an 18-ft. powerboat to tow behind a slow-moving houseboat for daytime cruising and exploring, or other water equipment, such as waterskis and jet boats.

There are National Park Service-operated boat ramps and campgrounds at all the marinas, except Dangling Rope, and each also has a ranger station.

Sailboating is popular around Wahweap Bay and Bullfrog Bay, where the most reliable winds are found, although storms and high winds can, of course, make any sort of boating treacherous.

Scuba diving allows you to explore Indian ruins that were covered by water when the lake was created by flooding Glen Canyon.

Blue Water Adventures, 697 North Navajo, Page AZ 86040, ☎ 520/645-3087, is a full-service dive shop and offers guided trips for snorkelers and scuba divers, including overnight camping trips to Lake Powell.

Probably the most popular trip on Lake Powell is to Rainbow Bridge National Monument, 50 miles up the lake from Wahweap, and the same distance down the lake from Bullfrog or Hall's Crossing. The colorful, 290-ft.-tall, 275-ft.-wide natural bridge is the largest in the world and is instantly recognizable to anyone who has browsed through the local postcard displays. The actual site is accessible only by water, or by rugged foot or horseback trails through Navajo land. No camping is permitted at Rainbow Bridge.

Other worthwhile sites on the lake include Antelope Island, south of Rainbow Bridge, which was a campsite for the first white explorers in the area, and Cha Canyon, 10 miles east of Rainbow Bridge on the San Juan River Arm, which is filled with ancient Indian rock art.

Wilderness River Adventures, 50 South Lake Powell Boulevard, Page AZ 86040, ☎ 520/645-3279 or 800/528-6154, runs raft trips below Glen Canyon Dam and Lake Powell, on the Colorado River to Lee's Ferry. These excursions pass through the only land remnant of the original Glen Canyon.

The Jet Ski M.D., 136 Sixth Street, PO Box 3966, Page AZ 86040, ☎ 520/645-3121, provides sales, service and repairs, along with a rental hotline for waverunners and jet skis.

High Image Marine Center, 920 Hemlock Avenue, PO Box 2004, Page AZ 86040, ☎ 520/645-8845, provides sales and service for small and large boats plus all personal watercraft. They stock marine supplies and accessories as well as RV parts. A rental department offers boats, jet skis, waterskis, skurfers, kneeboards, tubes, hydrosleds, water worms, windsurfers, beach canopies, diving equipment, wet suits, and camping equipment.

Doo Powell, 130 6th Avenue, Page AZ 86040, ☎ 520/645-1230 or 800/350-1230, rents personal watercraft.

Outdoor Sports Lake Powell, 861 Vista Avenue, Page AZ 86040, ☎ 520/645-8141, provides sales and service along with rentals of boats, waverunners, water toys, kneeboards, waterskis, and rod and reel sets.

Lake Powell Tours, PO Box 40, St. George UT 84771, ☎ 520/645-2263, operates two- to five-day boat-camping tours of Lake Powell, Rainbow Bridge, Stevens Arch, and Hole-in-the-Rock. Guests are provided with all transportation, meals and snacks, plus camping and sleeping gear. Departures from April to October.

Lake Powell is 186 miles long, with 1,960 miles of shoreline. The many species of fish found here include largemouth, smallmouth, and striped bass (up to 30 pounds), carp, catfish, walleye, northern pike, perch, bluegill, and sunfish. March to November is the most popular fishing season, but the lake is open year-round and doesn't freeze, so fishing is possible any time.

Inquire at the marinas for the best places to fish. Experienced anglers head to the most remote waters up the various canyon arms, such as the extensive Escalante River Arm, past Hole-in-the-Rock, or the West Canyon Arm, 10 miles south of Dangling Rope. The ubiquitous houseboats seen on the lake are usually equipped with a fishing boat trailing behind on a tow line.

Since most of Lake Powell is in Utah, a Utah fishing license is required for those waters. To fish the Arizona portion of the lake, approximately the lower five miles, you need an Arizona fishing license. Appropriate licenses are available at the marinas.

Arizona Reel Time, PO Box 169, Marble Canyon AZ 86036, ☎ 520/355-2222, runs guided fishing trips for largemouth, smallmouth or striped bass on the lake plus trophy trout fishing trips below the Glen Canyon Dam at Lees Ferry.

GRAND CANYON

River Trips

This is the cat's meow as far as Southwestern river trips are concerned, offering adventure, exploration, and discovery. You travel though time on this stretch of the Colorado River, back a billion or so years into prehistory. You can touch and climb rocks millions of years old and visit prehistoric Indian sites. Watch for the wildlife such as bighorn sheep, deer, birds, and reptiles, along with contrasts in vegetation, from desert cacti on precipitous canyon slopes to cottonwoods and thirsty ferns near waterfalls. Retrace the steps of explorers and challenge the rapids.

Just about all the experts agree that the best times of year for the Grand Canyon are April to May and September to October. Be aware that on partial canyon trips, put-in or take-out will require hiking a 5,000-ft.-deep trail. Sometimes arrangements can be made for mule-back transportation and there are several guided trips offering helicopter transportation. To facilitate cooperative scheduling, arrangements should be made through your outfitter.

Only concessionaires licensed by the National Park Service are allowed to run trips through the canyon. A number of tour operators offer Grand Canyon trips but these are operated through licensed concessionaires.

It probably pays to shop around for the trip that best suits your interests. Outfitted trips are run in paddle- or oar-powered rafts, motorized rafts, and wooden dories. Their duration ranges from day-trips to three-week expeditions.

The main boat launching area for Grand Canyon river trips is at Lees Ferry, northeast of the National Park. The boat ramp there also provides access to the trophy rainbow trout fishing waters between Lees Ferry and the Glen Canyon Dam.

For additional information or reservations for any Grand Canyon river trips, contact the **River Subdistrict Office,** Grand Canyon National Park, PO Box 129, Grand Canyon AZ 86023.

Rivers & Oceans, PO Box 40321, Flagstaff AZ 86004, ☎ 520/525-4575 or 800/473-4576, is also a central reservation office for Grand Canyon river trips.

For experienced river runners it is possible to create your own private river trip through the canyon, but start planning early. There is quite a bit of Park Service bureaucracy to wade through for the appropriate permit, and the current wait for private permits is six to eight years. For information phone the **River Permits office,** ☎ 520/638-7843.

The following outfitters offer a variety of river running options through the Grand Canyon:

O.A.R.S. Inc., Box 67, Angel's Camp CA 95222, ☎ 209/736-4677, fax 209/736-2902, runs five- to 15-day river trips from April to October in wooden dories, oar-powered rafts, paddle-boats, or inflatable kayaks.

Colorado River & Trail Expeditions, PO Box 57575, Salt Lake City UT 84157-0575, ☎ 801/261-1789 or 800/253-7328, fax 801/268-1193, offers rowing through the canyon in April or August and motorized trips of four, six, or nine days from May to September. All trips include opportunities for off-river hiking explorations.

ARA's Wilderness River Adventures, PO Box 717, Page AZ, ☎ 520/645-3296 or 800/992-8022, offers motorized and oar-powered trips through the canyon. Itineraries include four- or six-day trips from Lees Ferry to Phantom Ranch, five or seven days from Phantom Ranch to Bar 10 Ranch, or seven or 14 days from Lees Ferry to Bar 10 Ranch. Also available are one-day float trips from Glen Canyon Dam to Lees Ferry. Customized trips and charters are also offered.

Arizona Raft Adventures, 4050 East Huntington Drive, Flagstaff AZ 86004, ☎ 520/526-8200 or 800/786-7238, fax 520/526-8246, runs river trips with participant involvement in rowing and paddling. The trips include hiking, swimming the small rapids, helping in the kitchen, learning the natural history, or just relaxing; you can do as much or as little as you want. Trips scheduled from April to October begin and end in Flagstaff and include eight-day itineraries in motorized rafts, or six- to 14-day trips with a choice of vessels.

Special interest trips include a Natural History Lab trip, emphasizing geology, origins, botany, climate, and environmental impacts of the Glen Canyon Dam. Also offered are professional seminars and psychologist-led outdoor retreats. Two- to six-day trips are offered from April to September on the San Juan River in Utah. Customized special interest trips may be arranged for groups of 16 or more.

Grand Canyon Dories, PO Box 216, Altaville CA 95221, ☎ 209/736-0805, runs river trips in dories, a compartmentalized, rough-water, motorless boats made of aluminum, fiberglass, or marine plywood. These vessels ride higher and drier than rafts, don't bend or buckle in the waves, and don't get soft when it's cold. A guide travels in each boat but you can take the oars and learn to run the rapids. Another option is to test your skill in a two-person inflatable kayak.

Groups are limited to a maximum of 20 people per trip. If you're seeking a longer, slower, quieter voyage, as compared with other Grand Canyon river trips, with time to observe, understand and savor the canyon from the water and the land, this is for you. A 277-mile trip takes 16 days. Five- to 11-day trips are also offered from Lees Ferry or Phantom Ranch. You do need to hike in or out of the canyon or arrange for mule-back transportation to participate in a shorter trip. Full-length trips start and end in Flagstaff. Also available: Grand Canyon rafting trips of six, eight or 13 days; six-day trips in June through Desolation and Gray Canyons on the Green River; nine-day trips in June on the Colorado River through Canyonlands National Park; eight-day trips on the San Juan River in May or June.

A 47-day trip retracing the complete voyage of John Wesley Powell is offered from Green River, Wyoming to the Virgin River arm of Lake Mead, in Nevada. The Powell trip is divided into four portions of eight, 10, 12 and 17 days that may be taken separately.

Grand Canyon Expeditions, PO Box 0, Kanab UT 87471, ☎ 801/644-2691 or 800/544-2691, fax 801/644-2699, runs the entire 277-mile length of the Grand Canyon from April to September on eight-day motorized or 14-day oar-powered dory and raft trips.

Trips emphasize comfort and safety in negotiating nearly 200 rapids while passing through one of the earth's most spectacular geological exhibits. They've had 25 years to perfect their skills while running specialized trips for the National Geographic Society, Smithsonian Institution, and Cinemax, among others. Scheduled special interest trips highlight canyon history, geology, photography, ecology, archaeology, and astronomy. Trips include round-trip transportation from Las Vegas, sleeping bags and pads, ground cloth and rain shelter, waterproof river bags for sleeping gear, cameras and personal items, all meals on the river, cold beer, soft drinks, wine or champagne with evening meals, and ice is available throughout the trip. Customized charters are also offered.

Outdoors Unlimited, 6900 Townsend-Winona Road, Flagstaff AZ 86004, ☎ 520/525-9834 or 800/637-7238, runs trips from May to October in oar- or paddle-powered boats that hold five to six passengers and a guide. Itineraries include 12-day trips from Lees Ferry to Lake Mead, five-day trips from Lees Ferry to Phantom Ranch, and eight-day trips from Phantom Ranch to Lake Mead. Trips starting at Lees Ferry include overnight accommodations at Marble Canyon. Trips ending at Lake Mead include shuttle service to Las Vegas.

Western River Expeditions, 7258 Racquet Club Drive, Salt Lake City UT 84121, ☎ 801/942-6669 or 800/453-7450, fax 801/942-8514, offers six-day motorized trips through the Upper Grand Canyon, or three- and four-day trips in the Lower Grand Canyon, including helicopter transfers to or from the Colorado River below Lava Falls. Once a year they run a 12-day rowing trip. Trips are scheduled May to September.

Museum of Northern Arizona Ventures, Route 4, Box 720, Flagstaff AZ 86001, ☎ 520/774-5211, runs Grand Canyon rafting trips.

American River Touring Association, 24000 Casa Loma Road, Groveland, CA 95321, ☎ 209/962-7873 or 800/323-2782, runs six- to 13-day Grand Canyon raft trips.

Arizona River Runners, Box 47788, Phoenix AZ 85068-7788, ☎ 602/867-4866 or 800/477-7238, runs three- to eight-day Grand Canyon rafting trips.

Canyoneers, Inc., Box 2997, Flagstaff AZ 86003, ☎ 520/526-0924 or 800/525-0924, runs two- through 14-day Grand Canyon trips in motorized rafts or paddle-powered rowboats. Seven-day, six-night trips in powered pontoon boats cover the whole 277 miles from Lees Ferry to Pierce Ferry. Two-day, two-night trips in the same motorized vessels cover 89 miles from Lees Ferry to Bright Angel Beach, near Phantom Ranch. A 14-day, 13-night paddle-powered row boat trip covers 225 miles from Lees Ferry to Pierce Ferry and includes round-trip transportation from Flagstaff.

Canyoneers also operates the Kaibab Lodge on AZ 67 north of the North Rim. Among a variety of tours they offer are winter cross-country ski trips.

Canyon Explorations, Box 310, Flagstaff AZ 86002, ☎ 800/654-0723, runs six- to 15-day Grand Canyon raft trips.

Diamond River Adventures, Box 1316, Page AZ 86040, ☎ 520/645-8866 or 800/343-3121, runs four- to 12-day motorized and oar-powered river trips through the Grand Canyon.

Expeditions, Inc., RR 4, Box 755, Flagstaff AZ 86001, ☎ 520/774-8176 or 602/779-3769, runs five- to 18-day Grand Canyon river trips. Five- to six-day trips cover 87 miles and entail a nine-mile hike out of the canyon at the end. Eight- to nine-day trips cover the second portion of the Grand Canyon for 139 miles and require a seven-mile hike to the put-in spot. Twelve- to 18-day trips cover 226 miles on the river.

Trips are in oar-powered rafts with options available for those who prefer paddle boats or kayaks. All trips include leisure time and hiking time for exploring side canyons. Also included is transportation from Flagstaff to Lees Ferry or the Grand Canyon, depending on the put-in point. Return transportation from Diamond Creek is provided at the end of the full Grand Canyon trip to Flagstaff. All trips include a sleeping bag and foam pad, vehicle and valuables storage at a Flagstaff warehouse, all meals, plus hotel and motel pick-up in Flagstaff.

Complete outfitting services, tent and pack rentals, and shuttle services for vehicles to the South Rim or Diamond Creek are available. Customized trips for special interests, such as kayaking clinics, management training seminars, art and photography workshops, and experiential education programs are also offered.

Georgia's Royal River Rats, Box 12057, Las Vegas NV 89112, ☎ 702/798-0602, runs three- to eight-day Grand Canyon river trips.

Moki Mac River Expeditions, Box 21242, Salt Lake City UT 84121, ☎ 801/268-6667 or 800/268-6667, runs six- to 14-day Grand Canyon oar-powered raft trips, or eight-day motorized raft trips.

Sleight Expeditions, Box 40, St. George UT 84770, ☎ 801/673-1200, offers five- to 12-day Grand Canyon raft trips.

Ted Hatch River Expeditions, Box 1200, Vernal UT 84078, ☎ 801/789-3813, or 800/433-8966, has seven-day Grand Canyon rafting trips.

Tours West, Inc., Box 333, Orem UT 84059, ☎ 801/225-0755 or 800/453-9107, offers three- to 12-day Grand Canyon rafting trips.

Wild & Scenic, Inc. , Box 460, Flagstaff AZ 86002, ☎ 520/774-7343, or 800/231-1963, runs trips of a half-day to 13 days in rafts or sportyaks on the Colorado River through the Grand Canyon.

Hualapai Tribal River Trips & Tours, PO Box 246, Peach Springs AZ 84634, ☎ 520/769-2219 or 602/769-2210, runs one- or two-day raft trips from Diamond Creek on the Colorado to Pearce Ferry on Lake Mead. Two-day trips include one day of rapids.

If the number of rafting tour operators on the Grand Canyon seems daunting, a one-stop free booking service known as **River Travel Center,** ☎ 800/882-RAFT, represents 16 Grand Canyon river outfitters with 3-18 day itineraries in oar, paddle or motor rafts. The service can provide information, brochures and confirm reservations for a variety of departure dates.

The national park's **River Permit Office,** ☎ 520/638-7843, can provide a complete list of licensed river concessionaires.

Fishing & Boating

Some of the prime waters for rainbow trout fishing are along the 15-mile stretch of the Colorado River between the Glen Canyon Dam and Lees Ferry. There is a boat ramp at Lees Ferry and a Park Service-maintained fish cleaning station.

You need a trout stamp and an Arizona fishing license to fish in the national park. These are available from the **Park Service,** ☎ 520/638-2262, from **Babbitt's Store,** in Grand Canyon Village, or from several concessionaires who run guided fishing trips.

Fishing in the trophy waters north of Lees Ferry is an adventure. There are several endangered species of fish in these waters and these must be thrown back. For details contact the ranger station next to the Lees Ferry Campground (see below, under Camping), or contact the various lodges in Lees Ferry that offer guided fishing trips (see below under *Accommodations*).

Ambassador Guide Service, ☎ 520/355-2228 or 520/771-8627, offers guided fishing trips of a half-day or full day at Lee's Ferry. All trips are catch and release, with lunch included on full day trips.

Large rainbow trout can sometimes be found in Bright Angel Creek, accessible from the North Kaibab Trail off the North Rim. Other creeks below the North and South Rims may have good fishing at times, especially in the fall and winter months. Consult with park personnel regarding conditions.

VERDE

River Trips

Canyon River Equipment Outfitters, PO Box 3493 Flagstaff AZ 86003-3493, ☎ 520/526-4663 or 800/637-4604, fax 520/526-4535, runs guided whitewater raft, cataract, canoe, inflatable, and kayak trips on the Verde River, as well as the Lower Colorado River through the southern part of the Grand Canyon and the San Juan River in Utah. They can also provide complete outfitting for private river runners, including food, equipment rental (rafts, canoes, kayaks or inflatables) and shuttle packages.

River Otter Canoe Company, 458 South 1st Street, PO Box 2655, Camp Verde AZ 86322, ☎ 520/567-4116, offers canoe rentals and Verde River tours.

WILLIAMS/FLAGSTAFF

Fishing & Boating

There is fishing and boating available at four Forest Service campgrounds in the vicinity of Williams. For details see below, under *Camping*.

Information on fishing and boating site regulations in the area is available from a local office of **Arizona Game & Fish Department**, 310 Lake Mary Road, Flagstaff AZ 86001, ☎ 520/774-5045.

For information about the following areas contact the **Mormon Lakes Ranger District**, 4825 Lake Mary Road, Flagstaff AZ 86001, ☎ 520/556-7474.

Close to Flagstaff, **Upper and Lower Lake Mary**, eight miles southeast on Lake Mary Road, are stocked with catfish, walleye, and northern pike. There are boat ramps on both lakes. You can water-ski on the upper lake. There is a Forest Service campground.

Ashurst Lake, 18 miles southeast of Flagstaff on Lake Mary Road, and four miles east on Forest Road 82E, offers fishing for rainbow trout, a boat ramp, and two campgrounds.

You can also fish for rainbows in **Coconino Reservoir**, a mile south of Ashurst Lake. Under the same jurisdiction is **Mormon Lake**, 20 miles southeast of Flagstaff on Lake Mary Road, containing 2,000 acres stocked with northern pike and catfish. The average water level is only 10 ft. (sometimes lower), so there's no waterskiing or boat ramp. You carry your boat into the water and, if that's not enough exercise, there are short, easy hiking trails in the area. Two campgrounds, two lodges offering room or cabin accommodations, a café, and store are situated by the lake. The area is also popular for winter sports.

Kinnikinick Lake lies 25 miles southeast of Flagstaff on Lake Mary Road, near the south end of Mormon Lake, then 11 miles east on Forest Roads 125 and 82. There are trout in the lake. There is also a boat ramp and a free campground.

Stoneman Lake, 8½ miles farther south from the turn-off for Kinnikinick Lake on Lake Mary Road, then six miles east on Forest Road 213, has been the location for state record-setting catches of yellow perch. There is a boat ramp but no campground.

SEDONA

Fishing & Boating

Rainbow and brown trout are stocked in Oak Creek. Other cold water fish found mainly in **Upper Oak Creek** include cutthroat trout, grayling, sunfish, smallmouth bass, and bluegill. The water is warmer farther south and four species of warm water catfish – yellow, channel, black, and flathead – are found in **Lower Oak Creek,** along with largemouth bass and carp.

Grass-hopper Point, two miles north of Sedona, is a popular spot along Oak Creek for rainbow and brown trout.

There is fishing for a fee at **Rainbow Trout Farm, ☎** 520/282-3379, three miles north of Sedona off US 89A in Oak Creek Canyon. You don't need a license and they supply the gear.

Dead Horse Ranch State Park, on the north end of Cottonwood, east of Tuzigoot National Monument, offers fishing for bass, catfish, and trout. There is also a campground here.

Guided fishing trips in the Flagstaff/Sedona/Oak Creek area can be arranged by **Flagstaff Mountain Guides,** PO Box 2382, Flagstaff AZ 86003, ☎ 520/526-4655.

WINSLOW/HOLBROOK

Fishing & Boating

McHood Park, ☎ 520/289-3082, located five miles southeast of Winslow, offers swimming, boating, camping facilities and fishing for catfish, trout, and bass.

Twenty-four miles east of Winslow, off I-40 at Joseph City, is **Cholla Lake Park.** It offers boating and fishing in the shadow of a power plant.

On Snow

ARIZONA STRIP/GRAND CANYON NATIONAL PARK

There's an active winter sports area from Jacob Lake south on AZ 67 to the North Rim.

Canyoneers, Inc., Box 2997, Flagstaff AZ 86003, ☎ 520/526-0924 or 800/525-0924, operates the winter sports facilities in the Kaibab National Forest between Jacob Lake and the North Rim. From December to March there are various tour packages available that include accommodations, meals, and equipment rentals.

Guided tours and a helicopter service from the South Rim to Kaibab Lodge are also offered. Canyoneers-operated facilities include the following:

❏ The **North Rim Nordic Center** is a half-mile south of Jacob Lake on Forest Road 579 and offers 30 kilometers of groomed cross-country ski trails, guided backcountry tours, equipment rentals, and instruction. This is the only Kaibab Forest facility that you can reach by car. You can park here and ski to the following areas or Canyoneers can provide transportation.

❏ **Kaibab Lodge,** 26 miles south of Jacob Lake, is usually snowed-in during the winter but you can ski in or take a shuttle.

❏ Accommodations are available at the lodge or across the road at the **North Rim Winter Camp,** ☎ 520/638-2383, next to the North Rim Country Store. The winter camp provides mostly backcountry skiing access and accommodations in heated Mongolian yurts.

Most tours leave from the lodge, some from the winter camp. **Papillon-Grand Canyon Helicopters** (see below, under *In Air*) operates helicopter service to the Kaibab Lodge in winter from the South Rim.

All North Rim services within the park are closed in winter but you can ski in. There are no groomed ski trails in the national park. Camping is permitted with a backcountry permit.

WILLIAMS

The mountains near Williams offer cross-country skiing, snowmobiling, plus ice fishing for trout or catfish at **White Horse Lake**, 19 miles southeast of town.

The small **Williams Ski Area**, ☎ 520/635-9330, is on the 9,255-ft. **Bill Williams Mountain**, five miles south of town. Vertical drop is only around 700 ft. Downhill and cross-country ski rentals are available.

Cross-country skiing is popular on Forest Service land 20 miles northeast of Williams. For information and maps contact the Chalender Ranger District office (see above, under *Touring Flagstaff*).

Arizona Snowbowl, ☎ 520/772-1951, is 14 miles northwest of town and offers four chairlifts, more than 30 downhill trails, and a vertical drop of 2,300 ft. Conditions are highly variable throughout the December-through-March ski season, so it's a good idea to call ☎ 520/779-4577 for current reports. Equipment rentals are available and there is a ski school.

Cross-country skiing is offered at **Flagstaff Nordic Center**, ☎ 520/774-6216, providing 26 miles of groomed trails for all levels of skiers, telemark skiing areas, ski rentals, and instruction. The area is 15 miles northwest of Flagstaff on US 180.

Backcountry skiing is popular in the San Francisco Peaks. Several forest roads located 10 miles northwest of Flagstaff, and north of US 180, lead to such areas as Wing Mountain and Hart Prairie. For information contact the Peaks Ranger District Office (see above, under *Touring Flagstaff*).

Mormon Lake Ski Center, ☎ 520/354-2240, is 20 miles southeast of Flagstaff, then eight miles south on Mormon Lake Road, across from the Mormon Lake Lodge. The center offers 26 miles of groomed trails, equipment rentals, and instruction.

Montezuma Nordic Ski Center, ☎ 520/354-2221, four miles north of Mormon Lake at Montezuma Lodge, near Dairy Springs Campground, offers 13 miles of groomed trails, equipment rentals and instruction.

In Air

GRAND CANYON NATIONAL PARK

Grand Canyon scenic flights are not allowed to go below the rim, but they're still pretty spectacular.

Grand Canyon Airlines, Box 3038, Grand Canyon AZ 86023, ☎ 520/638-2463 or 800/528-2413, offers scenic flights over the canyon from the Grand Canyon Airline Terminal, Grand Canyon Airport, near Tusayan, six miles south of the South Rim visitor center. Hourly flights are operated by two pilots in a 19-seat, twin-engine Vistaliner. The wings are over the top of the plane so they don't obstruct the view.

Air Grand Canyon, Main Terminal, Grand Canyon Airport, PO Box 3339, Grand Canyon AZ 86023, ☎ 520/638-2686 or 800/247-4726, guarantees window seats and provides video camera hook-ups. Also: Customized flight itineraries are available.

Air Star Helicopters-Airlines, Main Terminal, Grand Canyon Airport, PO Box 3379, Grand Canyon AZ 86023, ☎ 520/638-2622 or 800/962-3869, runs scenic flights in fixed-wing aircraft or helicopter tours.

Windrock Aviation, Main Terminal, Grand Canyon Airport, PO Box 3125, Grand Canyon AZ 86023, ☎ 520/638-9591 or 800/247-6259, offers scenic flights over the Grand Canyon, Monument Valley, and Lake Powell, plus customized tours. Narrated flights are in high-wing aircraft and every seat is by a window.

The following operators offer scenic helicopter flights departing from Grand Canyon Heliport, on AZ 64, a mile and a half south of the lower entrance to the National Park.

Papillon Grand Canyon Helicopters, Box 455, Grand Canyon AZ 86023, ☎ 520/638-2419 or 800/528-2418, offers 30- or 50-minute scenic flights over the Grand Canyon. Also available are six-hour air and ground trips to Havasu Falls by helicopter and horseback, or overnight trips including accommodations at Havasupai Indian Village. Also offered are helicopter flights to Kaibab Lodge in winter for flight/ski packages.

Kenai Helicopters, Box 1429, Grand Canyon AZ 86023, ☎ 520/638-2412 or 800/541-4537, offers scenic flights over both rims of the Grand Canyon.

FLAGSTAFF

Alpine Air Service, ☎ 520/779-5178, has scenic flights to Meteor and Sunset craters, Sedona and Oak Creek Canyon from Flagstaff's Pulliam Field, five miles south of town off I-17.

SEDONA

Air Sedona/Scenic Airlines Sedona, 235 Air Terminal Drive, Suite 3, Sedona AZ 86336, ☎ 520/282-7935 or 800/634-6801, at the airport south of town off US 89A, offers local tours, longer scenic flights adding the Grand Canyon and the Havasupai Reservation, or deluxe tours to Meteor Crater, Lake Powell, Canyon de Chelly, and Monument Valley. Also: Charter flights and customized tours are available.

Other fixed-wing scenic flights and charters are offered by the following operators:

- ☐ **AeroVision,** #70 Hangar Drive, Sedona AZ 86336, ☎ 520/282-4498 or 800/779-8904, operates scenic flights over Sedona's red rocks, the Grand Canyon, Monument Valley, and Lake Powell. Also: Charters and special tour flights are available.
- ☐ **Air Safari,** 1225 Airport Road #2, Sedona AZ 86336, ☎ 520/282-3485.
- ☐ **Scenic Airlines Sedona,** 235 Air Terminal Drive, Suite 3, Sedona AZ 86336, ☎ 520/282-7935 or 800/634-6801.
- ☐ **Sedona Sky Treks,** 30 Cedar Court, Sedona AZ 86351, ☎ 502/284-2998.

A variety of helicopter tours based at Sedona Airport are offered by the following operators:

☐ **Arizona Helicopter Adventures**, PO Box 1729, Sedona AZ 86339, ☎ 520/282-0904 or 800/282-5141.

☐ **Action Helicopters of AZ**, Sedona Airport, PO Box 2699, Sedona AZ 86339, ☎ 520/282-7884.

☐ **Skydance Helicopters**, 125 Airport Road, Suite 5, Sedona AZ 86336, ☎ 520/282-1651 or 800/882-1651, runs flights over Sedona's red rocks, maneuvering through canyons, between rock pinnacles, hovering beside ancient Indian cliff dwellings. A multi-camera video system on board records the flight for you on high quality VHS tape.

You can float over the red rocks at dawn in your choice of guided hot air balloon flights. Contact the following:

☐ **Northern Light Balloon Expeditions**, PO Box 1695, Sedona AZ 86339, ☎ 520/282-2274.

☐ **Red Rock Balloon Adventure**, 3230 Valley Vista Drive, Sedona AZ 86339, ☎ 520/284-0040 or 800/258-3754.

☐ **Sky High Balloon Adventures**, 165 Zane Grey Drive, Sedona AZ 86336, ☎ 520/204-1395 or 800/551-7597, offers year-round sunrise flights and seasonal sunset flights, limousine pick-up and delivery, and a champagne picnic in a national forest.

☐ **Inflated Ego Balloon Company**, 3230 Valley Vista Drive, Sedona AZ 86351, ☎ 520/284-9483.

☐ **Aerozona Balloon Company**, PO Box 10081, Sedona AZ 86339, ☎ 520/282-1499.

And for those seeking an even more intimate experience of flying over northern Arizona's striking scenery, this can be arranged by **Arizona Hang Gliding Center**, 5721 Robert Road, #2B, Prescott Valley AZ 86324, ☎ 520/772-4114 or 800/757-2442.

Eco-travel & Cultural Excursions

A number of ecologically-oriented tours and cultural explorations are offered by various outfitters listed throughout individual adventure categories above, particularly some of the river tour operators.

Specialized tours are offered by the **Four Corners School of Outdoor Education**, PO Box 78, East Route, Monticello UT, ☎ 801/587-2156. These include a nine-day, eight-night, Grand Canyon Winter Traverse-North Rim to South Rim. The trip, offered only in mid-March, involves skiing 43 miles over a five-day period to reach the North Rim, carrying a backpack, camping, and eating meals prepared by the staff. At the rim you tie your skis to your pack and descend 14 miles to Phantom Ranch, while a geologist-guide explains the surrounding scenery. After a layover day on the canyon floor, you hike up 12 miles to the South Rim for the last night in a motel. Recommended only for people who can ski seven to nine miles per day with a 50-pound pack.

Another trip is called **High Desert Dynamics-North Rim Grand Canyon.** It is also offered only once a year in early October. The trip includes six days and six nights accommodations at the North Rim's Grand Canyon Lodge, with five- to eight-mile daily hikes led by a three-person team consisting of a biologist/river guide, an anthropologist/archaeologist, and a geologist. Evening seminars and slide shows are shown in the lodge.

Williams hosts a **Bill Williams Rendezvous** on a weekend in late May, featuring authentically-clothed and outfitted mountain men competing in cowchip throwing contests, black powder shooting, and other events. The town's **Arizona Cowpuncher's Reunion and Old-Timer's Rodeo**, held the first week in August, includes a rodeo, cowboy parade, and barn dance.

Coconino Center For the Arts in Flagstaff presents numerous exhibits and performances of cultural interest. These include the following yearly art exhibits: **Youth Arts Month**, in spring; **Trappings of the American West**, in June, focusing on the American cowboy; **Festival of Native American Arts**, from June to August, featuring fine arts and crafts created by Indians of the Four Corners, as well as contemporary and traditional Indian music; **Wood, Fiber, and Clay**, in fall, featuring works of Northern Arizona artists.

Northern Arizona University in Flagstaff offers frequent concerts, art shows, theatrical performances, and sporting events.

Flagstaff's **Museum Club** puts on local culture shows nightly. See above, under *Touring Flagstaff,* for information.

Boulder Outdoor Survival School, PO Box 3226, Flagstaff AZ 86003, ☎ 520/779-6000, is the oldest and largest primitive skills school in the country. Their programs include numerous backcountry excursions designed to teach self-sufficiency in the wilderness, in a number of settings throughout northern Arizona and the southwest.

Many consider **Sedona** something of a cultural phenomenon under normal circumstances. A number of Sedona jeep tours, for example, would probably qualify as cultural excursions, especially ones that visit vortex sites, cosmic medicine wheels (which are usually built illegally on forest service land), the mysterious Hopi mesas, Indian ruins, and other historic sites. Contact individual operators for tour details. The town also offers a variety of yearly special events, including Hopi Days, Fiesta del Tlaquepaque, and concert festivals featuring jazz, pop, or chamber music. For information contact **Sedona-Oak Creek Chamber of Commerce**, PO Box 478, Sedona AZ 86339, ☎ 520/282-7722 or 800/288-7336.

Jerome's Spirit Room, a bar in the Conner Hotel on Main Street, provides live music on weekends and genuine western culture all the time.

Where to Stay & Eat

LAKE POWELL AREA

The following offer modest individual trailer/housekeeping units with kitchens:

Hite Resort & Marina/ARA Leisure Services, Lake Powell UT 84533, ☎ 801/684-2278 or 800/528-6154; **Halls Crossing Resort & Marina/ARA Leisure Services**, Lake Powell UT 84533, ☎ 801/684-2261 or 800/528-6154, fax 801/684-2326; **Bullfrog Resort & Marina/ARA Leisure Services**, PO Box 4055, Bullfrog, Lake Powell UT 84533, ☎ 801/684-2233 or 800/528-6154, fax 801/684-2312. Fully equipped houseboat rentals are also available at the marinas.

Defiance House Lodge at Bullfrog Resort offers 48 better-than-average rooms done in Southwestern decor overlooking Lake Powell or a garden area.

Ticaboo Lodge, Restaurant & RV Park, UT 276, Ticaboo UT 84533, ☎ 801/788-2110, is 11 miles north of Bullfrog, Lake Powell, with 66 guest rooms, a restaurant, pool, hot tub, and some kitchenettes. The RV park has 35 hook-ups.

Anasazi Restaurant at Defiance House Lodge, the only restaurant for many miles, serves three meals a day. The steaks and Mexican dishes are average.

ARIZONA STRIP

Cliff Dwellers Lodge and Trading Co., Inc., US 89A, Marble Canyon AZ 86036, ☎ 520/335-2228 or 800/433-2543, is nine miles west of Navajo Bridge. It has 20 air-conditioned rooms, a restaurant, store, and gas station. Guided fishing trips, river rafting, scenic flights, and hikers' shuttle service are also available.

Lee's Ferry Lodge, 541½ US 89A, Box 1, Vermillion Cliffs AZ 86036, ☎ 520/355-2231, offers nine modest rooms, a restaurant, gift shop, and fishing store.

Marble Canyon Lodge, PO Box 1, US 89A, Marble Canyon AZ 86036, ☎ 520/355-2225 or 800/726-1789, fax 520/355-2227, has air-conditioning, 51 rooms, 10 suites, a coffee shop, and a dining room. Also: Guided fishing trips are available.

Jacob Lake Lodge, Jacob Lake AZ 86022, ☎ 520/643-7232, is 44 miles north of the North Rim, offering motel rooms, cabins, dining room, gas station, and post office.

Kaibab Lodge, North Rim Grand Canyon, Jacob Lake AZ 86022, has the closest accommodations to the North Rim and is 26 miles south of Jacob Lake, 18 miles from the National Park. Mailing address is c/o **Canyoneers, Inc.**, PO Box 2997, Flagstaff AZ 86003. To reach the lodge, ☎ 520/638-2389; for information, ☎ 520/526-0924 or 800/525-0924. The lodge has 26 units, jacuzzi, restaurant, gift shop, store and gas station. Also: Horseback riding, mountain bike rentals and guided tours, guided hikes and vehicle tours are available May through October.

The lodge becomes a cross-country ski center from December to mid-April. It has ski equipment rentals, lessons, tours, groomed trails, and set-track including skating lanes. Early reservations are suggested.

GRAND CANYON

Last-minute cancellations do occasionally crop up but reservations are usually needed at least six months to a year in advance to secure a room in the immediate Grand Canyon National Park area. The operator of the lodges and dining rooms in Grand Canyon Village, on the South Rim, accepts reservations up to 23 months in advance. Outlying areas, even as close as Tusayan, just a few miles from the South Rim, may be able to accommodate you on short notice. The farther away you go, the easier it is to get a room or campsite. Plan especially far in advance for the summer season, May through October, which attracts the largest crowds.

Grand Canyon Lodge, North Rim, Grand Canyon AZ 86023, ☎ 520/638-2611, provides the North Rim's only accommodations. It includes an appropriately grand 1930s stone and timber main lodge, with huge windows overlooking the North Rim. Standard motel rooms and three choices of cabins are available. Pioneer Cabins are close to the lodge and sleep five people. Frontier Cabins are closer to the rim and come with a double and a single bed. Western Cabins are the fanciest with two double beds and a porch with a choice canyon view. The lodge is open May to October. Reservations are accepted up to 23 months in advance. For information, contact the same company that manages the lodges inside Bryce Canyon and Zion National Parks, **TW Recreational Services**, PO Box 400, Cedar City UT 84720, ☎ 801/586-7686, fax 801/834-3157.

The **Grand Canyon Lodge Dining Room**, ☎ 520/638-0611, serves three meals a day in a stunning, spacious, log-beamed dining room with stone walls and enormous windows overlooking the canyon. Reservations are necessary for lunch and dinner. A cafeteria in the lodge serves three meals daily. Grand Canyon Lodge is an information center for all park activities.

Cameron Trading Post, PO Box 339, Cameron AZ 86020, ☎ 520/679-2231 or 800/338-7385, is an active trading post year-round, including a post office, store, gift shop, restaurant, a small museum, and a modest motel on a bank of the Little Colorado River.

Eight and a half miles south of Cameron, the **Anasazi Inn-Gray Mountain**, PO Box 29100, Gray Mountain AZ 86016, ☎ 520/679-2214, fax 520/679-2334, is a spartan 100-unit motel, with coffee shop, gift shop, and pool.

Grand Canyon National Park Lodges, PO Box 699, Grand Canyon AZ 86023, ☎ 520/638-2401, fax 520/638-9247, operates the following South Rim properties:

☐ **Desert View Trading Post Cafeteria** features a self-service cafeteria 23 miles east of Grand Canyon Village on the East Rim Drive.

☐ **El Tovar Hotel** is a dramatic structure four stories high, built from limestone and logs in 1905. It's the most elegant and expensive South Rim property, looking like a sporting lodge favored by Napoleonic-era European royalty, offering rooms and suites, some with staggering views, a gift shop, dining room, and concierge service.

☐ **El Tovar Dining Room**, ☎ 520/638-6292, serves steaks, seafood and Continental fare in a formal environment, although casual clothing is permissible. El Tovar's guests may make reservations, but others must wait for a table.

☐ **Bright Angel Lodge** is a less expensive alternative to El Tovar, yet retaining distinction in its 1930s-era stone and log construction. The property includes a steak house, coffee shop, gift shop, and beauty salon. Several rustic rim cabins are also available.

- [ ] **Bright Angel Restaurant,** ☎ 520/638-2631, serves three standard American meals daily, while the **Arizona Steakhouse** serves dinners only, including steaks, seafood and a salad bar. Open March through December.
- [ ] **Thunderbird Lodge and Kachina Lodge** are modern motels which do not have their own dining rooms, but you can walk to those at Bright Angel Lodge or El Tovar.
- [ ] **Maswik Lodge** has modern motel rooms and some cabins for the lowest available South Rim rates. On the premises, at the southeast corner of Grand Canyon Village, is the **Maswik Cafeteria** and a gift shop.
- [x] **Yavapai Lodge** is the largest South Rim lodge, situated across from the visitor center and a mile from the rim, offering standard motel rooms, the **Yavapai Cafeteria** and, serving faster food, the **Yavapai Grill.** It also has a gift shop.
- [ ] **Babbitt's Delicatessen,** in the general store near Yavapai Lodge, serves sandwiches and salads to eat-in or take-out.
- [ ] **Hermit's Rest Snack Bar** is at the end of the West Rim Drive, serving cold drinks, ice cream, candy, and hot dogs.
- [ ] **Phantom Ranch** provides the only accommodations in the bottom of the Grand Canyon, at the end of the North Kaibab Trail and across the river from the bottom of Bright Angel and South Kaibab trails. Guests stay in stone cabins beneath shading trees or in four 10-person hiker dormitories with bunk beds. The cabins are usually reserved for overnight mule-back travellers; the only other ways to get here are on foot or by river raft. Meals are available. Reservations are taken as much as a year in advance.
- [ ] **Moqui Lodge** is managed by the Grand Canyon Lodges, but actually situated outside the park. It's a modern, airy structure, with motel rooms, a dining room, gift shop, horseback riding and tennis.
- [ ] **Moqui Lodge Dining Room,** ☎ 520/638-2424, serves Mexican and American food. Summer chuckwagon cookouts with live western music are offered.

There are a number of motels and family-style restaurants, including a **McDonald's**, a few miles outside the park's South Rim in Tusayan.

Grand Canyon Squire Inn, PO Box 130, Grand Canyon AZ 86023, ☎ 520/638-2681, fax 520/638-2782, is a Best Western with 150 motel rooms, dining room, coffee shop, gift shop, pool, tennis, bowling, sauna, jacuzzi, and billiards.

Grand Canyon Red Feather Lodge, US 64, PO Box 1460, Grand Canyon AZ 86023, ☎ 520/638-2414 or 800/538-2345, opened in spring 1995, offering 130 rooms, a pool, fitness room and spa, and a Denny's restaurant on the premises.

Holiday Inn Express Grand Canyon, US 64, PO Box 1699, Grand Canyon AZ 86023, ☎ 520/683-3000 or 800/465-4329, opened in summer 1995. Children stay for free and a Continental breakfast is included. Located two miles from the National Park.

Quality Inn Grand Canyon, PO Box 520, Grand Canyon AZ 86023, ☎ 520/638-2673 or 800/221-2222, fax 520/638-9537, contains 185 rooms, a restaurant, coffee shop, a pool and two hot tubs.

Havasupai Lodge, Supai AZ 86435, ☎ 520/448-2111 is the only motel in the village of Supai. It has 24 rooms and reservations are necessary. A restaurant, creek swimming, hiking and horseback riding are available here.

Relatively near Supai, within 80 miles of the Indian village, **Grand Canyon Caverns**, PO Box 180, Peach Springs AZ 86434, ☎ 520/422-3223, offers 48 motel rooms, a restaurant, and a gift shop. Western cookouts and guided cave tours are available.

WILLIAMS

Grand Canyon Inn, PO Box 702, Williams AZ 86946, ☎ 520/635-2345 or 520/635-2809, is 28 miles north of Williams at the junction of US 180 and AZ 64 near Valle. The 61-room motel has a restaurant, gift shop, and gas station. Helicopter and fixed-wing scenic flight reservations can be made here.

Comfort Inn, 911 West Bill Williams Avenue, Williams AZ 86046, ☎ 800/228-5150, has 54 rooms, a pool, and a restaurant.

El Rancho Motel, 617 East Bill Williams Avenue, Williams AZ 86046, ☎ 520/625-2552 or 800/228-2370, offers 25 rooms and a pool.

The newest Williams property is the **Fray Marcos Hotel**, ☎ 800/843-8724 or 520/773-1976, fax 520/773-1610, located in the historic Williams depot for the Grand Canyon Railway. The 89-room property combines turn-of-the-century style with modern amenities, including casual dining on the premises, in **Spenser's** restaurant. With a single phone call you can book accommodations here and transportation on the Grand Canyon Railway.

Ramada Inn at the Mountainside, 642 East Bill Williams Avenue, ☎ 520/635-4431 or 800/462-9381, fax 520/635-2292, is situated within walking distance of the Grand Canyon Railway, offering 95 rooms, a pool, jacuzzi, restaurant, and room service.

Quality Inn Ranch Resort, Route 1, PO Box 35, Williams AZ 86046, ☎ 520/635-2693 or 800/221-2222, is six miles east of Williams, off I-40. The motel offers 69 rooms, a restaurant, coffee shop, pool, tennis, jacuzzi, and horseback riding. Locations for skiing and fishing are nearby.

FLAGSTAFF

Accommodations

Flagstaff is packed with chain motels and fast foods, as well as other standard accommodations and restaurants. There are three **Best Westerns,** ☎ 800/528-1234, two **Travelodges,** ☎ 800/255-3050, a **Howard Johnson's,** ☎ 800/654-2000, a **Quality Inn,** ☎ 800/228-5151, a **Ramada Inn,** ☎ 800/325-2525, two **Rodeway Inns,** ☎ 800/228-2000, and an above-average **Residence Inn by Marriott,** ☎ 800/331-3131, on the east side of town. Most have pools, many have restaurants, and some offer courtesy car service.

You can usually find a place with a vacancy unless some major event is in town. If you plan ahead, there are several unusual places to stay and dine.

Best Western Woodlands Plaza Hotel, 1175 West US 66, Flagstaff AZ 86003, ☎ 520/773-8888, fax 520/773-0597, is a cut above the average Best Western, offering 125 large rooms, several restaurants (see below), pool, indoor and outdoor jacuzzis, sauna, and an exercise room. Room service and complimentary limousine service are offered.

Monte Vista Hotel, 100 North San Francisco Street, Flagstaff AZ 86001, ☎ 520/779-6971, fax 520/779-2904, used to be frequented by western movie stars. Today it's a partly restored historic hotel, with 64 rooms, in a 1920s structure. You can actually stay in a room that was once occupied by Walter Brennan. Some rooms share a bath.

Little America Hotel, 2515 East Butler, PO Box 3900, Flagstaff AZ 86003, ☎ 520/779-2741 or 800/352-4386, fax 520/779-7983, offers 248 large rooms set on 500 acres of wooded grounds, including a two-mile jogging trail and pool. A restaurant and gift shop are open 24 hours a day.

The Inn at Four Ten, 410 North Leroux Street, Flagstaff AZ 86001, ☎ 520/774-0088, is an antique-filled B&B with three suites, including kitchen areas and private baths, or two rooms that share a bath. It is close to the downtown area and occupies a 1907 structure.

There are several character-laden youth hostels downtown. Contact the Chamber of Commerce for information.

Ski Lift Lodge, US 180 North & Snowbowl Road, Flagstaff AZ 86001, has 28 rooms and cabins plus a restaurant. Situated six miles from the Arizona Snowbowl Ski Area.

Arizona Mountain Inn, 685 Lake Mary Road, Flagstaff AZ 86001, ☎ 520/774-8959, has standard B&B rooms in a main house, and cabins with one- to five-bedrooms, fireplaces, and kitchens. The inn's location southeast of town provides good access to hiking and cross-country skiing.

Mormon Lake Lodge, PO Box 12, Mormon Lake AZ 86038, ☎ 520/774-0462, fax 520/354-2356, offers lodge rooms and cabins, a popular western-style restaurant featuring western music (see below), and a full slate of year-round activities, including hiking in summer, along with ice fishing, snowmobiling, and cross-country skiing in winter. The property includes a grocery store, fishing supplies, and gas station.

Restaurants

There are a lot of ordinary places to eat in Flagstaff and some more unusual ones. Chain restaurants are well-represented. Because of the college crowd there are plenty of spots for cheap eats. More upscale establishments are beginning to appear, including some imaginative choices.

- ❒ **Horseman Lodge Restaurant**, 8500 US 89 North, Flagstaff, ☎ 520/526-2655, serves good steaks in a large western log structure.
- ❒ **Cottage Place Restaurant**, 126 West Cottage Avenue, Flagstaff, ☎ 520/774-8431, serves Continental-inspired beef, poultry, and vegetarian dishes in a cozy, early-1900s cottage.
- ❒ **Sakura**, in the Woodlands Plaza Hotel (see above), serves sushi, tempura, and beef, chicken or seafood teriyaki
- ❒ **Woodlands Café**, also in the Woodlands Plaza Hotel, serves poultry, seafood, and beef dishes with a Continental flare in a Southwestern-style dining room.

- ☐ **Chez Marc Bistro,** 503 North Humphreys Street, Flagstaff, ☎ 520/774-1343, is in an old, historic house decorated in French country antiques, serving nouvelle cuisine, soups, salads, and sandwiches for lunch and dinner.
- ☐ **Main Street Bar & Grill,** 4 South San Francisco Street, Flagstaff, ☎ 520/774-1519, is a college hang-out, serving barbecued ribs, sandwiches, and Mexican food.
- ☐ **Little America Hotel** (see above) serves a popular Sunday brunch.
- ☐ **Macy's European Coffee House and Bakery,** 14 South Beaver, Flagstaff, serves good coffees, teas, and baked goods.
- ☐ **Café Express,** 16 North San Francisco Street, Flagstaff, ☎ 520/774-0541, serves good breakfasts, sandwiches, salads, and fresh baked goods.
- ☐ **Mormon Lake Lodge Steak House & Saloon,** at Mormon Lake Lodge (see above), has been an Old West steak house since the 1920s, servings beef, ribs, chicken, and fresh trout, all cooked over an open fire.

SEDONA

Accommodations

High season here is April to November and reservations are necessaryduring those months. Prices drop a little the rest of the year, but there are not many bargains. The well-situated or deluxe resorts are very expensive and the more modest properties charge top dollar for what they offer. There are a lot of places to stay in Sedona, but you have to look outside of town for less expensive lodgings, in the Cottonwood-Jerome area or around Camp Verde or Flagstaff, which is less than 30 miles north. Many, many restaurants, coffee shops, and bakeries, ranging in price from inexpensive to decidedly not, can be found in Sedona. For complete listings contact the Sedona Chamber of Commerce.

Upscale resort properties include the following:

Enchantment Resort, 525 Boynton Canyon Road, Sedona AZ 86336, ☎ 520/282-2900 or 800/826-4180, contains 162 units, including private two-bedroom adobe cottages called "casitas," and one-bedroom suites with kitchenettes. The beautiful resort, which blends harmoniously into the red rock scenery that dwarfs it, also offers six pools, a fine restaurant (see below), 12 tennis courts, croquet, and a six-hole pitch & putt golf course, all situated scenically beside the trailhead to the Boynton Canyon Vortex in a red rock canyon. This is probably Sedona's top resort in a competitive field, and among the best in all the Southwest. Its combination of a tranquil, natural setting, and sophisticated resort amenities is virtually unmatched in the region. It has been rated among the top 10 resorts in the world by the sophisticated readers of *Condé Nast Traveler*. Rates are expensive.

L'Auberge de Sedona Resort, 301 L'Auberge Lane, Sedona AZ 86336, ☎ 520/282-1661 or 800/272-6777, fax 520/282-2885, has 95 lodge rooms and luxurious cabins decorated in elegant French country style, with fireplaces and porches, on Oak Creek. The property includes a pool, a coffee shop, and a very good dining room (see below), all situated on 10 acres uptown. A different section of the resort, The Orchards at Auberge, offers modern Southwestern-style rooms. Rates are moderate to expensive.

Junipine Condo Resort, 8351 North US 89A, Sedona AZ 86336, ☎ 520/282-3375 or 800/742-PINE, fax 520/282-7402, is in Oak Creek Canyon, a mile north of Slide Rock State Park. It contains 38 modern wood and stone units, either one-bedroom, one-bath, or two-bedrooms, two-baths, each with a fireplace, kitchen, and deck. Facilities include a restaurant, jacuzzi, volleyball, basketball, and horseshoes. There's no pool but you can swim or fish in Oak Creek and explore hiking trails adjacent to the property.

Los Abrigados Resort & Spa, 160 Portal Lane, Sedona AZ 86336, ☎ 520/282-1777 or 800/521-3131, fax 520/282-2614, has 172 deluxe, modern Mexican-style, two-room suites with kitchens, fireplaces and patios. There is also a pool, restaurant, tennis, and health spa. Located next to the Tlaquepaque shops, the resort shares the same architectural inspiration. Its courtyards and walkways connect with the shopping area. Accommodations are available in a 1930s stone structure on the property which has been converted to a two-bedroom, $1,000-per-night, ultra-deluxe retreat.

Poco Diablo Resort, 1752 South AZ 179, PO Box 1709, Sedona AZ 86336, ☎ 520/282-7333 or 800/528-4275, fax 520/282-2090, is two miles south of US 89A and AZ 179. It contains 110 rooms, some with fireplaces and indoor jacuzzis, a good Southwestern restaurant, two pools, three jacuzzis, four tennis courts, nine-hole golf course, and racquetball.

Bell Rock Inn, 6246 AZ 179, Sedona AZ 86336, ☎ 520/282-4161, is seven miles south of US 89A and AZ 179. The adobe-style resort contains 96 units decorated in a Southwestern desert style, a pool, jacuzzi, tennis, and dining room. Guests receive nearby golf privileges. Rates are moderate.

Garland's Oak Creek Lodge, Oak Creek Route, PO Box 152, Sedona AZ 86336, ☎ 520/282-3343, offers creek-side accommodations, with breakfast and dinner included in daily rates, eight miles north of town in Oak Creek Canyon. Open April though October. The dining room is open to non-guests by reservation only. The lodge and the restaurant are often booked solid far in advance.

Chains and standard motels are best represented by the following properties:

Best Western Arroyo Roble Hotel, 400 North US 89A, Sedona AZ 86336, ☎ 520/282-4001, offers 53 rooms, six luxury villas, in-room coffee, tennis, racquetball, billiards, indoor/outdoor pool, exercise room, and jacuzzi. Villas contain two bedrooms, 2½ baths, fireplaces, and private balcony overlooking Oak Creek. Expensive.

Quality Inn King's Ransom, PO Box 180, Sedona AZ 86336, ☎ 520/282-7151 or 800/221-2222, has 65 units, heated pool (March 15 to November 30), jacuzzi, dining room, and coffee shop.

Railroad Inn at Sedona, 2545 West US 89A, Sedona AZ 86336, ☎ 520/282-1533 or 800/858-7245, fax 520/282-2033, is a standard motel, with a pool and restaurant. Special Room, Ride & Meal Deal packages are offered in conjunction with the Verde River Canyon Excursion Train. Rooms are moderately priced.

Individualistic, mostly moderately priced properties include the following:

Graham's Bed & Breakfast Inn, 150 Canyon Circle Drive, Village of Oak Creek AZ 86351, ☎ 520/284-1425, fax 520/284-0767, six miles south of Sedona, has five elegant Southwestern-style rooms, a jacuzzi, and provides a complimentary hot breakfast. Rates are expensive.

The Lodge at Sedona, 125 Kallof Place, Sedona AZ 86336, ☎ 520/204-1942 or 800/619/4467, has been voted "Arizona's Best Bed & Breakfast" several times by the readers of Phoenix's largest newspaper. It's an elegant, antique-filled, 13-room country inn on 2½ acres. Rooms have a jacuzzi and fireplace. Gourmet breakfast is included with expensive room rates, and dinners are available.

Bed & Breakfast at Saddle Rock Ranch, 255 Rock Ridge Drive, Sedona AZ 86336, ☎ 520/282-7640, was once the locale for movie productions amid red rock scenery. Its rooms now offer woodburning fireplaces, private baths, and good views of the canyons. There is a pool and spa.

The Canyon Wren, Star Route 3, PO Box 1140, Sedona AZ 86336, ☎ 520/282-6900 or 800/437-WREN, has four cabins designed for intimacy and dedicated to the enjoyment of couples or individuals only. Cabins come with a kitchen, fireplace, and whirlpool bath.

Canyon Villa Bed & Breakfast, 125 Canyon Circle Drive, Sedona AZ 86351, ☎ 520/284-1226 or 800/453-1166, offers 10 moderate to expensive rooms with fireplaces in a beautiful house set amid gorgeous red rocks.

Greyfire Farm, 1240 Jack's Canyon Road, Sedona AZ 86336, ☎ 520/284-2340, accommodates guests and their horses. There are many horseback riding, hiking and biking trails in the vicinity of this B&B south of town.

Red Rock Lodge, PO Box 537, Sedona AZ 86336, ☎ 520/282-3591, offers 14 rooms and one cottage, with in-room jacuzzis, fireplaces, and kitchens, near the north end of Sedona.

Cedar's Resort, PO Box 292, Sedona AZ 86336, ☎ 520/282-7010, has 38 units on Oak Creek, a pool, jacuzzi, and fishing.

Oak Creek Terrace Resort, 4548 North US 89A, Sedona AZ 86336, ☎ 520/282-3562 or 800/658-5866, beside Oak Creek, five miles north of town, offers 16 units with fireplaces, kitchenettes with refrigerators, and private patios with barbecues. Two-bedroom suites come with an in-room double jacuzzi. A Honeymoon Suite is in an A-frame house on Oak Creek.

Don Hoel's Cabins, Oak Creek Canyon, Sedona AZ 86336, ☎ 520/282-3560 or 800/292-4635, are 20 simple cabins in Oak Creek Canyon, nine miles north of Sedona. Rates are moderate.

New Earth Lodge, 665 Sunset Drive, Sedona AZ 86336, ☎ 520/282-2644, offers vacation cottages with kitchens decorated in Southwestern style, and spectacular red rock views.

Healing Center of Sedona, 25 Wilson Canyon Road, Sedona AZ 86336, ☎ 520/282-7710, offers accommodations in geodesic domes and a vegetarian dining room. It also offers a sauna, jacuzzi, flotation tank, acupressure massage, herbal or crystal treatments. Channeling and rebirthing assistance are available at the center. Room rates are inexpensive to moderate.

Recommended properties outside Sedona include the following:

Best Western Cottonwood Inn, 993 Main Street, Cottonwood AZ 86326, ☎ 520/634-5575 or 800/528-1234, fax 520/255-0259, has 64 rooms, a restaurant, pool, and jacuzzi.

The Jerome Inn, 311 Main Street, Jerome AZ 86331, ☎ 520/634-5094 or 800/634-5094, offers utilitarian accommodations amid Victorian decor in Jerome's oldest hotel. Some of the eight rooms share a bath.

Nancy Russel's Bed & Breakfast, 3 Juarez Street, PO Box 791, Jerome AZ 86331, ☎ 520/634-3270, overlooks the Verde Valley, with two antique-filled guest rooms in an old restored miner's house. Breakfasts include fruit from Ms. Russel's garden.

Best Western Cliff Castle Lodge, PO Box 3430, Camp Verde AZ 86322, ☎ 520/567-6611 or 800/622-7835, fax 520/567-9455, is at I-17 and Middle Verde Road, with 82 rooms, a pool and a restaurant.

Restaurants

The Yavapai Room at Enchantment Resort (see above), overlooks Boynton Canyon and serves a Southwestern menu, including selections of wild game. A champagne brunch, accompanied by live jazz, is offered on Sundays. Reservations are required.

L'Auberge Restaurant, ☎ 520/282-1667, in L'Auberge de Sedona Resort (see above), serves an elegant, expensive French prix fixe six-course dinner overlooking Oak Creek. The menu changes daily. Reservations are required. The resort also has a more casual choice, **Orchards Restaurant,** ☎ 520/282-7200.

The Willows at Poco Diablo, ☎ 520/282-7333, at Poco Diablo Resort (see above), serves Southwestern dishes in a dining room overlooking a small golf course and a red rock canyon. Reservations suggested.

Canyon Rose at Los Abrigados, ☎ 520/282-ROSE, serves Southwestern dishes indoors or outdoors. Reservations suggested. Also: Sunday brunch.

Rene at Tlaquepaque, ☎ 520/282-9225, is located in the ersatz Mexican village shopping area, serving French food in a Spanish colonial setting. Be prepared to pay dearly for a great meal. Reservations required. **El Rincon,** ☎ 520/282-4648, serves Mexican food in the same upscale shopping complex.

Irene's Restaurant, Castle Rock Plaza, Oak Creek Village, ☎ 520/284-2240, serves American home style cooking, including baked goods.

Also in Castle Rock Plaza, the **Mandarin House,** ☎ 520/284-2525, serves Chinese food.

Heartline Café, 1610 West US 89A, Sedona, ☎ 520/282-0785, has unusual salads and dishes made with fresh herbs, fruits, and vegetables.

Phil & Eddie's Diner, 1655 West US 89A, Sedona, ☎ 520/282-6070, is a throwback to the heyday of Route 66, serving classic diner fare, burgers, ice cream sodas, and breakfast any time.

Thai Spices Natural, 2986 West US 89A, Sedona, ☎ 520/282-0590, in the White House Motel, serves Thai food prepared with organic ingredients.

Rainbow's End Steak House & Saloon, 3235 West US 89A, Sedona, ☎ 520/282-1593, serves up flame-grilled steaks and has country-western music.

In Jerome, **House of Joy,** on Hull Street, ☎ 520/634-5339, still looks like the brothel it was at one time, but now serves popular Continental cuisine. Open only on Saturdays and Sundays for dinner. Reservations are suggested far in advance.

Jerome Palace, Clark Street, Jerome, ☎ 520/634-5262, serves up barbecue with a view. The Verde Valley unfolds beneath the second-story dining room windows.

Macy's European Coffee House & Bakery, Main Street, Jerome, ☎ 520/634-2733, offers a similar menu, featuring coffees, teas, sandwiches and pastries, as their shop in Flagstaff. Open for breakfast and lunch.

WINSLOW/HOLBROOK

Chain motels are often, though not always, the best bet in this area. Food will be modest, especially if you're coming from Sedona, and it's going to be mostly standard American fare, meat and potatoes, scarce vegetables – that sort of thing.

Best Western Adobe Inn, 1701 North Park Drive, Winslow AZ 86047, ☎ 520/289-4638, fax 520/289-5514, has 72 rooms, a restaurant, and an indoor pool.

Casa Blanca Café, 1201 East 2nd Street, Winslow, ☎ 520/289-4191, serves Mexican and American food.

Wigwam Motel, 811 West Hopi Drive, Holbrook AZ 86025, is reason enough to stay overnight in Holbrook; accommodations are in 15 stucco tipis. How often do you see one of those, let alone sleep in it? Rooms contain handmade wooden furniture.

Best Western Arizonian Inn, 2508 East Navajo Boulevard, Holbrook AZ 86025, ☎ 520/524-2611 or 800/528-1234, has 70 rooms and mini-suites, free HBO movies, a pool, restaurant and coffee shop. Also: This is one of the few properties in Holbrook that specifies no pets.

Comfort Inn, 2602 Navajo Boulevard, Holbrook AZ 86025, ☎ 520/524-6131 or 800/228-5150, offers 61 rooms, a heated pool and a complimentary continental breakfast.

Budget Inn Motel, 602 Navajo Boulevard, Holbrook AZ 80625, ☎ 520/524-6263, has 38 rooms and a pool.

Aquilera's Café, 200 Navajo Boulevard, Holbrook AZ, ☎ 520/524-3806, serves big plates of Mexican and American food.

Camping

NORTH LAKE POWELL AREA

Camping is permitted almost anywhere on the shoreline of Lake Powell, but not within one mile of developed areas (the marinas and Lees Ferry), and no camping is permitted at Rainbow Bridge National Monument. There is a 14-day consecutive limit for interior sites; the limit is 30 days for camping along the Lake Powell shoreline. You can't camp in roadside pull-outs, picnic areas or on posted beaches.

There are public campgrounds at Halls Crossing (65 spaces, cold water showers), Bullfrog Basin (87 spaces), and Hite Crossing (12 spaces). There are also primitive campgrounds close to these areas. Contact local ranger stations for directions.

The BLM operates several campgrounds in the Henry Mountains. The sites may or may not have water and the rough dirt roads leading to them may not be in very good shape; at the best of times they are probably only suited to four-wheel-drive vehicles. Contact the BLM office in Hanksville (see above, under *Touring*) for road conditions and details on the following sites:

Starr Springs Campground, 23 miles north of Bullfrog Basin and 43 miles south of Hanksville, off UT 276, is open year-round with water available May to October.

Lonesome Beaver Campground, 27 miles south of Hanksville on 100 East, is open May to October, but there is no water.

ARIZONA STRIP

Lees Ferry has four campgrounds situated in Marble Canyon, just south of the Lees Ferry Historic District. Boat camping is permitted at a site north of Lees Ferry, below the Glen Canyon Dam. For information contact the **Lees Ferry Ranger Station**, ☎ 520/355-2234.

Heart Campground, operated by the Paiute Tribe, offers campsites and RV spaces a quarter-mile north of Pipe Springs National Monument, off AZ 389.

Jacob Lake Forest Camp, 44 miles north of the North Rim on AZ 67 is open May through October.

De Motte Forest Camp, just south of Kaibab Lodge off AZ 67, 18 miles north of the North Rim, is open June through September.

GRAND CANYON NATIONAL PARK AREA

The following phone numbers provide information about Grand Canyon National Park, Box 129, Grand Canyon AZ 86023: visitor activities & programs, ☎ 520/638-9304; park information, ☎ 520/638-2245; park headquarters, ☎ 520/638-7888.

Backcountry camping requires a free permit available from the **Backcountry Reservations Office,** Box 12, Grand Canyon AZ 86023, ☎ 520/638-7875. Permits are limited and reservations are necessary. For a **Backcountry Information line,** ☎ 520/638-7888. During high season it may be easier to find camping sites outside the park. Reservations for Grand Canyon campgrounds may be made with a credit card by writing to **MISTIX,** PO Box 85705, San Diego CA 92138-5705, or ☎ 800/365-2267.

There is a primitive campground at **Toroweap Point** on the North Rim of the Grand Canyon. A permit is required and is available at the North Rim Ranger Station, located a few miles north of the campground or, by mail, from the Backcountry Reservations Office.

On the North Rim, **North Rim Campground,** is a mile and a half north of the Grand Canyon Lodge and is usually open only from May to October.

Below the South Rim two campgrounds, **Bright Angel** and **Cottonwood,** are for backpackers only, who may stay only two days. Reservations are often required months in advance.

Desert View Campground, on the East Rim Drive, 25 miles east of Grand Canyon Village, does not accept reservations. Camping limit is seven days. Open May through September.

Mather Campground, south of the visitor center on the South Rim, has tent sites and trailer sites with year-round hook-ups in the adjacent Trailer Village. Flush toilets and showers are available. There is a seven-day limit. You can make reservations up to eight weeks in advance for the busy March 1 to December 1 season. The rest of the year the campground functions on a first-come, first-served basis. For reservations see the above contacts, or Grand Canyon Lodges, listed above under *Where to Stay & Eat*.

Ten-X Campground is three miles south of Tusayan, near the South Rim. It's open from May through October.

Havasu Campground is the only place you can camp in Havasu Canyon. The camping area starts below Havasu Falls and stretches for nearly a mile along Havasu Creek to Mooney Falls. There are no fires permitted. Campers need a cook stove. There is a small grocery store in the village of Supai, 2½ miles away.

WILLIAMS/FLAGSTAFF

There are four campgrounds near Williams, all on fishing and boating lakes.

Cataract Campground, two miles northeast of Williams, is only open May through October. The others are open year-round but may have water only in the summer. These include, **Kaibab Campground,** four miles northeast of Williams, **Dogtown Campground,** seven miles southeast of Williams, and **White Horse Lake Campground,** 19 miles southeast of Williams.

Bonito Campground, at Sunset Crater National Monument, is open May through October, with 44 sites for tents and RVs.

Fort Tuthill County Park, ☎ 520/774-3464, three miles south of Flagstaff off US 89A, has a 103-site campground amid 355 acres of wooded nature trails. Lakeview Campground, across from Upper Lake Mary, 15 miles south of Flagstaff on Lake Mary Road, is the closest campground to Upper and Lower Lake Mary. Drinking water is available. Ashurst and Forked Pine Campgrounds are situated on opposite shores of Ashurst Lake, 18 miles southeast of Flagstaff on Lake Mary Road, and four miles east on Forest Road 82E.

Pinegrove Campground is 18 miles southeast of Flagstaff on Lake Mary Road and a mile east on Forest Road 651.

There are two Forest Service campgrounds at Mormon Lake, **Dairy Springs** and **Double Springs,** with a combined total of 45 sites. To reach the campgrounds drive 20 miles southeast of Flagstaff on Lake Mary Road, then turn east and south on Mormon Lake Loop Road, which follows the west shore of the lake. You'll come to Dairy Springs in four miles. Double Springs is two miles farther south.

SEDONA AREA

There are six Forest Service campgrounds in Oak Creek Canyon, all situated along US 89A within a 12-mile stretch starting six miles north of town. The campgrounds are usually open March through September and they are the only spots where camping is permitted in **Oak Creek Canyon**. Most of the 173 campsites are issued on a first-come, first-serve basis.

Eleven sites at **Cave Springs Campground** are available for reservation, ☎ 800/283-CAMP. Several of the Forest Service campgrounds can accommodate trailers but no electrical hook-ups or showers are available. Private campgrounds nearby provide hook-ups.

Dead Horse Ranch State Park, north of Cottonwood, has a year-round campground with hookups for RVs and showers.

Two campgrounds are located near Camp Verde. **Beaver Creek** is 12 miles north of town and east off I-17. **Clear Creek** is five miles south on Main Street.

A small campground is at **Clints Well,** near the junction of Lake Mary Road and AZ 87.

WINSLOW/HOLBROOK

There's a campground at McHood Park, six miles southeast of Winslow.

Overnight backpacking or horsepacking trips are permitted in the 50,000-acre **Petrified Forest National Wilderness,** but not in the National Park. A free permit must be obtained at least an hour before the park closes at the Painted Desert Visitors Center or the Rainbow Forest Museum. Backpackers must depart from the Flattops trailhead or the Kachina Point trailhead. Remember there are no trails, and no established campgrounds in the wilderness area.

The Navajo Reservation & Hopiland

A large part of Northern Arizona is made up of the Navajo Nation, the largest Indian reservation in the United States. It contains 26,000 square miles and 250,000 residents. Hopiland, far smaller and surrounded by Navajo land, is home to perhaps the most culturally intact Indian tribe in America.

These cultures have long influenced the surrounding areas. You'll see Indian ruins, Indian goods for sale, exhibits pertaining to Indian museums and visitor centers, and you'll see actual Indians everywhere you go in Northern Arizona. The reservation lands present unique perceptions of the world; some liken visiting them to seeing a foreign country.

No place could be more American. This chapter explores all aspects of the Navajo Reservation and Hopiland. These Indian tribal lands are a special part of Arizona (also spilling over into portions of neighboring Utah and New Mexico), and considered by some to be the very heart of the southwest. This arid, high desert plateau country, ranging from 4,000 to more than 7,000 ft. in elevation, is the central spot where many believe human occupation of the Colorado Plateau started. At the least, this is where travellers experience the most direct link with the prehistoric past.

Geography & History

The Navajo religion teaches that there are two classes of beings: Earth People and Holy People, with Holy People possessing the power to help or hurt Earth People. Centuries ago the Holy People taught the "Dineh," the Navajo people, how to live correctly and conduct the acts of everyday life, including how to live in harmony with Mother Earth, Father Sky, and all the other elements, such as man, animals, plants, and insects.

The Holy People defined Navajoland by specifying its limits within an area enclosed by four sacred mountains. Thus, in Navajo lore, the eastern border of their lands is Mount Blanca, east of Alamosa, Colorado. The southern border is Mount Taylor, near Grants, New Mexico. The western edge of Navajoland is in the San Francisco Peaks, close to Flagstaff, Arizona, and the northern limit is Mount Hesperus west of Durango, Colorado.

These points delineate the boundaries of this book, an area where the past is never far away. It is very close in Navajoland, and even closer in neighboring Hopiland.

The **Navajo Nation** covers 26,000 square miles. This includes practically all of northeastern Arizona lying east of the Grand Canyon and north of I-40. It also includes a slice of northwest New Mexico, roughly from the Arizona border to Farmington and south to I-40, plus the area of southeastern Utah from Page, Arizona to the Colorado border, south of the San Juan River.

Sweeping panoramas of epic space unfold across the Navajo Reservation, perched atop the Colorado Plateau. Navajoland contains two National Monuments located in canyons occupied long ago by the Anasazi, a tribal park consisting of desert flats and sand dunes sprouting protrusions of random rock monoliths, buttes and mesas the size of a skyscraper, or larger, numerous historic sites, and ever-popular fishing lakes situated among forested mountains along the New Mexico border.

You can visit ancient Anasazi Indian sites at **Navajo** or **Canyon de Chelly National Monuments**. Then you can see how the ancient ways link with the present beneath the 500-ft. tan cliffs of Monument Valley Navajo Tribal Park, where Navajo ranchers herd sheep as they have done for centuries. Or sink a line into the cold, clear waters of Wheatfields Lake in the Lukuchukai Mountains, one of a dozen major fishing lakes operated by the Navajo people.

The Dineh consider the land to be their mother and themselves an integral part of a universe in which they must do everything possible to maintain balance and harmony on Mother Earth.

Of course, in 1864 the United States Army took historical exception to some of the Navajos' efforts. The tribe had a well-known antisocial habit which entailed maintaining an even distribution of wealth by helping themselves to newcomers' possessions, including those of white settlers.

US troops forced the Long Walk, which was the involuntary relocation of the Navajo People from these lands their ancestors had farmed and lived on for hundreds of years, to even bleaker surroundings in eastern New Mexico. The experimental effort at acculturation predictably failed, but not before many Navajos died and many spirits among the Dineh were broken. In 1868, the Navajo people were permitted to return to this area. They had to start from scratch as their homes and farms were destroyed from neglect and their minds subtly infiltrated by the white man's ways.

Among various modern proscriptions enforced to protect and control the reservation lands granted the Dineh by the federal government are certain restrictions to backcountry travel:

- ☐ No biking or jeeping on back roads.
- ☐ A fee charged for a hiking permit.
- ☐ Wandering on your own in Canyon de Chelly, Monument Valley, or Navajo National Monument is discouraged, guided tours are the only option for backcountry travel.

Adventure takes an introspective turn in these parts. You may still ride a horse, a bike, or a jeep, but you do so as a guest in a different cultural milieu.

Among the contrasts you may see in Navajoland are some you might notice in any dramatically poor, chronically unemployed, Third World country trying to balance inherent contradictions.

On the one hand the Navajos like cashing in on their scenery, history, and traditions. And they'd like to maintain the dignity of their traditions, which is where many challenges lie. Conflicts are inevitable when attempting to balance economic growth and historic reserve while incorporating the changes wrought by an increasingly modern way of life.

Everything is symbolic in Navajo tradition. A basket, for example, represents the well-being of an individual. The Holy People created the First Man and First Woman, who made baskets for ceremonial uses. Each part of a basket has significance. Navajo people still use baskets ceremonially but workshops churn out hundreds a day for sale and today Navajos also use them for decorative touches at home.

Sand paintings are another symbolic art that originated with the Holy People for ceremonial usage. The paintings represent numerous rituals and sacred songs. Today, many Navajo artisans mass-produce these ceremonially significant objects for commercial sale throughout Navajoland. Every gallery, gift shop, and gas station is equipped with a display rack for sand-painted refrigerator magnets.

And then there is the Navajo love affair with the media. Filmmakers, television producers, and advertising art directors have long treasured the burnished, dramatic vistas stretching across the mother of the Dineh.

No problem, no conflict here. The Navajo impose fees for commercial photography; individuals vehemently decline to participate in your snapshot, but you can snap away all you like for a dollar.

What seems perfectly rational to you may not seem so to a Navajo and vice versa, so don't expect a perfectly oiled tourism machine in these parts. Some of the kinks are still being worked out. Time, for example, tends to have a different, non-specific meaning on the reservation. Slow down; a stranger putting on airs is not taken seriously anyway.

The Navajo people consider adapting to the demands of nature, as defined by themselves, a higher calling than conforming to the dominion of man, at least non-Navajo man. Treating those concerns with respect is the only way to gain more than a superficial understanding of this place, and even that might not be enough to open the doors.

According to the Navajo Tourism Department, rules and regulations regarding visits to the Navajo Reservation are as follows:

- ❏ Respect the privacy and customs of the Navajo people. Enter home areas only upon invitation.
- ❏ Do not wander across residential areas or disturb property.
- ❏ Obtain permission before taking pictures. A gratuity may be expected.
- ❏ Please keep Navajoland clean. Do not litter! Do not burn or bury garbage. Please place all refuse in trash containers.
- ❏ Do not disturb or remove animals, plants, rocks, or artifacts as these are protected by "Tribal Antiquity" and federal laws enforced on the Navajo Reservation. Rock hunting is prohibited.
- ❏ Possession and consumption of alcoholic beverages is prohibited.
- ❏ The use of firearms is not allowed on the reservation.
- ❏ The Navajo Nation is not responsible for any injuries, accidents, or thefts of personal property while travelling through the reservation.

❐ Appropriate dress is required. Please, no swimwear or bikinis.

❐ Please maintain pets on a leash or in a confined area. All actions of pets are the responsibility of the owner.

Hopiland is even harder to crack. It is bisected by AZ 264, running between US 160 in the west and US 191 in the east, and is surrounded by the southwestern corner of the vastly larger Navajo Reservation.

The Hopi Reservation was established in 1882, four years after the creation of the Navajo Reservation, granting the Hopi lands along the southern end of Black Mesa, where their families had lived for at least 650 years.

Hopiland includes three angular, flat-topped mesas jutting over the rock-strewn, scrub and cacti desert. Hopi villages include one called **Oraibi** which was settled in 1050, making it the oldest consistently occupied community in North America. Other villages, comprised of small clusters of homes, are located on **First Mesa, Second Mesa** or **Third Mesa.**

Despite the long-time proximity of their reservations, Hopis and Navajos come from different roots and differ in cultural beliefs. Navajo people are descended from nomadic Athabascan tribes that filtered into this area from Canada, around 600 years ago.

The Hopi are considered to be linked with the vanished Anasazi and have resided on the remote mesas for the past 1,000 years.

Protracted and embittered boundary feuds concerning the low-lying, arid gullies, lonely pastel buttes, and radiant, phantasmagoric mesas twinkling in the torrid desert like distant ships at sea, are still a problem with no readily apparent solution.

Ranging as high as 7,200 ft., Hopiland is a very different place than the Navajo Reservation. For one thing, the Hopi people are more clearly protective of their privacy. They tend to live close together in small villages, while the Navajo like more space between themselves and their neighbors.

In addition, no photographs, recordings, or drawings are permitted in the Hopi villages and backcountry travel is prohibited.

Particular ceremonies or dances are open only to tribal members. Other less significant ceremonies, often held on summer weekends, including distinctive dances, are considered public events, although would-be photographers are liable to have camera equipment confiscated by tribal police.

Officials will not hesitate in asking you to leave if they catch you violating their customs.

Complete guidelines for visitors to Hopiland are as follows:

- ☐ The Hopi ask you to be mindful while attending ceremonies; they call for the same respect due any sacred event – neat attire and a respectful disposition.
- ☐ Disruption of shrines or removal of articles/artifacts are strictly prohibited and possession of such items may subject the possessor to federal prosecution. All archaeological sites on the reservation are protected by federal laws and Hopi tribal ordinances.
- ☐ Photography, recording, and sketching villages and ceremonies are strictly prohibited.
- ☐ Overnight camping is allowed, but there are no facilities available.
- ☐ Alcoholic beverages and drugs are strictly prohibited by law on the Hopi Reservation.
- ☐ Before spending any length of time in the villages, permission should be obtained from the village leader. Non-Indians may not reside on the reservation without consent of the respective chief or official.
- ☐ Please observe all rules and regulations established by the villages. The villages are autonomous and have the authority to establish their own governing policies supported by the Hopi Tribal Council. It is advisable to check with village Community Development offices before going into the village to visit or witness a ceremony.

Policy signs are posted outside each village. For information about specific Hopi Villages contact the following village offices:

INFORMATION

Bacavi, ☎ 520/734-2404.
First Mesa, ☎ 520/734-2670.
Hotevilla, ☎ 520/734-2420.
Kykotsmovi, ☎ 520/734-2474.
Mishongnovi, ☎ 520/737-2520.
Moenkopi, ☎ 520/283-6684.
Shungopavi, ☎ 520/734-2262.
Sipaulovi, ☎ 520/734-2570.

Getting Around

Private vehicles or organized tours are just about the only way to travel in this area of Indian country. There are a few private landing strips, but no commercial airports.

There are fewer than 1,000 hotel rooms in all of the Navajo Nation and Hopiland. Reservations are highly recommended, particularly in summertime when hotels near popular Monument Valley and Canyon de Chelly are likely to be fully booked.

Coming from the Petrified Forest National Park area on I-40, it's 43 miles east on the interstate to a junction with Tribal Route 12 north, just a few miles west of the New Mexico border.

Window Rock, the Navajo capital and a good place to start, is 26 miles north on Tribal Route 12. There are several interesting shops and attractions in Window Rock and several possibilities for overnight accommodations.

Twenty-nine miles west of Window Rock on AZ 264 is **Hubbell Trading Post National Historic Site**, an original and still-operating trading post, where you can buy corn flakes, barbed wire, or Indian rugs. It is managed by the National Park Service. From Hubbell, it's 35 miles north on US 191 to Chinle, Arizona.

Three miles east of Chinle on Tribal Route 7 is **Canyon de Chelly National Monument**. A paved South Rim Drive ends at a rugged dirt road better suited to intrepid mountain bikers than cars. A North Rim Drive leading to overlooks along the rim of the upper **Canyon del Muerto** also leads east 25 miles to Tsaile, Arizona, location of **Navajo Community College**, the **Ned Hatathlie Cultural Center** and the main access to adventurous possibilities in the **Chuska** and **Lukachukai Mountains**, straddling the Arizona-New Mexico border.

From this area it is possible to travel south to the volcanic **Black Pinnacle** or **Wheatfields Lake**, east to **Shiprock**, New Mexico and the Four Corners National Monument, then west to **Kayenta**, Arizona, the gateway to Monument Valley.

Monument Valley lies 24 miles north of Kayenta off US 163 or 25 miles south of Mexican Hat, Utah. From there continuing to explore the Navajo Nation, you have to backtrack to Kayenta and travel 19 miles west on US 160 and nine miles north on AZ 564 to Navajo National Monument. **Tuba City** is 40 miles west on US 160 and is on the way to the **Navajo Mountain-Rainbow Bridge** area near Lake Powell.

Navajo Indian Reservation & Hopiland

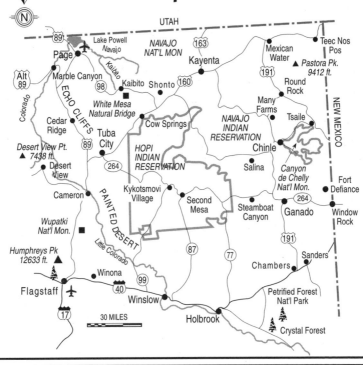

Hopiland is accessed from the west by AZ 264 which meets US 160 in Tuba City. The two-lane state highway crosses to the eastern border of the small reservation 60 miles west of Window Rock.

INFORMATION

Navajo Times, PO Box 310, Window Rock AZ 86515, ☎ 520/871-6641 or 520/871-7357, fax 520/871-6177, is the tribal newspaper which contains, among reservation and other news, information about special events.

Commercial photographers in Navajoland need a permit from **Office of Broadcast Services,** PO Box 2310, Window Rock AZ 86515, ☎ 520/871-6655 or 520/871-6656.

Permits are required for visits by non-Navajos to archaeologically, historically and culturally significant Navajo reservation sites, as well as for any archaeological or anthropological research. If you question whether or not a place you want to visit fits into one of these categories, it's probably better to ask first.

For information or required permits contact **Navajo Natural Historic Preservation Department,** PO Box 2898, Window Rock AZ 86515, ☎ 520/871-6437.

In addition, **Navajo Tribal Rangers,** responsible like their counterpart US Park Rangers for certain lands, may be reached at the following numbers: **Window Rock** AZ, ☎ 520/871-6701; **Chinle** AZ, ☎ 520/674-5250; **Crownpoint** NM, ☎ 505/786-5532; **Shiprock** NM, ☎ 505/368-4522; **Tuba City** AZ, ☎ 520/283-4644; **Montezuma Creek** UT, ☎ 801/651-3673.

Touring

Time is of a special essence in Arizona, which does not acknowledge daylight savings time. Mountain standard time is observed year-round. The exception is the Navajo Reservation, which sets its clocks ahead one hour in May, then back one hour in October. To confuse this issue, the Hopi Reservation, which is completely surrounded by the Navajo Reservation, does not change its clocks for daylight savings time.

It may help to think of it this way: in summertime, most of Arizona is on the same time as California; in winter, it's on the same time as Colorado, New Mexico, and Utah; the Navajo Reservation is on the same time as Colorado, New Mexico, and Utah year-round.

Window Rock

Window Rock, the capital of the Navajo Nation with a population of more than 3,000, is situated at 6,750 ft., 17 miles west of Gallup. The town boasts a modern motel, a relative rarity in Navajoland. You can also find several fast food options, including a Dunkin' Donuts, food markets, and gas stations, making Window Rock a functional base for day trips to Hubbell Trading Post and the Chuska Mountains.

In Window Rock you can see the octagon-shaped Navajo Nation Council Chambers, built to resemble a traditional, ceremonial hogan or Navajo home, on the short drive from downtown to **Window Rock Navajo Tribal Park**. The park and the Council Chambers are a half-mile north of AZ 264 on Tribal Route 12, and a half-mile east. This is the site of a large, red, sandstone outcrop containing a hole 47 ft. in diameter. This is the window after which the town was named. The park has a picnic area and a hiking trail.

Tours of the **Council Chambers**, which are decorated with murals illustrating Navajo history, may be arranged, ☎ 520/871-7171 or 520/871-6417. If the 88-member council, representing 100 chapters and communities, is in session, you may be able to listen to debates spoken in Navajo, the baffling language used to successfully transmit military codes during World War II.

Navajo Tribal Museum, PO Box 308, Window Rock AZ 86515, ☎ 520/871-6673, has a collection of arts and artifacts, plus exhibits describing the reservation lands, its ancient and current residents, with craft displays of various styles in silver jewelry and weaving. It is next to the Navajo Nation Inn, north of the junction of AZ 264 and Tribal Route 12 North.

Navajo Arts & Crafts Enterprises, ☎ 520/871-4090, shares the same building as the tribal museum and offers one of the more comprehensive collections in the Four Corners of high caliber natural turquoise, coral, onyx, lapis, and sterling silver jewelry, along with baskets, handwoven rugs, Navajo pottery, t-shirts, and postcards. NACE, a non-profit organization, was founded in 1941 by the Navajo Nation to promote traditional Navajo crafts. Today the operation has grown to offer works by other Southwestern Indians and craft supplies, such as beads, silver, and woolen yarns.

The same company operates a Navajo Arts & Crafts Enterprise store in Chinle, ☎ 520/674-5338, and the shop at Cameron Trading Post, ☎ 520/679-2244, in the western Navajo Nation near the Grand Canyon.

Tse Bonito Navajo Tribal Park is a half-mile east of Tribal Route 12 on AZ 264 in Window Rock. It marks the site where the Navajo people camped before starting the Long Walk to Fort Sumner, New Mexico, in 1864. There is a small campground, but no facilities.

Behind Tse Bonito park, **Navajo Nation Zoo & Botanical Park**, PO Box 308, Window Rock AZ 86515, ☎ 520/871-6573, near the Arizona-New Mexico state line on AZ 264 in Window Rock, features animals native to the Navajo Reservation and domestic animals that are culturally important to the Navajo people. You can see rattlesnakes, eagles, wolves, mountain lions, black bears, elk, coyotes, and Navajo sheep.

St. Michael's Historical Museum, three miles west of Window Rock on AZ 264, is a 1937 stone church containing exhibits relating to the history of the Catholic Church and the Navajo people.

Window Rock Enterprises, PO Box 1389, Window Rock AZ 86515, ☎ 520/871-4294 or 520/871-4562, provides tours, transportation, and information about the Window Rock area.

Navajo Transit System, ☎ 520/729-5449, operates a bus service connecting Window Rock with communities throughout the Navajo and Hopi Reservations.

For further information contact the **Navajoland Tourism Department**, PO Box 663, Window Rock AZ 86515, ☎ 520/871-7371, fax 520/871-7381.

Hubbell Trading Post

Situated 29 miles west of Window Rock on AZ 264 and a mile west of Ganado, **Hubbell Trading Post National Historic Site** is operated by the US National Park Service, but in much the same way as the property has been run for more than 100 years, as a functioning trading post. In these parts that means you can find crafts and fine arts that have been traded here for corn, beans, flour, hardware, and tools. You can also buy or presumably trade for these things yourself.

Many things changed for the Navajo people after the Long Walk in 1864, followed by the Navajo's return in 1868 to these ancestral lands. For one, the Navajo people had to start from scratch, eking out subsistence livings from the land that had been left unattended. For another, where they had once been able to live modestly and self-sufficiently, they had now been introduced to the ways of the white man. They were becoming reliant on sweets, coffee, canned foods, tools, needles, thread, cloth, and other items. But, having never been part of the cash culture, Indians could only trade the common items of their lives such as blankets, rugs, pottery, baskets, and jewelry. Cash was never exchanged at trading posts run by entrepreneurial whites.

Long into the 1900s Hubbell Trading Post and other scattered outposts across the reservation provided the sole connection between rural Indians and the encroaching society that had altered for all time their ancient ways of life.

John Lorenzo Hubbell opened the doors to his trading post here in 1878 and the property remained in continuous operation by the same family until 1965, when it was sold to the Park Service.

J.L. Hubbell died in 1930. His grave is on the side of a hillock surveying the trading post and his original homestead. A free tour is offered several times daily of his antique-decorated home, kept up in the historically accurate style of the 1880s frontier. After the short tour you can step into the trading post to buy a cold drink, a candy bar, a quart of milk, motor oil, a hammer, canned green beans, a silver bracelet, a kachina doll, or perhaps one of high quality, hand-spun and dyed, Navajo rugs.

The really fine work is stored in a big, old vault. Beware the hefty price tags. Asking prices are intentionally high here to leave room for negotiations. Selling prices may be considerably lower depending on the negotiating skill of the buyer.

In addition, during the summer months, Navajo weavers and silversmiths display their skills at demonstrations in a small museum and gift shop adjacent to the trading post.

Canyon De Chelly Monument

Five miles northwest of Hubbell Trading Post on AZ 264 then 35 miles north on US 191, is **Chinle**, a fairly large community that has developed with the growing popularity of **Canyon de Chelly National Monument**, PO Box 588, Chinle AZ 86503, ☎ 520/674-5436. There are several motels, restaurants, a Burger King, gas stations, and markets.

Canyon de Chelly National Monument is actually two main canyons, the 35-mile-long **Canyon del Muerto** to the north and the 26-mile-long **Canyon de Chelly** to the south, which converge at their lowest depths in Chinle.

The canyon walls are only 34 ft. high near Chinle, but they reach a height of 1,000 ft. at the eastern end of the National Monument. Enclosed within those vertical sandstone walls are 83,800 acres containing numerous primitive Indian sites. Yet modern Navajo farmers still tend flocks of sheep and cultivate bean fields on the fertile canyon bottom. There may be nowhere else in Indian country where the natural continuum between ancient and modern Indian life is so clearly visible in such an unaffected way.

A visitor center is located three miles east of Chinle on Tribal Route 7. There is a small museum with a full-size round log hogan (the traditional log and mud homes that many Navajos continue to live in) outside. Information is available about the rim drives to overlooks into the canyons and Navajo-guided tours are offered. Museum exhibits in the visitor center describe elements of the span of Indian occupation of the canyons.

The earliest occupants were nomads who discovered the area more than 2,000 years ago. The Anasazi periodically used the canyons before eventually settling to live in hole-in-the-ground pit houses and farm the canyon bottom around 500 AD. Successive generations evolved primitive masonry skills, eventually constructing kivas and above-ground pueblos. By the 12th-14th centuries, when they attained their cultural peak, a population of 1,000 was scattered in numerous small villages. Then, like the rest of their mysterious Anasazi brethren, they disappeared into the sands of time.

Some may have gone to nearby Hopiland. For the next 300 years only Hopis farmed the canyon bottom. The Navajos arrived in the 1700s and appreciated the many places they could hide in the canyons after looting forays against other local residents, including Spanish settlers and other Indians. In retaliation for these lootings, counter-attacks were launched that killed many Navajo braves and captured women and children for slaves.

Kit Carson, leading US Army troops, cleared out the last contentious canyon dwellers in 1864 by burning fields and killing livestock to starve the Navajo into submission. The Canyon de Chelly Navajos joined many others in the walk to New Mexico.

Survivors began filtering back in 1868. Today, their descendants still live in summer hogans to farm or raise livestock in the bountiful, moist canyon bottom right beside incredible Anasazi pueblo ruins. The main difference is that the farmers now retreat during the cold and sometimes snowy winters to live in homes with satellite dishes on the canyon rim or in Chinle.

An additional difference is the limited tours that may pass through the canyon. In general, visitors are not permitted to enter, explore, or camp in Canyon de Chelly without a park ranger or a Navajo guide.

There is one trail, to **White House Ruin**, that can be hiked unescorted, but that's it as far as exploring the inner canyon on your own is concerned. You can cruise the rim drives and stop at scenic overlooks. If you want to get inside you can hire a private guide or take one of the many tours that are offered.

The pair of 21-mile, one-way drives along the stark sandstone rims of this Navajo spiritual center begin at the visitor center. Well-marked parking areas provide access to scenic overlooks revealing 11 million years of geological history and 20 centuries of Indian habitation. These are distinguished by approximately 100 primitive ruins, many of which you can see far below the rim drive turn-offs.

On the South Rim, sites include **Tunnel Canyon Overlook, Tsegi Overlook**, and **Junction Overlook**, where Canyon del Muerto veers north. Six miles from the visitor center is **White House Overlook**.

In the deep canyon the vertical walls that appear to have been sliced neatly, as if with a chisel, blend somehow gracefully into eccentric, bulging rock forms, some forming arched rock overhangs that once offered protection against the elements to the Anasazi.

Intriguingly, amid all this rock, prosperous cultivation occurs on the canyon bottom, but even on the near-sheer walls, where trees and shrubs seem to sprout from boulders, natural cycles continue. Canyon de Chelly is a special place for observing that sort of thing.

Other stops on the South Rim Drive include **Sliding House Overlook, Wild Cherry Overlook**, and **Face Rock Overlook**.

The last stop, before the paved rim drive goes beyond the Park Service boundaries and turns into a rugged, impassable-when-wet, dirt road, is the famous **Spider Rock Overlook**, a spot that figures prominently in Navajo religious tradition. Spider Rock is an 800-ft.-tall spire rising from the canyon floor. From the 1,000-ft.-high overlook you can see this Navajo deity and a slightly smaller spire next to it, **Speaking Rock**.

The North Rim Drive follows Tribal Route 64 northeast from the visitor center along the rim of Canyon del Muerto. Stops include **Ledge Ruin Overlook, Antelope House Overlook**. Both sites reveal easily visible but tiny-looking ruins in the canyon far below. **Mummy Cave Overlook**, 18½ miles northeast of the visitor center, is a ruins site where two mummified corpses were discovered by 19th-century canyon explorers. The name Canyon del Muerto, which means Canyon of the Dead, also came from this early archaeological find.

Massacre Cave Overlook, the last stop on the North Rim Drive, is where more than a hundred Navajo were killed by Spanish soldiers in 1805.

You can return to Chinle on the North Rim Drive or continue on paved Tribal Route 64 for 13 miles to the small town of Tsaile, at the junction with Tribal Route 12. Tsaile is the modest, northerly jumping-off point for access to Tsaile Lake and Wheatfields Lake, and it is the location of Navajo Community College, home to the **Ted Hatathlie Museum & Gallery, ☎ 520/724-3311.**

The entrance to the college is a mile west of Tribal Route 12 off Tribal Route 64 and the Hatathlie Museum is on the east side of the small campus in a six-story cultural center shaped like a hogan. Exhibits explain primitive and modern Indian cultures. There is a gift shop and bookstore.

Wheatfields Lake is 10 miles south of Tsaile off Tribal Route 12. It's a popular fishing lake in a mountainous location. There is a campground and the Lakeside Store.

Tsaile Lake, Assayi Lake, Bowl Canyon Recreation Area and several other lakes are in the mountains south of Wheatfields Lake and north of Window Rock. These areas are detailed below, under *Fishing* and *Camping*.

Fifteen miles south of Wheatfields Lake on Tribal Route 12 is a junction with NM 134, which can be followed for 20 miles northeast across the scenic **Chuska Mountains** to US 666. From there it's 43 miles north on US 666 to Shiprock NM, a large Navajo community named after **Shiprock Peak**.

The 1,500-ft. volcanic rock is visible 10 miles southwest of town, looming high over the desert. There are no services near the landmark; the Navajo spiritual site is off-limits to hikers and climbers and can only be viewed from a distance.

Shiprock is not a particularly interesting town. One good thing in town is a supermarket. It is not a gas station/convenience store, but a real market. There are also several trading posts in the vicinity offering a range of Indian goods, including **Foutz Trading Company**, Shiprock NM 87420, ☎ 505/368-5790, three miles west of town on US 64. Two other trading posts are 15 miles east of town on US 64 in Waterflow, New Mexico.

From Shiprock, following US 64 west for 26 miles leads to **Teec Nos Pos**, a tiny, practically invisible community with a small motel and the **Teec Nos Pos Trading Post**, noted for sales of distinctive, locally made rugs.

Six miles northeast of Teec Nos Pos on US 160 is **Four Corners Monument Navajo Tribal Park**, a small park marking the only site in the United States where the borders of four states – Arizona, New

Mexico, Colorado, and Utah – meet. Strangely, there's little to see here in the actual center of this amazing territory of mountains, canyons, rivers, and deserts that form the Four Corners region. The exact spot is marked by a stone slab in the ground which you may stand on, officially being in four states at one time. A typically disconsolate assortment of Indian vendors offers t-shirts and mass-produced souvenirs from rickety wooden stalls.

From the Four Corners Monument it's 40 miles north on US 160 to Cortez, Colorado, and 28 miles north to the Ute Mountain Casino, providing insight into another aspect of modern Indian culture and perhaps even insight into the drab Four Corners monument.

Continuing west in Navajoland on US 160 it's 70 miles to **Kayenta**, the next reservation town of any magnitude and the gateway to **Monument Valley**.

Monument Valley

Kayenta is at the junction of US 160 and US 163, 23 miles south of Monument Valley Navajo Tribal Park.

The town provides basic services, several motels, restaurants, a market, and gas stations. It may not seem like much to offer, but there is only one motel and a campground in the extremely popular Monument Valley. Many travellers secure accommodations in Kayenta as a base for excursions north and to the **Navajo National Monument**, 28 miles west of town.

One of the more interesting sites in Kayenta is located in the Burger King. It is an exhibit of memorabilia relating to the Navajo code-talkers of World War II. Navajo servicemen relayed vital information in their native language, which baffled enemy cryptographers.

Eight miles north of Kayenta, on the way to **Monument Valley Navajo Tribal Park**, PO Box 93, Monument Valley UT 84536, ☎ 801/727-3287, lunar-looking **Agthala Peak**, a 1,500-ft. volcanic outcrop, looms to the east over desert flats, hinting at the magnitude of the geological wonders to come.

The 30,000-acre Navajo tribal park straddles the Arizona-Utah border east of US 163, 23 miles north of Kayenta and 25 miles south of Mexican Hat, Utah. You have to enter the park through Utah, on a three-mile entry road east of US 163, but the main scenic attractions are back across the border in Arizona. Near the highway the side of the entry road supports a row of stands offering frybread, Navajo tacos, mutton sandwiches, silver jewelry, and rugs.

At the end of the road there is a visitor center with bathrooms, gift and book store, campground, tour guides and traditionally dressed models who will pose for photographers at a small cost. Otherwise, the closest services are at Goulding's Lodge. The lodge, a mile west of US 163 across the highway from the park entrance, includes a motel, restaurant, gift shop, museum, tour services, landing strip, grocery store, and gas station.

The next closest services are in Kayenta or Mexican Hat. If you're shopping for antique Indian arts and crafts try the **Oljeto Trading Post**, nine miles northwest of Goulding's. Follow the paved road running past the Goulding's complex for some unusual finds.

Monument Valley's year-round visitor center is adjacent to a campground, open in summer only. From this area you can look out over red buttes, mesas, and pinnacles rising off the valley floor in distinctive individual majesty, like a proud tribe turned to stone. If it all seems somehow familiar, it's probably because the vistas, back roads, washes, gullies, and canyons have appeared as settings in dozens of western movies, television shows, commercials, and print ads. Monument Valley is particularly known as one of the favorite locations of Hollywood director John Ford, who filmed several John Wayne movies here. Other stars such as Henry Fonda appeared in Ford's classics *Fort Apache* and *My Darling Clementine,* made here. *The Searchers, The Trial of Billy Jack,* and The *Legend of the Lone Ranger* are among other features filmed in Monument Valley. There is a 17-mile loop road through the valley that is open to private vehicles, but no backcountry exploration is permitted without a Navajo guide. That deserted-looking back road that beckons is probably a Navajo family's driveway.

There are numerous turn-offs that offer views within the park and ample opportunity to stop and admire craft items displayed at strategic locations in open-sided, thatch roof sheds or simply spread on a blanket.

The scenic drive, a rather confusing and virtually unmarked sandy track filled with numerous opportunities for wrong turns, passes named sites, some with special spiritual significance to the Navajo people, as well as **John Ford Point**, honoring the movie maker who masterfully employed the valley's mystique to immortalize his film legacy and the epic scenery at the same time. Other activities on the valley floor, aside from car, bus, and jeep tour traffic, includes Navajo herdsmen trailing sheep through gullies and canyons studded with juniper, pinyon, and wind-blown, dusty sage, overshadowed by the mammoth, vertical rocks.

Even without being allowed to wander very far on your own, the views from the valley bottom drive are impressive. But a lot of people want to see more, hence the booming local industry in guided tours. An encampment of operators outside the visitor center offers a variety of scheduled or customized tour services throughout the day and night. Special photography tours depart before dawn or in the late afternoon to capture long valley shadows. Full moon evening tours are scheduled and wildlife tours depart at certain hours, depending on the animals being sought. You can generally book a scheduled tour on the spot for the same day, although the valley does get crowded in the summer and tours are in great demand.

The elegantly expansive valley seems to stretch forever into time, the eons marked by the dominating monoliths, volcanic steeples, isolated buttes, and mesas. The **Mittens**, **Merrick Butte**, **Elephant Butte**, **Three Sisters**, **Camel Butte**, **Sentinel Mesa**, **Totem Pole**, and **Yei Bei Chei**, are just some of the massive, independent-standing, angular stone sentinels that form the archetypal landscape instantly recognizable as the Southwest.

The fascinating details incorporated in that image, found in the nooks and crannies of Monument Valley, encourage the allotment of a day or more for surveying prehistoric Indian ruins, pictographs, hidden arches, and sandstone pinnacles standing atop the desert landscape. If you only see one Arizona sunset, this is the place to plant yourself on a rock escarpment and watch the shadows lengthen across the desert flats, the slanting rays of late-day sun coloring the rocky sandstone, bringing out a subtle range of pinkish hues, darkening into shades of red. A feverish glow radiates under a fading blue sky, finally relenting the remaining daylight in bright bands of mauve, pink, purple, and red. Near the horizon, colors transpose from the silhouetted rocks.

Monument Valley is popular in summertime. There may be crowds around the visitor center, campground, and Goulding's Lodge. The busiest part of the scenic drive is the first mile or so from the visitor center. After the sharp descent into the valley bottom there are different ways to go, so the traffic disperses. Still, you are not likely to have a private experience in here unless you arrange for some sort of guided tour into the hinterlands of the tribal park. The park's popularity and the lack of extensive accommodations in the area mean you should not count on a last minute reservation at Goulding's between May 15 and September 15. During this period it also gets extremely hot here (in the 100° range). Even if you're just going out for an hour or two on the scenic drive, carry water and food.

Springtime is beautiful in the desert, with wildflowers; fall is comfortably warm.

A good book on the area is *A Traveler's Guide to Monument Valley*, by Stuart Aitchison, Voyageur Press, 1993.

Navajo Monument & Reservation

Twenty miles west of Kayenta on US 160, then nine miles north on AZ 564, is the largest of the prehistoric Indian pueblo-type ruins in Arizona, at **Navajo National Monument**, PO Box 3, Tonalea AZ 86044, ☎ 520/672-2366 or 520/672-2367.

There is a visitor center with a small museum, a small but tasteful gift shop, and information on guided tours, which are the only way you can get close to the ruins in this park. The museum offers a free film on the Anasazi and artifacts, such as pottery, are on display.

A paved, half-mile trail from the visitor center leads to an overlook, from which you can see the **Betatakin Ruins**, carved into a mammoth 450-ft.-tall, 370-ft.-wide, and 135-ft.-deep alcove, set in a slender, steep-walled canyon. The only way you can visit the 135-room ruins is on a daily, ranger-guided, five-mile round-trip hike offered May through August and limited to 20 people. The round-trip hike is scheduled to take five hours and entails a 700-ft. descent from the 7,300-ft. canyon rim. Bear in mind that you will have to hike that same distance back to the rim.

Keet Seel Ruins are open from late May to early September and can only be reached by a strenuous eight-mile trail from the monument's visitor center. Because of the fragile condition and remote location of the ruins only 20 hikers a day are allowed to visit. A round-trip in a day is possible for strong hikers. You can also choose to camp near the isolated ruins and return the following day. Backcountry permits are required and are available at the visitor center. Arrangements can also be made there for a horseback trip with a Navajo guide. The horseback trips reach the ruins and return the same day.

Bring water and food on any hikes in this area. Be sure to plan sufficiently ahead and make reservations. Although cancellations do occasionally occur on the day of scheduled hikes, the limited numbers of people allowed to view these ruins makes planning ahead a virtual necessity. Horseback trips are a little easier to secure on short notice, but numbers on these are also restricted.

Navajo Mountain, northwest of Navajo National Monument, is the tallest peak on the reservation at 10,388 ft., rising east of **Rainbow Bridge National Monument**, near the shore of the San Juan Arm of Lake Powell. The road access is 13 miles west of AZ 564 on US 160, then northwest 12½ miles on AZ 98 to a turn-off north on Tribal Route 16. Route 16 is paved for 13 miles, then turns to dirt for the rest of the 24 miles to the west side of the mountain or the 29 miles to the east side. You can hike to Rainbow Bridge National Monument from trailheads on either side of Navajo Mountain.

On the east side of Navajo Mountain, **Navajo Mountain Trading Post** (Tonalea AZ 86044), offers guided horseback and hiking tours of Navajo Mountain and Rainbow Bridge National Monument. Backcountry permits issued by the Navajo Tribe are required for any off-road travel in this area and these are available by mail or in person from the **Navajo Parks & Recreation Department** (PO Box 308, Window Rock AZ 86515, ☎ 520/871-4941, extension 6647) or in person from the **Cameron Visitor Center**, at the junction of US 89 and AZ 64, on the western edge of the Navajo Nation.

If you were to continue northwest on AZ 98 past the turn-off for Navajo Mountain, 60 miles further you would reach Page, Arizona.

Continuing west on US 160 leads instead to **Tuba City** on the western edge of Navajoland, hardly a metropolis, though it does boast a population of more than 5,000. Situated 70 miles west of Kayenta on US 160, it's a good place to get gas or groceries, have a meal, or spend a night, but there's little to see and do in town.

Five miles west of town, on the north side of US 160, are some purported dinosaur tracks. Five miles beyond the dinosaur tracks is US 89. Fifteen miles south on US 89 is Cameron. From here, you can access the Grand Canyon to the west or Wupatki and Sunset Crater National Monuments and Flagstaff to the south.

Hopiland

Tuba City provides access to the western edge of Hopiland. In Tuba City turn south from US 160 on to AZ 264, which leads south and west for 40 miles across bare desert to Third Mesa. This is the start of the main Hopi settlements stretched along the two-lane highway for the next 40 miles or so to **Keams Canyon**.

Old Oraibi, thought to be the oldest continually occupied village in the United States, dating to 1100 AD, is on **Third Mesa**, a short distance south of AZ 264. Many historians think the Hopi people are descendants of the Anasazis. The stone houses clustered here on the rim of the mesa resemble nothing so much as the ancient ruins scattered all over Arizona, except with 20th-century people living in them. Several craft shops are found in dilapidated-looking structures in this tiny village.

Kykotsmovi is two miles east of the Old Oraibi turn-off on AZ 264. This is the site of the Tribal Government offices, which are a mile south of the highway. Several shops and a small grocery store are located in town and the **Hopi Civic Center** is just east of town on the highway. It's a community center, gymnasium, and the site for special events such as the **Reggae Inna Hopiland** shows, detailed below under *Eco-travel & Cultural Excursions.*

Six miles east of Kykotsmovi on **Second Mesa** is the **Hopi Cultural Center**, a modern complex with a motel, restaurant, campground, and a museum featuring exhibits that explain aspects of the Hopi culture and way of life. The displays are circumspect. The Hopi continue to be publicly reticent to divulge certain features of their customs or beliefs. There are several craft shops in the Cultural Center complex and on the adjacent highway. Other shops are farther east on Second Mesa, in the villages of **Secakuku** or **Shungopavi**. Look for a small sign in the front window indicating sales from individual homes.

Hopis are particularly recognized for silver overlay jewelry, enclosing polished stones behind intricately hand-cut silver silhouettes. You can also find rugs or cottonwood-carved kachina dolls representing Hopi spiritual beings, colorful woven sashes, hand-coiled pottery, and coiled baskets. Serious shoppers probably need to spend a few days here. Inquire locally about the finest crafts people and arrange personal visits for the best selections or custom-ordered work.

A good place to start is the **Hopi Arts and Crafts Silvercraft Cooperative Guild**, PO Box 37, Second Mesa AZ 86043, ☎ 520/734-2463. This shop, next to the Hopi Cultural Center, represents the work of hundreds of Hopi artists, offering silver jewelry, weavings, baskets, pottery, and kachina dolls. You can usually see artisans at work here and make arrangements to meet them privately.

First Mesa is the location of **Walpi**, another very old Hopi village that appears to have developed organically out of the mesa rim and has never had running water or electricity. Visitors are not permitted to enter without a guide. Half-hour tours leave from a visitor center outside this village. Craft work is often offered for sale by villagers. For information about tours or this tiny, 30-person village, ☎ 520/737-226 or 520/737-2670.

Keams Canyon anchors the eastern edge of Hopiland. It has a motel, restaurant, trading post and federal government offices. The modern town is seemingly made of trailers and is utterly without charm.

Keams Canyon Arts & Crafts, PO Box 607, Keams Canyon AZ 86024, ☎ 520/738-2295, offers a wide variety of souvenirs and also has a back room with extremely high quality Indian goods.

For information on Hopi ceremonies phone the **Hopi Indian Agency** in Keams Canyon, ☎ 602/738-2228. For information about the Hopi Villages contact the tribal headquarters, **Hopi Tribe**, PO Box 123, Kykotsmovi AZ 86039, ☎ 520/734-2441.

Villages tend to have their own sets of rules in addition to the tribal rules and these are generally posted just outside each village. In some cases, as when visiting Walpi, this means you cannot enter the village without a local guide. For specific information, the phone numbers for each village are given above, under the introduction to *The Navajo Nation & Hopiland*.

Adventures

Where backcountry activities on Navajo land are allowed, permits and fees are required. Information is available from **Navajo Parks & Recreation Department**, PO Box 308, Window Rock AZ 86515, ☎ 520/871-4941, extension 6647. The office is next to the zoo. Permits are available by mail or in person. There is a walk-in permit station at the Cameron Visitor Center, south of Cameron Trading Post on US 89 at the junction with AZ 64.

On Foot

Rock climbing and off-trail hiking are prohibited on the Navajo Reservation. In many places, loose, fragile rock and unfamiliar terrain may make climbing and hiking hazardous.

If you get a permit at the visitor center and hire a Navajo guide, you can hike through Canyon de Chelly National Monument and even camp overnight within the canyon. Ranger-led hikes are also offered by the center in the summer. Reservations are accepted.

In Canyon de Chelly summer weather is quite hot. Bring water, insect repellent and wear a hat. Winters can be snowy and cold.

Early spring is usually wet. May-June and September-October are the best months for hikers.

The only hiking you can do on your own in Canyon de Chelly is the **White House Ruin Trail**. The trailhead is at the White House Overlook, six miles east of the visitor center on the South Rim Drive. The trail descends 500 ft. in 1½ miles to White House Ruin, an Anasazi site containing remnants of more than 50 rooms and several kivas.

Hiking without a licensed guide is not permitted in Monument Valley. Guided hiking tours in Monument Valley, Mystery Valley and Hunts Mesa are offered by **Fred's Adventure Tours**, PO Box 310308, Mexican Hat UT 94531, ☎ 801/739-4294, and **Black's Hiking and Van Tours**, PO Box 393, Mexican Hat UT 84531, ☎ 801/739-4226. Otherwise inquire of the local tour operators around the visitor center for hiking guide services by the hour or extended overnight backpack trips. A number of these operators are listed below, under *Jeeping*.

At Navajo National Monument the eight-mile hike to **Keet Seel Ruins** offers an overnight backpack trip through Keet Seel Canyon to Arizona's largest Anasazi ruin. Elevation change is 700 ft. from the 7,000-ft. canyon rim to the ruins below and most of this change occurs in the first mile from the visitor center. The majority of the trail follows the canyon bottom and is considered easy. It is open from late May to early September and access is limited to 20 people per day. Reservations may be made as far as two months in advance through the visitor center. There is a primitive campground near the 160-room ruins, but you should bring your own water. Any water found in this area would need to be treated before consumption.

Ranger-guided hikes to Navajo National Monument's **Betatakin Ruins** are detailed above, under *Touring*.

Provided you have the appropriate permits, hiking and backpacking are permitted around Navajo Mountain or to **Rainbow Bridge National Monument**. To reach the trailheads follow the directions from AZ 98 (see above). The east fork of the road leads to the Navajo Trading Post and the trail from there to Rainbow Bridge is 14 miles each way. If you start on the west side of Navajo Mountain you can drive as far as the **Rainbow Lodge Ruins**. The trail from there is 12 miles one-way to the National Monument. You can't camp at Rainbow Bridge, but you can camp out along the trails, which are poorly marked and unmaintained. A topographical map is recommended if you do not have a Navajo guide. No services are available anywhere along either trail.

The trail from Rainbow Lodge is considered the classic hike to Rainbow Bridge and is the route used by most guided trips. Allow at least two days for the round-trip hike, which starts at an elevation of 6,300 ft., in the shadow of Navajo Mountain, and descends to 3,300 ft. at Rainbow Bridge. The canyon country is rugged and the trail is not well-marked. Many hikers take three days to complete this trip.

The trail from the east side of Navajo Mountain is longer, less used and even rougher, skirting the northern edges of Navajo Mountain and the red rock canyons between the mountain and Lake Powell.

Four Corners School of Outdoor Education (PO Box 78, East Route, Monticello UT 84535, ☎ 801/587-2156), offers a six-night llama/hiking tour in mid-September, called "Stories From Navajo Bridge & Rainbow Mountain." The trip covers a 30-mile hike around and through side canyons on rough trails with significant changes in elevation. Llamas carry the gear. As you circle the base of Navajo Mountain and explore side canyons stretching to Rainbow Bridge, an archaeologist-naturalist guide team directs discussions emphasizing the natural and cultural history of Navajo Mountain – an area that has figured into Navajo mythology and legend for thousands of years.

The **Antelope Creek Canyon** area south of Page off AZ 98, also known as **Corkscrew Canyon**, offers rugged unmaintained trails for experienced hikers through marble-walled canyon country. This is the area where some of the narrowest and most evocative slot canyons can be found, including the most impressive looking ones that always end up in art or travel photographs. Hiking permits are available at the Lee Chee Chapter House, three miles southwest of Antelope Creek Canyon on Tribal Route 20.

By Horse

Two Navajo-run stables offer horseback trips in Canyon de Chelly. You can also ride your own horse if you hire a Navajo guide to travel with you. Information is available from the visitor center or the following outfitters:

❐ **Justin's Horse Rentals**, PO Box 881, Chinle AZ 86503, ☎ 520/674-5678, is located near the start of the South Rim Drive and offers guided horseback trips by the hour or multi-day, overnight pack trips.

◻ **Twin Trail Tours**, PO Box 1716, Window Rock AZ 86515, ☎ 520/674-5985, offers trips into Canyon del Muerto. These include full-day trips featuring a 700-ft. descent into the canyon and visits to such sites as Mummy Cave, Standing Cow Ruin, and Antelope House Ruin. Overnight pack trips are available.

Horseback trips into other parts of Navajoland are offered by the following outfitters:

Bigman's Horseback Tours, PO Box 1557, Kayenta AZ 86033, ☎ 520/677-3219, offers a variety of trips in the areas around Mitchell Butte, Mystery Valley, Rain God Mesa, and Big Chief, all south of Monument Valley.

Monument Valley Horseback Trailrides, PO Box 155, Mexican Hat UT, 84531-0155, ☎ 801/739-4285 or 800/551-4039, offers customized horseback trips for four to 25 riders in Monument Valley, Mystery Valley, Hunts Mesa, and Horse Canyon.

With Navajo guides you explore these areas for an hour, a day or on camping trips lasting up to five days, riding through ancient Anasazi and Navajo lands.

On longer trips the guides lead you to remote places visited by few non-Indians, where broken pottery shards litter the ground beneath boulders packed with petroglyphs, while coyotes howl at night in the moon shadows of the monoliths.

Monument Valley Horseback Trailrides is a Navajo-run company. Two or more guides accompany each trip. Overnight packages include food, sleeping bags, and tents (if you bring your own gear there is a dramatic difference in price). A truck meets the group nightly with supplies and food. Trips are offered year-round.

Triple Heart Ranch Tours, Mexican Springs Trading Post, Mexican Springs NM 87320, ☎ 505/733-2377, offers horseback trips in the vicinity of Mexican Springs, the Chuska Mountains, Chinle, Rough Rock, Kayenta, and Monument Valley.

Don Donnelly Stables, 6100 Kings Ranch Road, Gold Canyon AZ 85219, ☎ 520/982-7822 or 800/346-4403, runs trips exploring the beauty of Arizona and Utah from the comfort of a well-made western saddle, including a Monument Valley ride offered in spring and fall. The trip starts with airport pick-up in Gallup and features comfortable camps set up with spacious tents, cots, toilets, hot showers, a dinner tent, gourmet chef, and evening entertainment. Indians and ranchers sometimes drop by to share stories around the campfire. Gear and equipment are transported by four-wheel-drive truck.

Rainbow Trails & Tours, PO Box 7218, Shonto AZ 86045, ☎ 520/672-2397, offers horseback trips to Rainbow Bridge National Monument.

On Wheels

The Navajo Tribe asks that visitors please restrict travel to designated trails and established routes. Travel by four-wheel-drive vehicles, dune buggies, jeeps, and motorcycles is prohibited on backcountry roads.

JEEPING & FOUR-WHEEL-DRIVE TRIPS

Other than hiking or horseback riding with an Indian guide, a four-wheel-drive tour is the only way to see the bottom of Canyon de Chelly. Most people take the organized, guided tours in large, open-sided, almost amphibious, jeeps or trucks. These are able to negotiate the boggy low spots and deceptive sandy washes containing quicksand and other obstacles that typically challenge travellers on the canyon bottom.

You can drive your own four-wheel-drive vehicle if you obtain a permit from the visitor center and hire a Navajo guide to ride along with you. Contact the Canyon de Chelly Visitor Center for information.

Thunderbird Tours, at Thunderbird Lodge, offers year-round, half-day or full-day tours of Canyon de Chelly and Canyon del Muerto in heavy-duty, six-wheel, four-wheel-drive touring vehicles. These are commanded by knowledgeable Navajo guides who know their way around the canyons' quicksand and muck. The guides point out deep red walls, natural monuments of sculpted sandstone, steep cliffs, ancient dwellings built in seemingly inaccessible caves, and the hand and toe holds by which these sites were reached. The tour takes you close to such sites as Mummy Cave and Antelope House Ruin.

Four-wheel-drive vehicle tours in Monument Valley and other areas generally inaccessible otherwise are offered by the following tour companies:

INFORMATION

Goulding's Tours, PO Box 1, Monument Valley UT 84536, ☎ 801/727-3231, fax 801/727-3344, offers half-day or full-day tours with Navajo drivers well-versed in cultural, geological, and historical information. Tours are scheduled March 15 through October and are available on request during winter months.

Golden Sands Tours, PO Box 458, Kayenta AZ 86033, ☎ 520/697-3684, operates jeep tours of Hunts Mesa, Hoskinni Mesa, and Monument Valley.

Tours of the Big Country, PO Box 309, Bluff UT 84512, ☎ 801/672- 2281, offers naturalist-guided vehicle tours of Monument Valley, based out of the Recapture Lodge.

Crawley's Monument Valley Tours, PO Box 187, Kayenta AZ 86033, ☎ 520/697-3463, offers vehicle tours of Monument Valley, Mystery Valley and Hunts Mesa.

Totem Pole Guided Tours, PO Box 306, Monument Valley UT 84536, ☎ 801/727-3230, offers vehicle tours of Monument Valley, Mystery Valley, Hunts Mesa, Poncho House, Paiute Farms, and Hoskinni Mesa.

Navajo Guided Tours, PO Box 456, Monument Valley UT 84536-0375, offers vehicle tours of Monument Valley and Mystery Valley.

Black's Hiking & Van Tours, PO Box 393, Mexican Hat UT 84531, ☎ 801/739-4226.

Fred's Adventure Tours, PO Box 308, Mexican Hat UT 84531, ☎ 801/739-4294.

Jackson's Guided Tours, PO Box 375, Monument Valley UT 84536-0375, offers vehicle tours of Monument Valley, Mystery Valley and Poncho House.

Bennett Guided Tours, PO Box 360285, Monument Valley UT 84536, ☎ 801/727-3283, offers vehicle tours of Monument Valley and Mystery Valley.

Jeep Tours/Roland C. Dixon, PO Box 131, Kayenta AZ 86033, ☎ 800/377-9370, offers jeep tours of Monument Valley.

MOUNTAIN BIKING

Backcountry mountain biking is prohibited on both reservations, but there are still some pretty good bike routes.

The rim drives at **Canyon de Chelly** are well-suited to biking. A round-trip on either drive from the visitor center runs about 40 miles. On the South Rim Drive, at the end of the paved road near the Spider Rock Overlook, the dirt **Tribal Route 7** continues for 35 miles to Tribal Route 12, six miles north of Window Rock.

In the Chuska Mountains, **Tribal Route 12** from Tsaile to Window Rock is a 52-mile stretch of paved road through mountainous terrain, fishing lakes, and pine-studded high country.

The **Monument Valley Loop Road** covers 17 miles one-way over sandy, dusty terrain mostly in the valley bottom, but with some short, steep climbs.

The nine miles of **AZ 564** between US 160 and Navajo National Monument are all uphill to the visitor center, but there are lots of trees and shady spots for cool rest stops overlooking scenic Tsegi Canyon.

Tribal Route 16 north from AZ 98 in western Navajoland to Rainbow Lodge covers 40 miles to Navajo Mountain and Lake Powell. A camping permit would be needed from **Navajo Parks & Recreation Department** (PO Box 663, Window Rock AZ 86515, ☎ 520/871-4941, extension 6647) for overnight travel in this area.

You might not be able to gain access to certain villages with a bicycle, but the route from Tuba City through Hopiland on **AZ 264** to US 191 is sufficient, at best, for a bicycler. There's not much shade and two-wheelers will have to share the narrow road with motorized traffic. There are several motels and free campgrounds in Hopiland so it's possible to make a multi-day road ride out of the 120-mile stretch.

On Water

The Navajo tribe operates 12 major fishing lakes. All are open to fishing year-round unless otherwise noted. Among the ones reported to be the best are the following:

- ❐ **Ganado Lake** is two miles east of Ganado on AZ 264 then a mile north on Indian Route 27. Camping is permitted but there are no facilities.
- ❐ **Tsaile Lake**, just south of Navajo Community College in Tsaile, offers fishing for bass, catfish, and trout.
- ❐ **Wheatfields Lake**, 10 mile south of Tsaile on Tribal Route 12 is a popular lake for rainbow and cutthroat trout fishing.
- ❐ **Whiskey Lake**, five miles south of Wheatfields Lake, is stocked with rainbow and cutthroat trout, open May 1 to November 30.

- **Asaayi** and **Berland Lakes**, off Tribal Route 12 between Wheatfields Lake and Window Rock, and Chuska Red Lake, north of Gallup off US 666 in New Mexico, are stocked with channel and warm water catfish.
- Try **Morgan Lake**, east of Shiprock off US 64, which is near the mammoth Four Corners Power Plant, a coal-burning, smoke belching behemoth. The plant tends to detract from the wilderness experience, but not from the trophy-size largemouth bass. Many Farms Lake, 14 miles north of Chinle, off US 191, might be a better bet for peace and quiet. You can fish for channel catfish and largemouth bass.
- **The Navajo Adventurers**, c/o Anthony Lee, PO Box 124, Bloomfield NM 87413, ☎ 505/632-3893, specializes in personalized, step-on fishing guide services in the Carrizo, Chuska, Lukachukai, and Beautiful Mountains east of Canyon de Chelly. This means you provide the vehicle and Mr. Lee rides along, imparting his local wisdom, directing you toward views spreading as far away as Navajo Mountain or the San Francisco Peaks, pointing out scenery that might otherwise go unnoticed, and leading you straight to where the fish are biting. All trips are customized to the client's specifications.

A permit is required for fishing any lakes or streams under jurisdiction of the Navajo Nation. These and information on fees and dates, as well as boating regulations, are available from **Navajo Fish & Wildlife Office**, PO Box 1480, Window Rock AZ 86515, ☎ 520/871-6451 or 520/871-6452. You don't need a state license to fish on the Navajo Reservation, only the Navajo-issued license.

Considering the size of the Navajo Reservation there are relatively few places offering information on fishing, boating, or permits. Use the following sources:

- **Lakeside Store Wheatfields**, PO Box 2309, Window Rock AZ 86515, ☎ 602/724-3262.
- **Fed Mart Store**, PO Box 269, Window Rock AZ 86515, ☎ 602/871-4724,
- **K-Mart Store**, #7361, 1312 West I-40 Frontage Road, Gallup NM 87301, ☎ 505/722-7261.
- **Swift's Sporting Goods**, 1725 South 2nd Street, Gallup NM 87301, ☎ 505/863-9331.
- **Wal-Mart**, 1308 West Metro, Gallup NM 87301, ☎ 505/722-2296.
- **Wal-Mart**, 700 Mike's Pike Boulevard, Winslow AZ 86047, ☎ 602/289-4641.

- ☐ **Ross Sporting Goods**, 204 West Main, Farmington NM 87401, ☎ 505/325-1062.
- ☐ **Zia Sporting Goods**, 500 East Main, Farmington NM 87401, ☎ 505/327-6004.
- ☐ **Four Corners Windsurfing**, PO Box 751, Fruitland NM 87406, ☎ 505/598-6688.
- ☐ **Kirtland Pawn Shop**, PO Box 166, Kirtland NM 87417, ☎ 505/598-6969.
- ☐ **Handy's Bait & Tackle**, 504 Aztec Boulevard, Aztec NM 87410, ☎ 505/334-9114.
- ☐ **Bonds & Bonds**, PO Box 640, Shiprock NM 87420, ☎ 505/368-4448.
- ☐ **Market City**, PO Box FF, Shiprock NM 87420, ☎ 505/368-4248.
- ☐ **Copper Village Development Corp.**, Sheep Springs Trading Post, Sheep Springs NM 87364, ☎ 505/732-4211.
- ☐ **Tsaile Trading Post**, PO Box 66, Tsaile AZ 86556, ☎ 602/724-3397.
- ☐ **Kayenta Trading Post**, PO Box 175, Kayenta AZ 86003, ☎ 602/697-3554.
- ☐ **CSWTA Inc., Environmental Consultants**, PO Box 790, Tuba City AZ 86045, ☎ 602/283-4323.
- ☐ **Cow Springs Trading Post**, Tonalea AZ 86004, ☎ 602/283-5377.
- ☐ **Red Barn Trading Post**, PO Box 245, Sanders AZ 86512-0245, ☎ 602/688-2762.

Four Corners School of Outdoor Education (East Route, Monticello UT 84535, ☎ 801/587-2859 or 801/587-2156) offers a week-long river trip in mid-May on the San Juan River, led by a Navajo biologist who interprets the meaning of the natural communities along the river to the Navajo people. Part of this trip is devoted to assisting the Navajo people in the ongoing study to identify and record non-native plants and animals that live in the riparian zone along the river.

The **Navajo Natural Heritage Program**, associated with The Nature Conservancy, is studying the ribbons of precious riparian habitat found along the river and its tributary creeks as part of an effort to protect native species and habitats found in otherwise austere country. While drifting the San Juan River in mid-May, participants help assess the changing ecological relationships caused by invasion of non-native flora and fauna.

In Air

Two Jays Helicopters, ☎ 801/727-3200, is based in an enviable position for a flightseeing operator, on UT 163, in between Gouldings and Monument Valley in Utah, offering tours of Monument Valley, Goosenecks of the San Juan, Lake Powell, Natural Bridges, Grand Gulch, Navajo Mountain and Rainbow Bridge.

Eco-travel & Cultural Excursions

Dances, festivals, rodeos, and tribal fairs are among the seasonal cultural events to be found in these areas.

Navajo Nation Fair, ☎ 520/871-6478, is held in Window Rock, Arizona early every September. The huge festival is billed as the World's Largest American Indian Fair. Although the people who run the Gallup Inter-Tribal Ceremonial might disagree with that claim, this is undeniably a big event, attracting around 200,000 participants and visitors during its five-day run. Navajo people from 110 far-flung, big and mostly little communities spread across the 26,000-square-mile reservation gather to celebrate, dance and socialize.

Activities at this over-sized county fair include a free beef brisket barbecue dinner for 8,000 guests, a Saturday morning parade, animal exhibits, carnival rides, rodeos, nightly country-western concerts featuring nationally known acts, traditional Indian song and dance contests, and Pow Wow dances performed by traditionally outfitted Indians from all over North America, including members of the Navajo, Apache, Sioux, Taos, Tewa, Ute, and Zuni tribes.

A beauty pageant to crown Miss Navajo Nation is held and crowns are presented to Navajo beauty pageant royalty in the persons of Miss Teen Navajo and Miss Northern Navajo. Indian foods, such as mutton and frybread are available from vendors – mainly women wearing traditional clothing and jewelry. There's a contest for the best frybread. In addition, prize-winning pottery, jewelry, rugs, baskets, and paintings are displayed and offered for sale.

Also in Window Rock each October is a popular **Coyote Calling Contest**. For information contact the Navajo Fish & Wildlife Department.

Shiprock Navajo Nation Fair, PO Box 1893, Shiprock NM 87420, ☎ 505/368-5108, 505/368-4679 or 505/368-4892, also known as the **Northern Navajo Fair**, is the oldest Navajo tribal fair. It is held in the reservation's largest city during the first week in October to celebrate the harvest. The fair coincides with an ancient Navajo healing ceremony: *The Night Way* or *Yei Bei Chei*, a nine-day chant. This complex, detailed ritual is usually held after the first frost and the public is permitted to view parts of the ceremony during the fair. Among the colorful rituals are *Yei's Come*, a Saturday afternoon dance, and masked *Yei Bei Chei Dancing*, starting on Saturday night and continuing until dawn on Sunday morning.

You can watch, but don't even think about taking photographs. "There is absolutely no pictures to be taken in the YEI BEI CHEI," according to tribal literature.

There's a free barbecue to open the fair on Thursday, a rodeo, an ongoing midway and carnival, 10K run, and a western dance. Other activities include social, as opposed to ceremonial, dancing and singing groups. You will also see Pow Wow contestants from all over the Navajo Nation and North America, outfitted in their best traditional attire. There are exhibits of livestock, arts and crafts, and there is an Indian Market where arts and crafts, as well as farm produce, are offered for sale. A big parade is held on Saturday morning, featuring local, regional, off-reservation, and national entries.

Other regional Navajo fairs, similar in style, though a bit smaller in size than the two above, include the following:

- ❐ **Western Navajo Fair**, ☎ 602/283-5452, held in Tuba City AZ, in late October.
- ❐ **Southwestern Navajo Nation Fair**, held in Dilcon AZ, ☎ 520/657-9244 or 520/657-3376.
- ❐ **Central Navajo Fair**, ☎ 520/647-5877, held in Chinle AZ, near Canyon de Chelly, in August.
- ❐ In addition, there is a **Chinle Agency Navajo Song and Dance Pow Wow Festival**, ☎ 520/674-5201, extension 201, held each March.
- ❐ **Eastern Navajo Fair**, held in Crownpoint NM, in July, ☎ 505/786-5841 or 505/786-5244.

Fairs and rodeos aside, there are aspects of Navajo and Hopi culture that are virtually impossible for an outsider to penetrate. It may be nearly impossible for an outsider to gather significant insights into Hopi culture, but Navajo religion and philosophy lecturers who may be able to help answer questions about Navajo society and its manners include the following:

- ❑ **Benny Silversmith**, St. Michael's AZ 86511, ☎ 520/871-7229.
- ❑ **Eddie Tso**, PO Box 442, St. Michael's AZ 86511, ☎ 520/871-6378 or 520/871-4531.
- ❑ **Herbert Bennally**, Navajo Community College, Shiprock NM 87420, ☎ 505/368-5291.
- ❑ **Carl N. Gorman**, PO Box 431, Window Rock AZ 86515, ☎ 520/729-2218.
- ❑ **Andrew Becenti**, Navajo Academy, 1200 West Apache, Farmington NM 87401, ☎ 505/366-6571.
- ❑ **Wilson Arnold**, Navajo Community College, Tsaile AZ, ☎ 520/724-3311.
- ❑ **Alfred Yazzie**, Rough Rock Demonstration School, PO Box 217, Chinle AZ 86503, ☎ 520/728-3311.
- ❑ **Steve Darden**, 2160 North 4th Street, Flagstaff AZ 86004, ☎ 520/536-2911.
- ❑ **Ed McCombs**, Navajo Community College, Tsaile AZ, ☎ 520/724-3311, organizes personalized Navajo culture tours. For example, a trip combining three days hiking and two nights camping in the Chuska Mountains, focusing on native healing plants and Navajo lore, might be arranged.

Special interest tour guides and other useful institutions are listed below.

Four Corners School of Outdoor Education (PO Box 78, East Route, Monticello UT 84535, ☎ 801/587-2156) offers a 10-day study tour in April, July and August called "Native Cultures of the Southwest." The tour focuses on Hopi, Ute, and Navajo cultures, explores mythology and native arts and includes visits with educators and tribal elders. The group attends dances and visits with moccasin makers, basket weavers, potters, kachina makers, weavers, buckskin makers and others. This trip provides an unusual opportunity to learn legends and gain understanding of aspects of Indian culture that would be impossible without meeting these people in their homes, among their families, perhaps while munching on piki bread prepared with bare hands and cooked on a 400° sandstone slab.

Canyonlands Field Institute, PO Box 68, Moab UT 84532, ☎ 801/259-7750, offers two van tours with motel accommodations, that include the Navajo and Hopi Reservations. Tours begin and end in Bluff Utah.

An "Ancient Skywatchers: Archaeo-Astronomy" tour runs for five days in late September, around the time of the Autumnal Equinox, and studies what astronomy can teach us about ancient people. The trip includes a predawn visit to Hovenweep National Monument to observe sunrise alignments at the site. A full day at Chaco Canyon includes stops at a famous pictograph of a thousand-year-old supernova that was also recorded in China. There's a stop at Aztec Ruins National Monument to consider the Great Kiva. Driving across the Chuska Mountains to the Navajo Museum at Tsaile allows time for a discussion of the astronomical features of hogans, distinctive landforms, and sand paintings, followed by a day exploring Canyon de Chelly's prehistoric and modern Indian sites.

The Hopi tour, offered in May, runs for three days and two nights and explores Hopi culture, history, and religion, along with Anglo influences and other contemporary issues. Tribal members explain Hopi history and lifestyle, as well as the techniques and symbolism incorporated into renowned Hopi silver, pottery, and kachina carving.

CFI also offers a four-day, three-night "Monument Valley Photography" tour twice a year in March and October. The tour is recommended for intermediate photographers and includes intense field sessions at Hovenweep National Monument, and the Goosenecks of the San Juan Monument Valley Tours are run with a Navajo guide from a base at Recapture Lodge in Bluff UT. Overnight film processing is available. You should be prepared to hike one to five miles with camera gear.

Special Expeditions, 720 Fifth Avenue, New York NY 10019, ☎ 212/765-7740 or 800/762-0003, fax 212/265-3770, offers a 13-day tour of the Grand Canyon, focusing on Anasazi, Navajo and Hopi cultures, and ending in Monument Valley. Groups are limited to a maximum of 10, who explore the mystique of the Southwest through prehistoric ruins, geology, arts and crafts, and traditions of contemporary Pueblo and Navajo people. Trips are scheduled in May, September, and October, and include transportation and accommodations in lodges or inns.

Western Indian Tours, 11431 North 23rd Street, Phoenix AZ 85028, ☎ 602/992-4845, fax 602/482-2256, operates cultural and scenic tours of Navajoland, including Monument Valley and Canyon de Chelly. Tours begin in Phoenix, Albuquerque or Las Vegas.

Discovery Passages, 1161 Elk Trail, PO Box 630, Prescott AZ 86303, ☎ 520/717-0519, operates trips identified as "cultural, environmental adventures to American Indian Country." Aside from direct encounters with native peoples and their beautiful lands, the tour features small groups, native guides and anthropologists, horsepacking and riding, rafting, hiking, camping, ceremonies and festivals. Customized trips can be arranged. Weekend packages are offered, featuring workshops and seminars in nature appreciation, wilderness survival, and Aboriginal living skills. Among regularly scheduled trips are the following:

- ❑ **The Canyon and the Pai** includes 10 days among the Haulapai, Havasupai and Yavapai Indians who live in and around the Grand Canyon, hiking and swimming in Havasu Canyon, and an easy raft trip on the Colorado River.
- ❑ **Sacred Mountains and the Navajo** is a 10-day itinerary covering Canyon de Chelly, Monument Valley, and Navajo Mountain, with accommodations in Navajo hogans, including cultural demonstrations.
- ❑ **The Hopi and Their Ancestors** is a 10-day insider's trip through Hopiland.

As for the far more secretive Hopis, people find unusual things on their desert mesas. Some find inspiration or spirituality in the remote open spaces and ancient villages. Others lay claim to renowned Hopi arts or observe traditional ceremonies, but it may be safe to say that no one ever expected to find dreadlocks in Hopiland; these appear in leonine profusion during irregularly scheduled **Reggae Inna Hopiland** shows.

Jamaican reggae is urban-bred, street-wise island music. The Hopi are private and traditional-minded, nothing if not laid-back, land-locked dirt farmers in far-off northeastern Arizona. Yet the world's top reggae bands have been quietly slipping into Hopiland to play since 1984. As many as 10 shows are scheduled yearly, featuring groups such as Third World, or the late Bob Marley's band, The Wailers. Freddie McGregor, a Jamaican mega-star, traveled more than a thousand miles out of his way by bus and accepted a reduced fee to play Hopiland in between shows in Los Angeles and New Orleans.

Hopis greet the Jamaicans with tribal drummers chanting in ancient rhythms. Traditionally clothed Hopi dancers move on to the floor, stepping to the beat of the prehistoric Indian reggae as it fills the Hopi Community Center, actually a gymnasium.

Visiting musicians, many sporting the long, dark tangles of hair known as dreadlocks, peer over stacked equipment from the small stage, entranced. Hypnotic chants and steady drumming energize the dancers, their colorful feather and bone garments trailing in sweeping arcs.

Black Jamaicans, weather-worn Hopis, and a select few pale faces coalesce; racial and cultural differences vanish in the moment.

"One love," as the Jamaicans might say, "one destination."

A typical inter-cultural reggae show, such as one that featured Sugar Minott of Kingston, Dread Flimstone of Los Angeles, and the Wailing Coyotes, a local group comprised of Hopi and Navajo musicians, will draw 1,000 or more on a weekend. More than 500 people materialized out of the desert to see McGregor on a weeknight. Even the biggest international reggae bands play Hopiland for fees far lower than usual. Why?

Outside the community center before a show, horses graze in the parking lot. The moon rises over the nearest mesa where lights twinkle amid sandstone outcrops on the hillside. It is warm and quiet, a conversation can be carriedon by whispers.

"We love the music," said a tribal member, "and the musicians appreciate an opportunity to be in this special place."

During a first set by Maxi Priest, Freddie McGregor sat smiling on a folding chair in the middle of the gym. While the audience swayed and danced, children flowed around and over him, scaling his knees and fingering his tight dreadlocks. Many of the youngsters wore long hair, too.

"We play for the love of the people," McGregor said later, "not for the money. These people, they don't have a lot and we used to be there. This is sort of a gift. And we are appreciated here."

"These Hopis were moved here, forced here, and we Jamaicans were all slaves. We come to Hopiland because of the spirit of the people. The Hopi people and our people share the struggle. How would you like it if someone came into your home and tell you to move, if you were pushed out here to this dirt? We see everything on tour, the good, the bad and the evil, and I tell you something, I'd like to come out here for a week, it's so quiet and peaceful. Hopiland is the best stop on the tour, one of the best places to play.

"We know the money isn't here, but the love of the music is. It's an experience, for the love and the culture."

Unfortunately, these wonderful shows are pretty much a hit-or-miss proposition these days. Scheduling is, to say the best, erratic, and information sometimes hard to come by. The reggae shows are not especially favored by tribal authorities.

For Reggae Inna Hopiland information contact the Tribal Office (PO Box 123, Kykotsmovi AZ 86039, ☎ 520/734-2441).

For more traditional dancing in Hopiland, the Hopi practice their beliefs through the year with different ceremonies for various phases of the annual cycle. Visitors are welcome. The Hopi believe the ceremonies are intended for the benefit of all people although, while on the reservation, remember that you are guests of the Hopi and act accordingly.

Some of the more popular ceremonies or dances are the **Social Dances** held in January and February, the **Bean Dance** held in February, and the **Kachina Dances**, held throughout the summer, ending with the **Home Dance** in August. The **Snake Dance** and **Flute Dance** are held in August in alternating years in Shungopavi and Mishongovi only. The Flute Dance is also held in Walpi every two years. Typically, rhythmic drumming and chanting set the pace for the elaborate steps performed by dancers wearing intricately feathered and beaded costumes, often with masks or painted headgear.

Where to Stay & Eat

Window Rock

Navajo Nation Inn, US 264, PO Box 1687, Window Rock AZ 86515, ☎ 520/871-4108 or 800/662-6189, fax 520/871-5466, offers modern rooms and suites decorated in a utilitarian Southwestern/Navajo-style and there's a heated pool. A restaurant and coffee shop serve traditional Navajo dishes, including Navajo tacos, blue corn pancakes, and frybread, plus American food.

Step-on tour guides are also available here. You provide and operate your own vehicle. A guide comes along to narrate a tour of the Window Rock area, Hubbell Trading Post or Canyon de Chelly. **Paulina Watchman**, PO Box 278, Navajo NM, ☎ 505/777-2703, offers B&B accommodations or straight room rentals.

Los Verdes, ☎ 520/871-5105, in St. Michael's three miles west of Window Rock, serves Mexican combination plates stuffed sopapillas, chimichangas, menudo, chile rellenos, and taco salads. It also has American, Mexican, and Navajo sandwiches.

Chinle

Canyon de Chelly Motel, PO Box 295, Chinle AZ 86503, ☎ 520/674-5875, is a comfortable, modern motel with 68 rooms, a heated indoor pool, and a clean coffee shop, the **Junction Restaurant**, ☎ 520/674-8443. The restaurant offers three meals a day, including Mexican food, Navajo tacos, sandwiches, burgers, and steaks.

Thunderbird Lodge, PO Box 548, Chinle AZ 86503, ☎ 520/674-5841 or 602/674-5842, is the classic place to stay at Canyon de Chelly, offering 71 modern motel rooms in standard and deluxe categories, as well as one- to four-person suites.

The lodge's restaurant, **Thunderbird Lodge Cafeteria**, offers daily lunch and dinner specials or a choice of five lunch entrées served cafeteria-style. It's located in the original trading post built here in 1896 and features an all-Navajo staff. The lodge also has a gift shop and a rug room with a complete line of Indian jewelry, crafts, and Navajo rugs.

Thunderbird Tours, based at the lodge, offers year-round tours of Canyon de Chelly and Canyon del Muerto.

Holiday Inn Canyon de Chelly, PO Box 1879, Chinle AZ 86503, ☎ 602/674-5000 or 800/465-4329, features 120 air-conditioned rooms, a heated pool, and a gift shop.

Garcia's, in the Holiday Inn, serves three meals a day from a menu that includes a blue cornmeal breaded rainbow trout with pinyon nut butter, lamb stew, vegetable lasagna, Mexican food, steaks, burgers, and sandwiches.

Coyote Pass Hospitality, PO Box 91, Tsaile AZ 86556, ☎ 520/724-3383 or 520/674-9655, offers B&B accommodations near Navajo Community College, the Chuska Mountains, and Canyon de Chelly. It's not your typical B&B. Guests are accommodated in a dirt-floor hogan and the restrooms are situated in an outhouse.

This may be the closest experience you can find on the reservation to what typical living conditions are like for many of the Navajo people. Tours of the Navajo Nation and cultural consulting are available.

Kayenta/Monument Valley

Navajo Trails Motel, Teec Nos Pas AZ, ☎ 520/674-3618, offers humble motel rooms that might serve in a pinch (depending on how sleepy you are).

Holiday Inn, PO Box 307, Kayenta AZ 86033 ☎ 520/697-3221, features 160 rooms, a gift shop, and the **Wagon Wheel Restaurant,** serving three meals a day, including Navajo specials, frybread with honey, steaks, salmon and vegetable lasagna, and sandwiches.

Wetherill Inn, PO Box 175, Kayenta AZ 86033, ☎ 520/697-3231 or 520/697-3232, fax 520/697-3233, offers 50 air-conditioned rooms a block north of midtown Kayenta.

Golden Sands Café, ☎ 520/697-3684, next to the Wetherill Inn, serves Navajo and American specials and possibly the only Oriental food on the reservation. The café's open for three meals a day.

Goulding's Lodge, PO Box 1, Monument Valley UT, 84536, ☎ 801/727-3231, is just north of the Arizona-Utah border on the west side of US 163, three miles west of Monument Valley Tribal Park.

Established in 1924 by Harry Goulding and his wife Mike, Gouldings's has grown from a small trading post housed in a tent, into the only full-service, year-round motel in Monument Valley. The hillside property includes 62 rooms with balconies, an indoor heated pool, a gift shop open March through October, and a campground with RV hook-ups.

Goulding's Stagecoach Dining Room serves three meals daily, including traditional Navajo and American food, Mexican food made with blue corn meal, huevos rancheros, roast leg of lamb and salads.

Goulding's Museum & Trading Post, adjacent to the motel complex, is housed in the original trading post. It includes exhibits of Anasazi artifacts and historical photos. And it contains motion picture memorabilia from the Gouldings' long-time association with director John Ford, actor John Wayne and others who trekked out here to work among the sage and monumental stone backdrops on such classic films as *Stagecoach* and *Fort Apache.* A set from *She Wore A Yellow Ribbon* is on display. The museum is open April through October.

The lodge offers nightly showings of a 20-minute multi-media photo and sound production, *Earth Spirit,* describing the creation of Monument Valley. Monument Valley and Mystery Valley tours, escorted by Navajo guides, are available.

Additional motel rooms close to Monument Valley are available in Mexican Hat Utah, 25 miles north of the park. These include the following:

- ❒ **Burch's Valley of the Gods Inn & Indian Trading Company**, PO Box 310-337, Mexican Hat UT 84531, ☎ 801/683-2221.
- ❒ **Canyonlands Motel**, Mexican Hat UT 84531, ☎ 801/683-2230.
- ❒ **Mexican Hat Lodge**, Mexican Hat UT 84531, ☎ 801/683-2222.
- ❒ **San Juan Inn & Trading Post**, PO Box 535, Mexican Hat UT, ☎ 801/683-2220.
- ❒ **Valley of the Gods Bed & Breakfast**, PO Box 307, Mexican Hat UT 84531, ☎ 303/749-1164.

Anasazi Inn at Tsegi Canyon, Kayenta AZ 86033, ☎ 520/697-3793, is situated 10 miles west of Kayenta on US 160 at the junction with AZ 564, nine miles south of Navajo National Monument. Fifty-two modest rooms overlook scenic red rocks and undulating, rugged cacti-studded terrain in Tsegi Canyon. A restaurant serves homemade soups, pies, breakfast all day, American food, and Navajo specialties. There is a gift shop.

Tuba City

Tuba Motel & Trading Post, Main Street, PO Box 247, Tuba City AZ 86045, ☎ 520/283-4545 or 520/283-4546, is a modern motel decorated in Indian-style. It includes the Mexican-American **Pancho's Family Restaurant.**

The classic, old-time **Tuba Trading Post**, a two-story octagon structure made of native stone in the early 1900s, is next door. The store carries groceries, snacks, souvenirs, hand-made rugs, jewelry, and pottery.

Greyhills Inn, 60 Warrior Drive, Tuba City AZ 86045, ☎ 520/283-6271, extension 36, is operated by Navajo hotel management students as a 32-room hostel with shared baths.

Tuba City Truckstop, ☎ 520/283-4975, on US 160, is open 24 hours a day, serving Navajo tacos and sandwiches, stews, burgers, and breakfast anytime.

Hopiland

Hopi Cultural Center Restaurant and Motel, PO Box 67, Second Mesa AZ 86043, ☎ 520/734-2401, is in the center of the Hopi universe at the Cultural Center. The motel contains 33 comfortable, standard rooms. A restaurant prepares steaks, burgers, grilled cheese sandwiches and hot dogs, as well as traditional Hopi dishes such as blue corn pancakes, Chil-il ou gyava, a bean chili, or Nok Qui Vi, a stew of lamb and corn, hominy soup, Hopi tacos, and tostadas.

Keams Canyon Motel, PO Box 545, Keams Canyon AZ 86043, ☎ 520/738-2297, has 20 modest rooms. You might want to look at one before you checkin.

Keams Canyon Café, ☎ 520/738-2296, on AZ 264 in Keams Canyon, is open till 9 PM week nights, but only until 6 PM on weekends, serving Navajo sandwiches, such as hot beef on frybread with onions and green chiles, barbecue beef ribs, Mexican and Oriental foods.

Camping

Fires are permitted only in grills, fireplaces or similar control devices. No open ground fires are permitted in campgrounds. Campers must provide their own firewood or charcoal. Please observe quiet hours from 11 PM to 6 AM at all camping areas.

Bring water and everything else you'll need. Most of the camping areas provide few facilities, although many do offer picnic tables and shaded sites.

Antelope Lake, located eight miles north of Pine Springs Arizona, 24 miles southwest of Window Rock via some rugged dirt roads, offers primitive camping but RVs are not recommended.

Summit Campground, eight miles west of Window Rock, is open year-round and can accommodate RVs, but has no facilities.

Ganado Lake, three miles northeast of Ganado, on Tribal Route 27, allows camping, but there are no facilities at the fishing lake.

Red Lake, 15 miles north of Window Rock on Tribal Route 12, allows primitive camping at the fishing lake.

Camp Asaayi Lake Campground is 11 miles northeast of Navajo New Mexico, and 35 miles north of Gallup off US 666 on a convoluted series of rough dirt roads deep in the Chuska Mountains. Open year-round. RVs are not recommended due to the poor roads.

Washington Pass Campground is six miles northeast of Crystal, New Mexico, on NM 134. The site is generally open year-round, depending on the road conditions in the winter. RVs can be accommodated.

Berland Lake Campground is a few miles north of Crystal, and is usually open year-round, depending on road conditions. No facilities are available and RVs are not advised to attempt the rugged dirt road to the campground.

Wheatfields Campground is 44 miles north of Window Rock and two miles south of Tsaile, Arizona, off Tribal Route 12 and usually open year-round. RVs can be accommodated.

Tsaile Lake Campground is a half-mile west of Navajo Community College in Tsaile, on the northeastern edge of Canyon del Muerto at Canyon de Chelly National Monument.

Canyon de Chelly National Monument has a large campground with water and bathrooms. However, disconcerting posted signs are plastered all over Canyon de Chelly warning visitors not to leave valuables in sight in their car or at the campsite.

Many Farms Lake Campground is a mile south of Many Farms, Arizona, 15 miles north of Chinle off US 191.

Morgan Lake, next to the Four Corners Power Plant in Fruitland New Mexico, 10 miles west of Farmington, allows camping, but there are no facilities available and the road is bad, so RVs are not recommended.

Mitten View Campground-Monument Valley, Monument Valley Tribal Park, PO Box 93, Monument Valley UT 84536-0289, ☎ 801/727-3287. Located a half-mile from the visitor center, the 100-site campground generally fills up by late afternoon in the summer and reservations are accepted only for groups of 10 or more. Plan to check in early for a choice campsite.

The camping area offers little privacy. It is on a sloping promontory overlooking the spacious valley, Sentinel Mesa, West Mitten Butte, Merrick Butte, and East Mitten Butte. The panorama from the campground ranks high among choice scenes to see from your tent in the soft, desert morning light. Showers and RV hook-ups are available.

Navajo National Monument has a small, tree-shaded campground close to the visitor center with restrooms and water. Several spots are large enough to park an RV, though there are no hook-ups.

For additional information regarding campgrounds or backcountry camping on the Navajo Reservation contact **Navajo Parks & Recreation Department**, PO Box 308, Window Rock AZ 86515, ☎ 520/871-4941, extension 6647.

Camping is permitted anywhere on the **Hopi Reservation**, but there are no camping facilities. There are free campgrounds – essentially, worn spots in the sagebrush – at Oraibi Hill, Oraibi Wash, and Second Mesa, adjacent to the parking lot at the Hopi Cultural Center. You can use the bathrooms at the Cultural Center if you camp at Second Mesa. Another possible camp site is Keams Canyon Community Park, which is the only one of these spots with water.

The High Country

Introduction

Lush meadows, sparkling streams, clear lakes, and mountain peaks make up the wild and beautiful High Country south of the Mogollon Rim known as "Arizona's mighty backbone." The land is covered with ponderosa pine and spruce, fir and aspen, pinyon pine, juniper, sycamore and oak.

The Rim, named for Juan Flores Mogollon, the Spanish governor of Arizona and New Mexico when they were part of New Spain, is formed by a series of sedimentary plateaus of rock deposited one upon the other. In the gorges of the White Mountains, wall after wall of horizontal rock layers are dramatic proof of the great upheaval that took place millions of years ago during the Paleozoic Age. The Mogollon Rim (there are various pronunciations, from Moe-GO-yun to Muggyun, depending upon the locale) forms a natural separation between the northern Colorado Plateau and the southern Basin and Range Region. Extending diagonally into central Arizona from southwest New Mexico, the 2,000-ft. (609-m) escarpment looms just north of the Hualapai, Mazatzal and Gila Bend Mountains, whose elevations range from 7,000 ft. (2,135 m) to 11,000 ft. (3,355 m). To the east, the Coronado Trail defines the state's boundary with New Mexico, and on the western border with California the boundary is delineated by the Colorado River.

Although to many the star of Arizona is the spectacular Grand Canyon, the regions of the lower three-fifths of the state have a great deal to offer the adventurous traveler.

There are the heights and valleys of the White Mountains, with seemingly more lakes and hiking trails than can be counted; dozens of national historic sites like Fort Bowie and the 1,000-year-old Kinishba Ruins; historic parks such as Tumacacori and Organ Pipe Cactus; and national monuments like Chiricahua, Casa Grande and Coronado National Memorial. There are many Indian reservations: Papago, San Xavier, Apache, and Gila River among others. And there are wildlife refuges of Cabeza Prieta, Cibola and Kofa. Both downhill and cross-country skiing are enjoyed in the White Mountains, and all of southern Arizona offers wonderful touring, hiking, fishing and camping opportunities.

Geography & History

There are 14 Indian tribes and 20 reservations within the Arizona borders, representing about 160,000 people. Reservations cover more than 19 million acres, and tell of people and a culture that has withstood the adversity of time while helping to shape American history. About half of the High Country land is **Apache Indian Reservation**. Although the Indians call their land the White Mountain Apache Indian Reservation, the federal government prefers to call it Fort Apache Indian Reservation, so don't get confused – White Mountain Apache and Fort Apache reservations are one and the same. The tribe is noted for basketry and beadwork.

The reservation is bounded on both sides by designated US national forest land – **Sitgreaves** and **Tonto National Forest** to the west of the White Mountain Apaches, and the Apache National Forest to the east.

Some of the state's best recreational opportunities are to be found on the 1.6 million acres of the reservation as well as in the wilderness of the adjoining national forests. Fishing, hiking, camping, boating, and winter sports can be enjoyed here in abundance. Each of the four seasons offers a new adventure. Summer in the High Country means fishing and camping, boating and swimming. During fall, Indian Summer provides weather for pleasant hikes in the crisp cool days and evenings while the bull elks trumpet their mating calls. Winter and the first snow brings skiers, skaters, and tobagggoners. In spring, the masses of wild flowers blossom and the brook and rainbow trout appear in great numbers.

Getting Around

Although you can fly into Phoenix or Tucson and begin the route from there, for a sort of continuity with the preceding chapters, we begin here from **Montezuma's Castle** and **Fort Verde**

State Historic Park and go east to the **High Country** and the small town of **Strawberry** before continuing on AZ 87 to **Payson** of Zane Grey fame.

AZ 87 is the route to the High Country from **Phoenix** and the **Valley of the Sun**. It's nicknamed "The Beeline Highway" because it offers a fast escape to the cool pine forests from the Valley when the desert is baking under the hot summer sun.

Continuing from Payson the route takes AZ 260, which follows the Mogollon Ridge through the Tonto and Sitgreaves National Forests and the towns of Heber and Show Low to the White Mountain areas of **Pinetop-Lakeside** and **Greer** to **Eager** and **Springerville**.

Scenic Airlines fly to Show Low from Phoenix and Scottsdale, ☎ 800/535-4448.

Motor Coach: Payson Express provides van service for people and packages between Payson and the greater Phoenix Metro area. In Phoenix ☎ 602/256-6464; in Payson ☎ 520/474-5254.

The High Country

White Mountains Passenger Lines, Show Low, ☎ 520/537-4539, connects with Payson, Phoenix, Tempe and Mesa.
Car Rentals: Quantum Car Rental, ☎ 520/472-6000 and 800/613-6804.
Horne Auto Center Car Rental, ☎ 520/537-5500.
Fuller Ford, ☎ 520/537-5767.
Hatch Motor Car Rental, ☎ 520/537-8887.
Blakemore Auto Rental, ☎ 520/537-2880.

INFORMATION

Arizona Office of Tourism, 1100 West Washington, Phoenix AZ 85007, ☎ 602/542-8687 or 800/842-8257.
Arizona Game and Fish Department, 2222 West Greenway Rapid, Phoenix AZ 85023, ☎ 602/942-3000, fax 602/789-3924.
Arizona State Parks, 800 West Washington, Phoenix AZ 85007, ☎ 602/542-4171 and 542-4174, fax 602/542-4180.
Bureau of Land Management, 3707 North 7th Street, Phoenix AZ 85011, ☎ 602/640-5501, fax 602/640-2398.
Arizona Republic Weatherline, ☎ 602/271-5656 Ext. 1010

Touring

From Montezuma Castle National Monument take AZ 87 to the towns of Strawberry and Pine, three miles apart. **Strawberry** is a small village named for the wild strawberries that used to grow here. Snugly set below the Mogollon Ridge, the tiny town boasts Arizona's oldest schoolhouse, a one-room log cabin built in 1885. **Pine** was settled in 1879 by Mormon pioneers, and some of the original rock and log cabins have been restored by new residents. The **Pine and Strawberry Museum** is located in the Old Mormon Church, and contains artifacts from early pioneers, Indian artifacts from local archaeological digs, and historical photos from both towns.

The **Pine-Strawberry Chamber of Commerce** has a self-guided walking tour map of the towns (but is not always open during business hours.)

Continue south on AZ 87 as the road climbs the Mogollon Rim above **Tonto National Forest**, offering several spectacular viewpoints along the way, including Tonto Natural Bridge.

Tonto Natural Bridge State Park

Mineral springs here left deposits which have created the world's largest natural travertine bridge. It measures 400 ft. in length, spanning a canyon 183 ft. high and 150 ft. wide at its widest point. You can admire the view from points overlooking the sides of the arch, as well as from the three trails in the park. No one is permitted under the bridge. The gravel road access to the bridge is steep and winding, especially over the last mile and a half.

Continue on AZ 87 to **Payson**, 17 miles south, where the steep cliffs of the Mogollon Rim rise 7,000 ft. to the north.

Payson

The beautiful scenery and cool climate at an elevation of 5,000 ft. wasn't what brought the settlers here; it was the glittering promise of gold. Miners came around 1881 and set up camp, but ranching and lumbering soon proved more lucrative. Novelist Zane Grey built a cabin at the foot of the rim and drew inspiration from the scenery and wildlife for his books. Unfortunately, his rustic cabin burned in a recent forest fire.

The **Zane Grey Museum & Counseller Art** offers Zane Grey exhibits, video viewing, Western art and a book and gift shop. The **Museum of the Forest** tells the story of Northern Gila County: prehistory, pioneers, Apaches and Zane Grey, with rotating exhibits and special programs. The town makes a good base for exploring Mogollon Rim country.

Back on AZ 260 and heading east, the road goes through magnificent forest country around **Kohls Ranch** and **Christopher Creek** as it continues to climb the rim above Tonto National Forest.

Tonto National Forest

The forest contains 2,969,602 acres of different recreational opportunities year-round, from the cool pine to the north along the Mogollon Rim to desert lands in the south. Road conditions vary so inquire locally for information.

Follow AZ 260 through the towns of Heber and Overgaard, following the Mogollon Rim to Show Low.

Show Low

Show Low is one of the few locations in the area that can be reached by air and where, as in Payson, there are automobiles for rent. The town's name makes an entertaining story; it got its name from a poker game played in 1876. A famous Indian scout named Croyden Cooley and his partner Marion Clark established a ranch here, fencing in with barbed wire some 100,000 acres. But even that much land wasn't enough for the two of them. One night they played a game of poker to decide who would own the land. They played all night long until finally it was Clark who said "Show low and you win." Cooley, having the deuce of clubs, did just that – and he took the ranch.

Years later the property was purchased and taken over by Mormons and the place where the famous game took place is now occupied by the Mormon church. Show Low's main street is named the Deuce of Clubs.

Continue on AZ 260 to Pinetop-Lakeside.

Pinetop-Lakeside

Pinetop-Lakeside are twin towns surrounded by lakes and pine forests near the edge of the Mogollon Rim. Although they began as two towns, in expansion they've merged to become one. Lakeside (elevation 6,746 ft.), originally named Fairview by Mormon settlers around 1880, has numerous lakes. Pinetop (elevation 7,279 ft.) was named by soldiers from Fort Apache who stopped to rest on the long climb up the Mogollon Rim. Both are major recreation areas with many resorts and cabins. From Pinetop-Lakeside, turn south on AZ 73 at Hon Dah to reach Whiteriver.

Whiteriver

This is the administrative center of the White Mountain Apache, who own more than 1.6 million acres of this wonderful outdoor recreational land. Since this is tribal land, you'll need tribal (not state) permits for any activity such as boating or fishing, but costs are reasonable.

There are two historical sites of particular interest here. **Fort Apache,** on the Fort Apache Indian Reservation, was established in 1870 and abandoned in 1922. Here the First Cavalry and the 21st Infantry confronted great Apache warriors such as Victorio in 1879 and Geronimo from 1881 to 1886, although the local White Mountain Apache were friendly.

A small museum, the **Apache Cultural Center,** is there, as well as officer's quarters and old cavalry horse barns. In the cemetery interesting headstones reveal that Indians and soldiers lie buried together. (For information, ☎ 520/338-4625.)

One mile southwest beyond the fort are the **Kinishba Ruins,** where prehistoric Indians built two large pueblos around 1232 and 1320. Coronado visited them in his quest for the "Seven Cities of Cibola." Excavated by University of Arizona archaeologists, pottery and shell jewelry was found scattered in 700 rooms. Entry is prohibited for safety reasons. You will need a permit to view the ruins even from the outside. (☎ 520/338-4625 for tour information).

Return to AZ 260 and continue on to Greer. On the way there are short side trips on well-marked state roads (some closed in winter) that take you to Hawley Lake, Big Lake, and Sunrise Ski Resort.

Greer

This small community is set 8,500 ft. into a White Mountain valley on the edge of the forest where deer are seen regularly. In summer visitors come to Greer for hiking the cool mountain trails and fishing. Come winter, skiers head for the slopes of Sunrise Ski Area 15 miles east. On the edge of town are miles of marked cross-country ski trails. There are several country inns, lodges and rustic cabins in which to enjoy the peace and quiet of the White Mountains.

From Greer continue east on AZ 260 to the almost-twin towns of Eagar and Springerville.

Eagar/Springerville

Eagar is mainly a stepping-off place for the **Coronado Trail** but at **Springerville** both the Casa Malpais Museum and the ruins themselves just north of town are interesting. Springerville began in 1879 as a trading post. In town a large statue, the 18-ft. Madonna of the Trail, commemorates hardy pioneer women of the past. A collection of historic cabins, houses and a granary can be seen at the **White Mountain Historical Society Park**, three blocks south of Main on Zuni, ☎ 520/333-4300.

Casa Malpais

The House of the Badlands is on a rim of volcanic rock overlooking the Round Valley of the Little Colorado River. To the south there's a breathtaking view of the White Mountains. The people who lived here long ago are now called the Mogollon, although their pottery and architecture is similar to the Anasazi of the Four Corners region. It is believed that Casa Malpais was occupied for about 200 years, being abandoned mysteriously around 1400 AD. To tour Casa Malpais, check at the museum in Springerville, first to view artifacts excavated from the site and then to sign on for a tour, the only way to enter the ruins.

From Springerville return to Eagar and head south on US 191 for a hair-raising ride on the **Coronado Trail.** Although the distance is only 123 miles, the drive takes a full four hours because the road is full of hairpin turns (460 curves from Alpine to Clifton alone). Use extreme caution. Take your time, stop to enjoy the view, and be sure to fill up on gas and stock up on water, groceries and snacks you might want before leaving Alpine. There is absolutely nothing but wilderness on the remaining 90 miles to Clifton except for **Hannagan Meadow**, where there is a lodge, a small store (open June-December) and several hiking trails – information is available at the store. The trail follows the route taken by Coronado.

Still seeking the treasures of the Seven Cities of Cibola, Coronado and his men struggled through this wild mountainous region of eastern Arizona. As you drive you'll be able to imagine how greed alone could drive them. The beautiful high-forest country is unchanged since the 1540s when they clawed and chopped through the desert scrub. This turned into pinyon-juniper forest, until they reached heavy spruce and fir forest extending from an altitude of 3,500 ft. to 11,000 ft. on Mogollon Rim. The road, isolated, zig-zagging narrowly through the underbrush, winds through the rugged mountains, densely closed in on every side by majestic, primeval forests. Reaching Hannagan Meadow in the center is as welcome as an oasis in a desert.

Adventures

On Foot

STRAWBERRY/PINE

From Strawberry, the scenic attractions include good hiking along **Fossil Creek Road**, a primitive, narrow, winding road past Fossil Creek leading to the Child's Power Plant, the Verde River, and back to Camp Verde.

Pine Creek Trail, a half-mile hike leading to the Pine Creek natural area consists of about 400 ft. of developed and undeveloped creek bottom land.

TONTO NATURAL BRIDGE STATE PARK

There are three trails here and hiking shoes are recommended for all three:

At Tonto Natural Bridge State Park, **Waterfall Trail**, about 300 ft. long, leads to waterfall cave, and **Gowan Loop Trail**, about half a mile, leads to an observation deck in the creek bottom.

The scenic **Highline Trail**, begins at the western edge of the Mogollon Rim in Tonto National Forest. With 51 miles of wonderful views, it begins off Hwy 87 and ends on Hwy 260. The historic trail was established in the late 1800s to link ranches and homesteads along the Mogollon Rim. Hikers can either wander on trails in the cool woods or make more energetic treks to the **Mazatzal** and **Sierra Ancha Wilderness** areas in Tonto National Forest.

MAZATZAL & SIERRA ANCHA WILDERNESSES

There are 35 hiking trails in the Mazatzal Wilderness and 13 in the Sierra Ancha Wilderness; pick up information and descriptions at the **Payson Ranger District** (☎ 520/474-7900) and the **Pleasant Valley Ranger District** (☎ 520/462-3311) for Sierra Ancha.

PAYSON

The Payson Ranger District of the Tonto National Forest offers hikes which can be done in segments or loops, challenging day outings, and extended pack trips with or without horses. However, being struck by lightning is a very real possibility close to the Rim. During lightning storms avoid mountain tops, ridges, open areas, shallow caves, and do not rappel. Find shelter between rocks in a boulder field, in a forested area away from tall trees, or return to your car. Also, carry plenty of water, 3-4 quarts per person – all backcountry water MUST be treated.

There is a short exercise trail next to the Payson Ranger Station on Hwy 260 one mile beyond the intersection of Hwy 87.

Pine Trail, 15 miles north of Payson, is located on FR 297, off Hwy 87. There are corrals, toilets and parking.

Two-Sixty Trail, 27 miles east of Payson off Hwy 260, also has corrals, toilets and parking.

Hatchery Trail is located at the Tonto Fish Hatchery entrance four miles north of Hwy 260 at FR 284. No facilities, only a large parking lot.

For maps and more information, contact the Payson Ranger District, ☎ 520/474-7900.

SHOW LOW

There are trails for hiking along the shore at Fool Hollow Lake.

PINETOP-LAKESIDE

Woodland Lake Park Trails is six miles of trails (including a 1¼-mile, handicapped accessible, paved loop) within the town of Pinetop-Lakeside. On Woodland Lake Road off SR 260 a four-mile loop trail begins at the spillway and passes through Big Springs connecting with a scenic natural area and self-guided trails.

The **White Mountain Trail system** in the Apache-Sitgreaves National Forest covers about 180 miles between Pinetop-Lakeside, Linden and Vernon. Some of the multi-use trails include the following:

- ☐ **Country Club Trail**, five miles long, offers easy hiking.
- ☐ **Timber Mesa Trail**, a six-mile loop on the top edge of the mesa, is a moderate hike.
- ☐ **Buena Vista Trails** offer nine miles of easy hiking through oak, pine and manzanita country, with views of Baldy Mountain.
- ☐ **Blue Ridge Trail**, a 9½-mile loop, elevation 7,100 to 7,656 ft., with remarkable views of the Baldy Mountain region in the White Mountains, is a moderate to slightly difficult hike.
- ☐ The 10-mile **Panorama Trail** loops between Porter Tank, South Tank, the base of Porter Mountain and the Twin Knolls and is a moderate hike.
- ☐ **Land of the Pioneers Trail**, moderate, along beautiful canyons and over Ecks Mountain, is approximately 11 miles long.
- ☐ The 18-mile **Los Caballos Trail**, winding through open pinyon juniper country with scenic views of the Mogollon Rim, is a moderate hike.
- ☐ **Juniper Ridge Trail**, moderate and winding 16 miles through the lower Manzanita/Pine country, has spectacular views of Juniper Ridge.
- ☐ The 16-mile **Ghost of the Coyote Trail** follows old logging roads and single-track roads and is difficult for hiking.
- ☐ The **Mogollon Rim Nature Walk** is north of Lakeside on SR 260. The **Mogollon Rim Overlook**, two miles north of Lakeside, has trail signs giving brief descriptions of both local history and vegetation.

SHOW LOW

The **Delli Llamas** offer guided llama tours in the White Mountains half-day to multi-day. PO Box 1416, ☎ 520/537-0274.

GREER

The **Butler Canyon Trail** just north of town off AZ 373 is a one-mile, self-guided nature trail. The **Mount Baldy Wilderness** offers two trails, each about seven miles long. They lead into the wilderness, where big game is common, and they join near the top of the mountain.

The spur leading to the summit and the summit itself are on land belonging to the Fort Apache Indian Reservation and are off-limits. The summit has religious significance to the Indians and trespassers are subject to arrest.

SPRINGERVILLE

The 1½-hour tour of **Casa Malpais** involves a half-mile of walking and a climb of 250 ft. In summer be sure to wear a hat and bring water.

The **Acker Lake Trail** south at Hannagan Meadow starts at campsites #6 and #7 and leads to Acker Lake and remote areas of the Blue Ridge Primitive Area.

On Horseback

PAYSON

The Payson Ranger District of the Tonto National Forest offers trails which can be done in segments and loops as well as challenging day outings and extended pack trips. Tie horses to a picket line, not directly to trees, which removes bark and damages roots. Stay on the trail – cutting across switchbacks causes erosion. Being struck by lightning is a very real possibility close to the Rim. During lightning storms avoid mountain tops, ridges, open areas, and shallow caves. Shelter between rocks in a boulder field, or in a forested area away from tall trees. Carry plenty of water – three or four quarts per person. All backcountry water MUST be treated.

Highline Trail, with 51 miles of wonderful views, begins on Hwy 87 and ends on Hwy 260. The historic trail was established in the late 1800s to link ranches and homesteads along the Mogollon Rim.

Pine Trail, 15 miles north of Payson, is located on FR 297, off Hwy 87. Facilities include corrals, toilets and parking.

Two-Sixty Trail, 27 miles east of Payson off Hwy 260, also has corrals, toilets and parking.

Hatchery Trail is located at the Tonto Fish Hatchery entrance four miles north of Hwy 260 at FR 284. No facilities, only a large parking lot.

MAZATZAL & SIERRA ANCHA WILDERNESSES

There are 35 horse/packsaddle trails in the Mazatzal Wilderness and 13 in the Sierra Ancha Wilderness.

For further information contact **Payson Ranger District** (☎ 520/474-7900) or **Pleasant Valley Ranger District** (☎ 520/462-3311) for Sierra Ancha.

SHOW LOW/PINETOP-LAKESIDE

Pinetop Lake Stables, east of AZ 260 on Buck Springs Rd, ☎ 520/369-1000.

Porter Mountain Stables, 1½ miles east of AZ 260 on Porter Mountain Rd., ☎ 520/368-5306.

Wilderness Ranch Stables, off Porter Mountain Rd., ☎ 520/368-5790.

Country Club Trail, five miles long, offers easy horseback riding.

Timber Mesa Trail, a six-mile loop on the top edge of the mesa, is a moderate horseback ride.

Buena Vista Trails offer nine miles of easy horseback riding.

Los Burros Trail offers 13 miles of moderate horseback riding.

The 10-mile **Panorama Trail** loops between Porter Tank, South Tank, the base of Porter Mountain and the Twin Knolls, with easy riding.

Land of the Pioneers Trail along beautiful canyons and over Ecks Mountain, approximately 11 miles long, is difficult for horseback riding.

The 18-mile **Los Caballos Trail** is a difficult horseback ride.

Juniper Ridge Trail, difficult for horses, winds 16 miles through the lower Manzanita/Pine country with spectacular views of Juniper Ridge.

The 16-mile **Ghost of the Coyote Trail** follows old logging roads and single-track roads and is a moderate trail for horseback riding.

GREER

Greer **Stables** offer guided rides, hayrides and cookouts (on AZ 373 across from Molly Butler Lodge).

On Wheels

STRAWBERRY-PINE

Scenic attractions include the **Mogollon Rim Road**, part of the historical **General Crook Military Road** which runs along the edge of the Rim. Located just above the Rim off AZ 87 are **Battleground Monument**, site of the last battle between the Apaches and the US Cavalry, **The Railroad Tunnel**, left unfinished by early mining developers, and **Pivot Rock**, an unusual balancing rock formation.

PINETOP-LAKESIDE

At Lakeside Ranger Station (☎ 520/368-5111), self-guided tour cassettes are available for auto tours of Lake Mountain and Porter Mountain.

Country Club Trail, five miles long, offers easy mountain biking.

The 10-mile **Panorama Trail** loops between Porter Tank, South Tank, the base of Porter Mountain and the Twin Knolls. It's a moderate mountain bike ride.

The **Land of the Pioneers Trail** is a moderate mountain bike ride along beautiful canyons and over Ecks Mountain, approximately 11 miles.

Los Burros Trail, 13 miles, offers moderate mountain biking.

Timber Mesa Trail, a six-mile loop on the top edge of the mesa, is difficult for mountain bikes.

Buena Vista Trails offer nine miles of difficult mountain biking. The 18-mile **Los Caballos Trail** offers moderate biking.

The 16-mile **Ghost of the Coyote Trail** follows old logging roads and single-track roads and is difficult for biking.

PAYSON

The Payson Ranger District of the Tonto National Forest offers trails which can be done in segments and loops, as well as challenging day outings. Be aware that hikers and horses have the right-of-way over mountain bikes. Move aside when encountering riders and refrain from making sudden moves. Also, being struck by lightning is a very real possibility close to the Rim, so during lightning storms avoid mountain tops, ridges, open areas, and shallow caves. Shelter between rocks in a boulder field, in a forested area away from tall trees, or return to your car. Also, carry plenty of water – three or four quarts per person. All backcountry water MUST be treated.

The **Highline Trail**, with 51 miles of wonderful views, begins on Hwy 87 and ends on Hwy 260. The historic trail was established in the late 1800s to link ranches and homesteads along the Mogollon Rim.

Pine Trail, 15 miles north of Payson, is located on FR 297, off Hwy 87; there are corrals, toilets and parking.

Two-Sixty Trail, 27 miles east of Payson off Hwy 260, also has corrals, toilets and parking.

Hatchery Trail is located at the Tonto Fish Hatchery entrance four miles north of Hwy 260 at FR 284. No facilities, only a large parking lot.

For maps and more information contact the **Payson Ranger District**, ☎ 520/474-7900.

WHITE MOUNTAIN APACHE RESERVATION

Biking is allowed only on the established roads of the campgrounds and Paradise Area, south of Horseshoe Lake, bounded by Route 78 on the south and the North Fork of the White

River on the north, and Forestdale Area, including Routes 66, 67 and 68, all east of Forestdale.

On Water

WHITE MOUNTAIN APACHE RESERVATION

There are boat rentals at **Hawley Lake**. When river water is at a safe level, usually in April and May, rafters and kayakers can experience fast and challenging rapids on rivers in the reservation. A special use permit is necessary, and available on a limited basis. Contact the **Director of the Game and Fish Department**, PO Box 220, Whiteriver AZ 85941.

More than 400 miles of clear cold streams and more than 25 lakes are full of fighting rainbow and brown trout, plus the only native trout of the state, the Apache trout. **Horseshoe Lake** and **Hawley Lake** are among the most popular and productive; other lakes are **Christmas Tree Lake, Hurricane Lake, Tonto Lake, Bootleg Lake** and **Cyclone Lake**.

Winter fishing is becoming popular here on the lakes; be sure the ice is thick enough for safety and holes cut in the ice should be small.

PINETOP-LAKESIDE

There's sailing at Sunrise Park Resort, off AZ 260 east and south on AZ 273 to **Big Lake**.

There are more lakes and streams than can be counted in the White Mountains. Famous for trout, bass and other fish, many of the lakes and streams also offer campgrounds and are excellent for wildlife watching. Some lakes close by: **Woodland Lake**, in Pinetop-Lakeside's Woodland Lake Park, a quarter-mile south off AZ 260; **Rainbow Lake**, one block south of AZ 260, Lakeside; **Scott's Reservoir**, north on Porter Mountain Road; and **Fred's Lake**, a quarter-mile south off AZ 260 via Penrod Ave.

STRAWBERRY

Inquire at **Strawberry Lodge**, HCR 1, Box 331, Strawberry AZ, 85544, ☎ 520/476-3333.

SHOW LOW

Show Low Lake County Park, 100 acres at an elevation of 6,000 ft., offers shoreline fishing for walleye, largemouth bass, bluegill, catfish, and trout. There is a small bait shop, boat rentals and a boat launch.

Fool Hollow Lake Recreation Area has two boat launching ramps and fishing along the lake.

GREER

There's fishing in the **Greer Lakes**, three little lakes just north of town, and the **Little Colorado River**, famous for trout, bass and other fish.

There also is fishing in the **Mount Baldy Wilderness**, about five miles of fishing streams. Trails lead into the wilderness then join near the top of the mountain where big game is common. The spur leading to the summit and the summit itself are on Fort Apache Indian Reservation land and are off-limits. The summit has religious significance to the Indians; trespassers are subject to arrest.

INFORMATION

Blue Sky Expeditions, ☎ 520/425-5252.
Salt River Canyon Raft Trips, ☎ 520/461-9494.
Far Flung Adventures, ☎ 520/425-7272.
Sun Country Rafting, ☎ 800/272-3353.

On Snow

Snowshoeing is available just about anywhere there is snow, but bring your own snow shoes, as few, if any, ski shops rent them.

WHITE MOUNTAIN APACHE INDIAN RESERVATION

A cross-country skiing area is open, with numerous trails guaranteed to satisfy both beginner and experienced skier. Trails wind through tall pines and close to streams.

PINETOP-LAKESIDE/GREER

More than 65 downhill ski runs wind through the three peaks (Sunrise, Apache and Cyclone Circle) of the **Sunrise Ski Area**. You'll find an equal number of beginner, intermediate and advanced runs. The emphasis here is on family skiing. Two double chair lifts, three triples, and four surface lifts guarantee short lines. Snow machines add to the snowpack if needed, which runs from late November or early December through early April. Sunrise Ski Area, Box 217, McNary AZ 85930, ☎ 520/735-7669.

There is cross-country skiing all through the **White Mountain Trailsystem**.

In-season sleigh rides are available at **Greer Lodge,** ☎ 520/735-7216.

For snowmobiling, ☎ 520/368-TOWN.

HANNAGAN MEADOW

There are marked trails for cross-country skiing from late November until late March.

Eco-travel & Cultural Excursions

PAYSON

Shoofly Village Archaeological Site, in the northern edge of Tonto National Forest, five miles north of Payson off AZ 87, is a village that was built and occupied between 1000 and 1250 AD. These people had close ties to the Hohokam and Salado prehistoric cultures. The site was partially excavated in the 1980s by Arizona State University. There is an asphalt trail through the ruins, with interpretive signs and, during the day, guides from the Shoofly Chapter and the Forest Service to give additional information.

SHOW LOW

Pintail Lake, two miles north of Show Low at Pintail Lake Wild Game Observation off AZ 77, is a migratory rest area. There are observation platforms to view the ducks, geese and other waterfowl, as well as several wildlife species, depending upon time of year.

PINETOP-LAKESIDE

There are birdwatching and nature studies at **Big Spring Environment Study Area**, on Woodland Rd. off AZ 260.

Other good birdwatching areas are: **Woodland Lake Park**, Woodland Lake turnoff from AZ 260; **Jacques Marsh**, two miles north of Lakeside on Porter Mountain Rd., then west on Juniper to the end of the road; and **Whitewater**, on the Fort Apache Indian Reservation.

The **White Mountain Native American Art Festival and Indian Market** in July attracts Native Americans from all over the Southwest. The festival includes dancing, music, arts and crafts, demonstrations and food.

SPRINGERVILLE

Little House Museum is a unique collection of territorial history and trophy fly-fishing at Box 791, Springerville AZ 85938, ☎ 520/333-2286.

Casa Malpais Museum, 318 E. Main St., Springerville AZ 85938. ☎ 520/333-5375 (see *Springerville Touring*).

HANNAGAN MEADOW

An interpretive tape of the **Coronado Trail** is available from either the Alpine or Clifton Apache-Sitgreaves National Forest offices.

Where To Stay & Eat

STRAWBERRY-PINE

Strawberry Lodge, 12 rooms, all with private bath; restaurant open for breakfast, lunch and dinner. HCR 01, Box 331, Strawberry AZ, 85544, ☎ 520/476-3333.

Windmill Corner Inn looks like a Swiss chalet, has queen-size beds and cable TV. Northside Hwy 87, HCR 01 Box 203, Strawberry AZ 85544, phone and fax: ☎ 520/476-3064.

Sportsmans's Chalet boasts the only elevator in Strawberry. Cocktails, pool tables, steaks, seafood and pizza in the restaurant. Hwy 87, Strawberry AZ 85544, ☎ 520/476-2411.

Strawberry Hill High Mountain Resort has 14 cabins and a suite. HCR 1 Box 302, Strawberry AZ 85544, ☎ 520/476-4252 and 800/637-6604.

Black Bear Restaurant & Lodge, 120 Ralls Dr., Strawberry AZ 85544, ☎ 520/476-3141.

High Country Inn Restaurant & Motel, Mexican and German food. PO Box 2110, Pine AZ 85544, ☎ 520/476-2150.

Tara's Rim County Café & Motel, barbecue pork, beef, ham, turkey, and a Friday night all-you-can-eat fish fry. Hwy 87, Pine AZ 85544, ☎ 520/476-3292.

Cool Pines Café, daily home-cooked specials, beer, wine, and "good company." PO Box 154, Strawberry AZ 85544, ☎ 520/476-4480.

PAYSON

Accommodations

Best Western Paysonglo Lodge, luxury lodge with free continental breakfast, restaurant. 1005 S. Beeline Hwy, Payson AZ 85541, ☎ 520/474-2382 and 800/772-9766.

Christopher Creek Lodge-Motel, Star Route Box 119, Payson AZ 85541, 23 miles east of Payson, ☎ 520/478-4300.

Kohls Ranch Lodge, E. Hwy 260, Payson AZ 85541, ☎ 520/478-4211 and 800/331-KOHL.

Majestic Mountain Inn, 602 E. Hwy 260, Payson AZ 85541, ☎ 520/474-0185 and 800/408-2442.

Payson Pueblo Inn, 809 E. Hwy 260, Payson, AZ 85541, ☎ 520/474-5241 and 800/888-9828.

Star Valley Motel, HC Box 45A, E. Hwy 260, Payson AZ 85541, ☎ 520/474-5182.

Swiss Valley Lodge, 801 N. Beeline Hwy, PO Box 399, Payson AZ 85541, ☎ 520/474-3241 and 800/24-SWISS, fax 520/472-6564. Offers both food and lodging.

Restaurants

Payson has a great assortment of eating places with a variety of cuisine. Here are several:

The Oaks Restaurant, 302 W. Main St., Payson AZ 85541, ☎ 520/474-1929. Steak, chicken and prime rib.

El Rancho, 200 S. Beeline Hwy, Payson AZ 85541, ☎ 520/474-3111. Restaurant and lounge, homemade Mexican food.

Mandarin House Restaurant, 1200 S. Beeline Hwy, Payson AZ 85541, ☎ 520/474-1342. Chinese food.

Heritage House, 202 W. Main St., Payson AZ 85541, ☎ 520/474-5501. Lunches of gourmet sandwiches, soup and salad.

Mario's, 600 E. Hwy 260, Payson AZ 85541, ☎ 520/474-5429. Restaurant and lounge, home-made Italian food, special home-made bread.

260 Café, 803 E. Hwy 260, Payson AZ 85541, ☎ 520/474-1933. Truck stop famous for home-made pies and home cooking.

Donut Corral, 105 S. Beeline Hwy, Payson AZ 85541, ☎ 520/474-5936. Lunch – sandwiches and soup as well as 35 varieties of fresh pastries and doughnuts.

WHITE MOUNTAIN APACHE RESERVATION

There is a trailer park and motel at **Hawley Lake**.

PINETOP-LAKESIDE

Accommodations

Best Western Inn of Pinetop, PO Box 1006, Pinetop AZ 85935, ☎ 520/367-6667 and 800/528-1234.

Bartram's Bed & Breakfast, Rt. 1, Box 1014, Lakeside AZ 85929, ☎ 520/367-1408 and 800/257-0211.

Apache Pines Motel, 1290 Deuce of Clubs, Show Low AZ 85901, ☎ 520/537-4328.

Cozy Pines Cabins, PO Box 212, Pinetop AZ, ☎ 520/367-4558.

Reed's Motor Lodge/K5 Western Art, Books & Gifts, PO Box 240, Springerville AZ, 85938, ☎ 520/333-4323.

Meadows Inn and Dining Room, 453 N. Woodland Rd., Pinetop AZ 85935, ☎ 520/367-8200. Seven suites and gourmet meals.

Lake of the Woods Cabins, PO Box 777, Lakeside AZ 85929, ☎ 520/368-5353.

Moonridge Lodge & Cabins, PO Box 1058, Lakeside AZ 85929, ☎ 520/367-1906.

The Place Resort, Rt. #3, Box 2675, Lakeside AZ 85929, ☎ 510/368-6777.

Bonanza Motel, PO Box 358, Pinetop AZ 85929, ☎ 520/367-4440.

Double B Lodge, PO Box 747, Pinetop AZ 85929, ☎ 520/367-2747.

Whispering Pines Resort, PO Box 1043, Pinetop AZ 89529, ☎ 520/367-4386.

Restaurants

Chalet Restaurant & Lounge, PO Box 1784, Pinetop AZ, ☎ 520/367-1514. Steaks, seafood, prime rib, salad bar.

Christmas Tree Restaurant, PO Box 1617, Lakeside AZ 85929, ☎ 520/367-3107. Home-made specialties, reservations suggested.

Creasey's Restaurant, PO Box 366, Pinetop AZ 85935, ☎ 520/367-1908. Pasta, fish, steak, wild game.

Matta's Too-Mexican Restaurant, PO Box 1988, Lakeside AZ 85929, ☎ 520/368-6969. Texas-style breakfast, lunch, dinner.

Chuck Wagon Steak House, 4048 Porter Mountain Rd., Lakeside AZ 85929, ☎ 520/368-5800. Western family-style dining, steaks, chicken, pork, sandwiches, salads, burgers and desserts.

GREER

White Mountain Lodge, PO Box 139, Greer AZ 85927, ☎ 520/735-7568.

Molly Butler Lodge, PO Box 134, Greer AZ 85927, ☎ 520/735-7226.

Amberian Point Lodge, PO Box 135, Greer AZ 85927, ☎ 520/735-7553.

The Aspens, PO Box 70, Greer AZ 85927, ☎ 520/735-7232. Cabins.

Big Ten Resort, PO Box 124, Greer AZ 85927, ☎ 520/735-7578. Cabins.

Greer Point Trails End, PO Box 224, Greer AZ 85927, ☎ 520/735-7513. Cabins.

Greer Lodge, PO Box 244, Greer AZ 85927, ☎ 520/735-7515. Lodging and restaurant.

Greer Mountain Resort and Restaurant, PO Box 145, Greer AZ, 85927, ☎ 520/735-7560.

EAGAR

Best Western Sunrise Inn, 128 N. Main St., Eagar AZ 85938, ☎ 520/333-2540, fax 520/333-4700.

SPRINGERVILLE

Reed's Motor Lodge, 514 E. Main Hwy 60/180, PO Box 240, ☎ 520/333-4323, fax 520/333-5191.

HANNAGAN MEADOW

Hannagan Meadow Lodge, Box 335, Alpine AZ 85920,
☎ 520/339-4370.

Camping

STRAWBERRY

Tonto Pines in Strawberry offers tent camping (without
showers), ☎ 520/476-3392.

WHITE MOUNTAIN APACHE RESERVATION

There are more than 1,000 campsites, provided with picnic
tables, fireplaces and toilets. Many have running water. You may
use dead and down trees but not green trees. Camping is restricted
to campgrounds unless a special permit for foot travel into
backcountry areas is purchased. **Hawley Lake** has campsites, store,
service station, boat rentals, trailer park and motel. For camping
permits contact the Director of the Game and Fish Department, PO
Box 220, Whiteriver AZ 85941.

There are designated campgrounds at selected stream and lake
sites throughout the Reservation. All high country campgrounds,
except for those at Hawley, Horseshoe and Reservation Lakes, will
not receive services after September 30. Campers may continue to
use seasonal-service campgrounds at their own risk, and must pack
out all trash. Services resume on April 15, weather permitting.

Black River and **Salt River** are primitive camping areas from the
Eastern Boundary of the Reservation Hwy #60 Bridge.

West End primitive camping is in the portion of the Reservation
west of Hwy 60, excluding the town of Cibecue and Hwy 12.

Bonita Creek primitive camping is a quarter-mile below route
Y-55 to its junction with route Y-70.

SHOW LOW

Fool Hollow Lake Recreation Area has campgrounds with shower, toilets, dump station, water, picnic tables and fire ring grills, overlooking the lake.

Show Low Lake County Park, 100 acres at an elevation of 6,500 ft., offers campgrounds, with plans for showers, toilets, store and observation deck.

PINETOP-LAKESIDE

There are more than 40 campgrounds in the White Mountains. Check with the Lakeside Ranger Station in Pinetop-Lakeside and the Apache Tribe for locations and availability.

Canyon Point is just past the Woods Canyon Rec. Area at AZ 260 and 288, elevation 7,600, open May-September, 117 units. Water and waste disposal.

GREER

Rolfe C. Hoyer, elevation 8,500 ft., open May-October, 200 units, water, waste disposal, boating and fishing.

Big Lake, off AZ 273, elevation 9,000 ft., open May-September, 55 units, no water, but boating and fishing on the lake.

EAGAR/SPRINGERVILLE

Casa Malpais Campground, one mile northwest of Springerville on US 60, ☎ 520/333-4632.

HANAGAN MEADOW

The Hanagan Recreation area, open May-October, elevation 9,100 ft., has eight units with access to wilderness area.

INFORMATION

Arizona Game & Fish, ☎ 520/367-4281.
Apache Game & Fish, ☎ 520/338-4385.
Apache Tribe Tourism, ☎ 520/368-1320.
Apache-Sitgreaves National Forest, ☎ 520/339-4384.
Apache-Sitgreaves National Forest, Clifton,
☎ 520/687-1301.
Apache-Sitgreaves National Forest, Springerville,
☎ 520/333-4301.
Arizona State Parks, ☎ 520/542-4174.
Camping Information, ☎ 800/280-2267.
Casa Malpais Museum, Springerville, ☎ 520/333-5375.
Fort Apache, ☎ 520/338-4625.
Kinishba Ruins, ☎ 520/338-4625.
Lakeside Ranger Station, ☎ 520/368-5111.
National Park Service, ☎ 520/640-5250.
Payson Chamber of Commerce, ☎ 520/474-4515.
Pinetop-Lakeside Visitors Bureau, ☎ 520/367-4290.
Pine-Strawberry Chamber of Commerce,
☎ 520/476-3547.
Tonto National Forest, Payson, ☎ 520/474-7900.
Tonto National Forest, Phoenix, ☎ 602/225-5200.
Show Low Chamber of Commerce, ☎ 520/537-2326.
Sunrise Ski Area, ☎ 520/735-7669 or 800/772-SNOW.
Springerville-Eager Chamber of Commerce, ☎ 520-333-2123.
US Forest Service, ☎ 800/280-2276.
White Mountain Apache Recreation Enterprise, ☎ 520/338-4385.

The Old West

Introduction

With the exception of the grasslands and the mountains, Old West Country is mostly desert dominated by cacti, giant saguaro, organ pipe, and yucca, along with sagebrush, creosote bushes and mesquite trees. Numerous reptiles live in the desert – poisonous Gila monsters, several varieties of rattlesnakes, and lizards. The higher grasslands merge into forests of oak, pinyon, juniper, and other pines as the elevation rises. Next come the stands of ponderosa pines, topped at the highest altitudes by dense aspen, maple, spruce, and fir.

There is an immense variation of climate here. On the desert you can expect mild winters and very hot summers; it will be somewhat cooler and wetter in the grasslands; in the winter the four mountain ranges can have a great deal of snow.

In Old West Country, the Chiricahua, Huachuca, Santa Rita and Santa Catalina Mountains, with elevations from 4,400 ft. to 9,000 ft., extend southeast across the southern region of the state. The state's southern boundary is with Mexico, and an excursion to the international city of Nogales adds to the adventures found in southern Arizona.

Geography & History

Here in Southern Arizona almost three centuries ago Spanish explorers pushed northward into the New World well before the first Europeans landed on the Eastern seaboard.

Lured by the tales of the famed Seven Cities of Cibola and untold wealth in gold, they braved the Indians and the wilderness, only to meet defeat at the hands of both.

The Old West

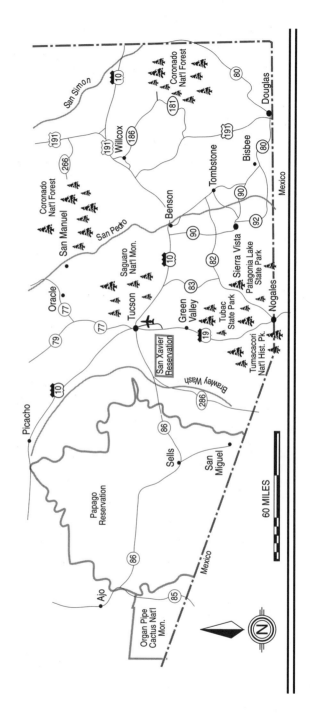

Before, during, and after the Civil War, the US Cavalry pursued Apache warriors led by their fabled chiefs, Cochise and Geronimo to protect hardy settlers. It was the mission of the Butterfield Overland Stage to transport both passengers and mail safely to the West.

Here, gunslingers at the OK Corral added to the myths of the Wild West. Mining towns that have become ghost towns evoke an era long gone, although the ruins linger.

Add to all this the fabulous scenery of the Sonoran Desert, the towering mountains, the grasslands and streams, and you have Arizona's Old West territory, full of adventure.

Getting Around

The route heads for **Old West Country** and winds down the hairpin turns (go slowly!) of the **Coronado Trail**, crossing Interstate 10 into **Willcox**. From there, the route leads south to **Fort Bowie National Historic Site** and south to **Chiricahua National Monument** in Coronado National Forest.

Tombstone is the next stop before back-tracking a little to **Bisbee**. From Bisbee the route heads east on AZ 90 to **Sierra Vista** and **Fort Huachuca,** then south on AZ 92 to the **Coronado National Monument**.

At **Nogales** on Interstate 19 you can enjoy a taste of Mexico across the border before heading north to **Tumacacori National Monument** and **Tubac Presidio State Historic Park**, site of the Spanish fort established in 1752.

Tucson and **Saguaro National Monument** are next on the list. Then you come to **San Xavier Indian Reservation** and **Old Tucson,** before heading to the West Coast through the Papago Indian Reservation to **Ajo** and **Organ Pipe Cactus National Monument**.

INFORMATION

Air

America West Airlines, ☎ 800/235-9292.
American Airlines, ☎ 800/433-7300.
Continental Airlines, ☎ 800/525-0280.
Delta Airlines, ☎ 800/221-1212.
Southwest Airlines, ☎ 800/435-9792.

Motor Coach

Greyhound Bus Lines, ☎ 520/882-4386 and 800/231-2222.
Bridgewater Transport provides service from Tucson Airport and Greyhound Station to Fort Huchuca, Sierra Vista and Bisbee, ☎ 520/432-5359.

Train

Amtrak has several trains weekly, ☎ 800/872-7245.

Auto Rental

All major automobile rental agencies have offices in Tucson.

Practicalities

Arizona Office of Tourism, 1100 West Washington, Phoenix AZ 85007, ☎ 602/542-8687 or 800/842-8257.
Arizona Game and Fish Department, 2222 West Greenway Rapid, Phoenix AZ 85023, ☎ 602/942-3000, fax 602/789-3924.
Arizona State Parks, 800 West Washington, Phoenix AZ 85007, ☎ 602/542-4171 and 542-4174, fax 602/542-4180.
Bureau of Land Management, 3707 North 7th Street, Phoenix AZ 85011, ☎ 602/640-5501, fax 602/640-2398.
Arizona Republic Weatherline, ☎ 602/271-5656, Ext. 1010.

Touring

From the High Country, head down the **Coronado Trail** (US 191) past Morenci and Clifton through Safford to Interstate 10 and west into Willcox.

Willcox

Willcox, established in 1880 with the construction of the Southern Pacific Railroad, has several museums of interest, and serves as a convenient base for exploring the historic and scenic attractions of this part of the Old West. There are about 20 historic buildings to be seen in a walking tour of Willcox's historic downtown.

Wyatt Earp's brother Warren is buried in the old Willcox Cemetery. Cowboy singer-actor Rex Allen grew up around Willcox, and the **Rex Allen Cowboy Museum** and **Cowboy Hall of Fame** is on Railroad Avenue, once Willcox's main street. Photos, movie posters, guitars, saddles, and all sorts of cowboy movie memorabilia are to be seen in the museum, which was originally an old saloon. There is a larger-than-life bronze of the cowboy across the street from the museum.

The **Willcox Chamber of Commerce** houses the **Museum of the Southwest**. In the Museum is a striking bust of Cochise, as well as exhibits on the Apache lifestyle. Also on display are cavalry weapons circa 1880, exhibits depicting important Indian wars, the route of the Butterfield Overland Stage, and much more.

From Willcox, AZ 186 leads 22 miles south to **Fort Bowie National Historic Site** (or, for a shortcut, take the unimproved road south from the town of Bowie east on I-10).

There are signs leading to the site. The first four miles are paved, then the road is unpaved for the remaining eight miles to the fort ruins. (Fill up with gas, especially if you plan to go on to Chiricahua Monument. None is available near the monument.)

Fort Bowie National Historic Site is the place where Apache chief Cochise finally made peace in 1872 and Geronimo surrendered in 1886, ending the Southwest Indian wars that had plagued the Old West for years. Located at 5,000 ft. in Apache Pass, between the Chiricahua and Dos Cabezas Mountains, the site is a 1,000-acre memorial to travellers, settlers and soldiers who played an important part in the history of the homeland of the Chiricahua Apache. As an unfailing source of water, **Apache Springs**, on the foot trail to the fort, was a watering place for Indians, emigrants, prospectors and soldiers.

The **Butterfield Overland Stage** had been operating through the area, carrying mail and passengers from St. Louis to San Francisco. A station was built at Apache Springs near Apache Pass. Skirmishes with Indians broke out led by Cochise, a Chiricahua Apache who was the craftiest and most feared of all Indians. After the Battle of Apache Pass, the first Fort Bowie was built, but in 1869 a larger fort was established as a base for extensive military campaigns against the Apache. With the surrender of Geronimo in 1886, the Southwest Indian wars ended. Since the fort had outlived its usefulness, it was abandoned in 1894. Visitors are asked not to climb or sit on the fragile walls of the ruins.

Returning to AZ 186, continue south 25 miles to the **Chiricahua National Monument**, where upper-Sonoran vegetation flourishes with grasslands, pinyon pine, oak and juniper in the Coronado

National Forest. The lava rock formations are fantastic. A world apart from the surrounding Sonoran and Chihuahuan Deserts, the cool forested land conceals not only plants and animals of the Southwest, but also a number of Mexican species. Influence from Mexico 50 miles to the south is strong. Many plants, animals and birds have crossed the border into the monument.

Chiricahua National Monument was created out of ash from a staggering volcanic explosion some 27 million years ago. This area of rock pinnacles, spires and balancing rocks has miles of the best hiking trails to be found in southern Arizona.

When the fallen ash hardened, it fused into the dark volcanic rock called rhyolite, and over the eons wind, water and ice sculpted the rock into odd formations.

The **Chiricahua Mountains** stand at a major geological crossroads: north, the southern Rocky Mountains; south, the northern Sierra Madre; east, the Chihuahuan Desert; and west, the Sonoran Desert. Surrounded by deserts and grasslands, the area is a repository of plant and animal species that have retreated to these highlands in response to gradual climatic changes.

The visitor center offers a short audiovisual program, exhibits that tell the story of the monument, as well as guided walks, short talks, with evening programs presented nightly from March through July and on weekends during late summer and fall. Restrooms, drinking water and a public telephone are also provided. Picnic areas are found at **Bonita Creek, Faraway Ranch, Massai Point** and **Echo Canyon** and **Sugarloaf** parking areas.

The route returns on AZ 186 to Willcox and goes west on Interstate 10, turning south on US 80 to **Tombstone.**

On the way, stop at the **AMERIND Foundation Museum** in Dragoon, devoted to an in-depth study of American Indian culture. Exhibits include ritual masks, tribal costumes, weapons, children's toys and art work. Dragoon is south of I-10 at Exit 318.

Tombstone

Tombstone likes to call itself "the town too tough to die," though it got its name from prospector Ed Schieffelin, who was told he would only find his tombstone in the Apache-infested San Pedro Valley. He named his first silver claim Tombstone, which later became notorious for saloons, gambling houses, and the Earp-Clanton shoot-out, re-enacted at the **OK Corral** and the **Helldorado Amphitheater** regularly.

Tombstone didn't die after the silver boom ended in 1886. Not after the Great Depression, either, and not even when the county seat was moved to Bisbee. In the 1930s Tombstone felt entitled to the claim of being too tough to die. Tombstone's many original historic buildings reflect the city's pride in its western heritage. The **Tombstone Courthouse**, built in 1882, is now a state historic park, housing artifacts and photographs of the good old days. Other historic attractions include **Arizona Territorial Museum** and **Bird Cage Theater**, an 1881 dance hall, gambling house, and saloon. The name comes from the bird-cage stalls hanging from the ceiling, and the purported 140 bullet holes in the walls and ceilings are a testament to those good old days. **Rose Tree Inn** is not actually an inn. It claims the largest rose tree in the world, grown from a rose slip sent from Scotland as a wedding present in 1885. The rooms are furnished with antiques owned by an early pioneer, who came to Tombstone by wagon train in 1880.

Boothill Cemetery contains more than 276 graves, most of them the unmarked graves of gunslingers, hanging and lynching victims, and the losers of the O.K. Corral gunfight. But those that are marked carry entertaining messages.

The **OK Corral**, as all moviegoers know, was the scene of the shootout between Doc Holliday and Wyatt Earp and the Clanton boys in October of 1881. The scene is laid out with markers and life-size figures, if these are the footprints you hanker to walk in.

The *Tombstone Epitaph* is the town newspaper and has been since 1880, when John Clum got off the stagecoach from Tucson and asked advice from the passengers. "What shall I call the newspaper?" he supposedly asked. As luck would have it, one of the passengers was Ed Schieffelin, the very same who christened the town Tombstone. He suggested *Epitaph*, and the newspaper is still in business. The office is open with the original press and other exhibits.

The route continues south 24 miles on US 80 to **Bisbee,** where you can view the gaping red hole in the earth that is the famous **Lavender Pit Open Mine**. About 400 million tons were shoveled out of this mine in its heyday. There's a parking area off US 80, one mile south of downtown Old Bisbee.

Bisbee

Bisbee proclaims its name on the top of the copper-rich **Mule Mountains** surrounding the town; you can see it as you drive along

Tombstone Canyon into Old Bisbee. Like Show Low, Bisbee is another town that was lost – or won – on a bet. Prospector George Warren, accompanying Lt. John Rucker and his group of Army scouts searching for renegade Apaches, liked the look of the land (he suspected silver) and registered a claim in his name. While drunk, he made a fateful bet that he could outrun a horse. He figured it was easy since he'd seen Apache warriors do it often. But he miscalculated the distance it took to round the stake – and he lost what eventually became one of the richest mining claims in the world.

In 1881 Phelps Dodge Company was mining in earnest, and although only three or four years worth of copper was sighted at any one time, the copper in Bisbee has never run out. It all ended, in 1975, when mining operations on a large scale became too unprofitable. But instead of becoming just another Arizona ghost town, Bisbee evolved into a center for artists, writers, poets, silversmiths and other creative people. It's also an excellent movie location, as well as a busy, interesting tourist destination.

Narrow winding streets lined with well-preserved turn-of-the-century Victorian buildings are typically Bisbee. Up the hill past Brewery Gulch the Copper Queen Hotel, a historic treasure, is still the reigning hostelry in town.

The **Copper Queen Mine** is open for tours, and another place of interest is the Bisbee Mining and Historical Museum in the former Phelps Dodge General Office Building downtown in Queen Plaza. Minerals, mining dioramas, old photographs and artifacts tell the story of Bisbee, named for an investor who never set foot in town. But George Warren, luckless prospector, is remembered by the adjacent community of Warren. (Actually, the city today consists of the historic district and the communities of Lowell, Warren, San Jose and Naco.)

From Bisbee the route heads east on AZ 90 to Sierra Vista and **Fort Huachuca** beforeturning south on AZ 92 to the **Coronado National Memorial.**

Fort Huachuca

Fort Huachuca, a National Historic Landmark, began in 1877 as a temporary Army camp to protect settlers and travelers from raiding Apaches, as well as to block Apache escape routes. It wasn't until 1886, when the campaign against Geronimo intensified, that the fort became a headquarters for the army. It remained open to deal with outlaws and renegade Indians near the Mexican border, even though many other forts and camps in the territory were closed. Kept open during World Wars I, II, and the Korean War, it was converted in 1954 to a facility for testing electronics and communications material and still is an active military base today.

Interesting here is the **Fort Huachuca Museum**, with a large collection of memorabilia from the days of the Apache wars. The famous black Buffalo Soldiers were stationed here and the museum has a room dedicated to their history. There also are barracks and administrative buildings on the parade ground dating from the 1880s.

Coronado National Memorial was created to commemorate the first major European expedition into the American Southwest. You can follow the route of Francisco de Coronado and his group of 336 Spanish soldiers, four priests, several hundred Mexican-Indians and 1,500 stock animals on their trek through the San Pedro Valley from the southern edge of Huachuca Mountains, along the US-Mexican border, to Quivira, one of the Seven Cities of gold. Along the way, instead of golden cities, they found only rock pueblos full of Indians who were more than ready to fight.

All is peaceful now in these 4,750 acres of oak woodlands. The scenic overlook at **Montezuma Pass** presents a sweeping view of the San Pedro Valley, which your imagination might couple with Coronado and his horde on their historic journey.

The visitor center presents a nine-minute video about the Coronado Expedition, and other exhibits display armor and weapons used by the Conquistadors.

Vegetation in the park is typical of the upper-Sonoran Zone – desert grasses and shrubs in the lower elevations, desert willow and honey mesquite along drainages. In the upper canyon, oak, Mexican pinyon pine and alligator juniper forests dominate, with Arizona sycamore and walnut along drainages.

Either retrace your route north on AZ 92 to AZ 82 and drive west to **Nogales** on Interstate 19 if you want a paved highway, or cut across the monument on a dirt road, which will take several hours longer but will provide magnificent mountain views. From Nogales you can enjoy a taste of Mexico in the town's sister city of Nogales across the border before going north on the interstate to **Tumacacori National Monument** and **Tubac Presidio State Historic Park**, site of the Spanish fort established in 1752.

Nogales

Nogales is on the border of Arizona and Mexico. You'll find a difference – the orderly town of Nogales, Arizona and the disorderly, casual Nogales, Mexico.

Nogales Pass over the border was used by Indians for at least 2,000 years; the Hohokam Indians came through early on, and the Pima settled into the area around 1500 AD. Apaches knew the pass well, using it for raids well into the 19th century.

The town originally was named Isaactown for a Jacob Isaacson who built an inn there in 1880. It was soon renamed for the walnut trees growing in the area, *nogal* being Spanish for walnut. There was fighting in Nogales in 1916 and 1918 against Pancho Villa, but all is quiet now. The main attraction on both sides of the border is shopping, the Mexicans coming north for the supermarkets, the Gringos going south to the shopping arcades. In the attractive main plaza at Calle Hidalgo and Calle Absolo the bones of Spanish Missionary Padre Kino, the Jesuit who founded 25 missions in the northwest Mexican plains, are enshrined. He died here in 1711. There's a monument to him across from the renovated Franciscan temple, Santa Maria de Magdalena.

Back in Nogales, Arizona, the **Pimeria Alta Historical Society Museum** exhibits old photographs and artifacts telling the colorful history of southern Arizona and northern Sonora.

The building which once housed the Nogales City Hall still contains the old jail.

The route turns north along the Santa Cruz River on I-19 to Tumacacori National Historical Park and Tubac Presidio State Historic Park, site of the Spanish fort established in 1752.

Padre Kino, whose bones rest in Nogales, Mexico, established **Tumacacori National Historical Park** as a mission in 1691. Apache raids caused the converted Indians to retreat north to San Xavier del Bac, and Tumacacori fell into ruins before it became a national monument in 1908. Two other missions, the relatively recent additions of **Guevavi** and **Calabazas**, also on the 47-acre site, were not open to the public at the time of publication. A lovely garden, with a fountain and pool, is representative of early mission gardens: fruit trees, herb and spice plants, and plants native to the Sonoran Desert.

Both self-guided and ranger-guided tours of the grounds and the ruins are available. At the visitor center there is an audio-visual presentation of the area's early Native American and Spanish

Colonial heritage. A small picnic area is located just outside the visitor center.

Continue north on I-19 to **Tubac Presidio**, the first European settlement in what is now Arizona. The Spanish established a fort after a group of settlers were massacred here in 1751. Tubac claims to be the oldest city in Arizona, a city that has lived under six cultures (Hohokam, Ootam, Pima/Papago, Spanish, Mexican and Anglo) and under six flags (Spain, Mexico, New Mexico, Territory of Arizona, US Territory of Arizona, and the State of Arizona).

The Gadsden Purchase brought prospectors, lured by tales of old Spanish mines, and Tubac became a boomtown. During the Civil War, troops left the town unguarded to fight in the east. When the Apaches again moved in the inhabitants fled. Today, while no longer a boomtown, Tubac is a thriving art colony with attractive shops, studios and galleries.

At **Tubac Presidio State Park**, founded in 1959 as Arizona's first state park, a museum depicts the area's history since its founding in 1752, with models showing how the fort looked in its early years.

Travelling north on I-19 toward Tucson, make a stop on the **San Xavier Indian Reservation** to see Mission San Xavier del Bac, "the White Dove of the Desert." Considered one of the finest examples of Spanish colonial architecture in the United States, the lovingly preserved church still is used by the Tohono O'odham Indians as a legacy of Padre Kino.

Continue on I-19 to Tucson, one of America's oldest cities, and nearby **Saguaro National Monument**, passing miles of cactus-studded desert valleys, golden grasslands, and rugged canyons among tall pine-covered mountain peaks. Tucson is truly the Old West. Here the US Cavalry chased Apache warriors from their land while the lure of gold and silver tempted every sort of tough and rugged character to try his luck. Here in what the locals call "The Old Pueblo" you can still savor the flavors of Mexico and Old Spain.

The city rises 1,200 ft. above the floor of the Sonoran Desert, surrounded by five mountain ranges. The tallest, the Santa Catalinas, form a massive backdrop for the city. With a population of more than half a million, this is a modern metropolis. There are cultural activities at museums and theaters all around town as well as on the campus of the University of Arizona.

From Tucson you might want to take a look at **Colossal Cave**, east of the city. A dry or dormant cave (as opposed to living), it is now on the National Register of Historic Places. The cave is open for tours of about 45-50 minutes daily.

Saguaro National Monument

The huge saguaro cactus has been described as the monarch of the Sonoran Desert, as a prickly horror, a plant with personality, and as the supreme symbol of the American Southwest. Since 1933 this giant cactus has been protected within the Saguaro National Monument, established to protect a wide spectrum of the flora and fauna of the Sonoran Desert.

The monument surrounds Tucson and is divided into Saguaro East and Saguaro West. To tour Saguaro East (also called Rincon Mountain District), an eight-mile Cactus Forest scenic drive leads through the heart of an extensive saguaro forest. There's another scenic drive, the six-mile **Bajada Loop Drive**, in Saguaro West, which also passes through dense saguaro forests.

The route now heads west on AZ 86, through the **Papago Indian Reservation**. The Papago, now called the Tohono O'odham Indian Nation, are known for basketry and pottery. The reservation contains more than 2.75 million acres of cactus, mesquite, ironwood and palo verde trees, all of which you will pass on the way to **Ajo** and **Organ Pipe Cactus National Monument.**

Ajo

Ajo, an authentic Old West copper mining town, offers views of Arizona's huge open-pit mines. Ajo has stopped producing as recently as 1985. The **Ajo Historical Museum** displays artifacts, relics and photographs relating to Ajo's mining history. Mining began with the Tohono O'odham Indians – who did small-scale mining hundreds of years ago – and ended with the world-class mining operations of Phelps-Dodge.

Ajo's Plaza is a small jewel of Spanish architecture, and the scenic loop road and **Lookout Point** are areas to consider before heading south to **Organ Pipe Cactus National Monument.**

In the Organ Pipe Cactus National Monument there are more than 330,000 acres of the Sonoran Desert to explore; 95% of the monument is designated wilderness area. In one of the world's largest assortments of desert flora and fauna you'll find 53 species of mammals, four of amphibians, 43 species of reptiles, more than 278 bird species, and even one fish species.

UNESCO (United Nations Educational, Scientific and Cultural Organization) has recognized Organ Pipe National Monument as a "Man in the Biosphere Reserve," which is an international program of scientific cooperation dealing with human and environmental interactions throughout all the climatic and geographical areas of the world.

There are ranger-guided walks, campground presentations, and self-guided driving tours. There's an audio-visual presentation at the visitor center, as well as a bookstore, restrooms and water fountain.

Adventures

On Foot

While hiking, drink plenty of water, use sunscreen and wear a hat. Steep grades and uneven surfaces can create hazards. Rattlesnakes, honey bees and cactus spines can all be potentially dangerous.

FORT BOWIE

Fort Bowie ruins are reached by hiking a moderately strenuous 1½-mile foot trail. The trail runs parallel to the old military wagon road. On the way you'll see the **Butterfield Stage Station**, the **Indian Agency ruins**, the **post cemetery**, **Apache Springs** and the first **Fort Bowie**.

The trailhead is on Apache Pass Road, which is a graded dirt and gravel road with multiple washes. It crosses several miles of open range, so if you hike along it, be alert for cattle and wildlife on the roadway. While water is available at the fort, summer hikers should consider carrying a canteen.

The visitor center is located at the ruins of the second fort. A small museum exhibits various artifacts. A picnic area and pit toilet facilities are available at the trailhead. Ranger-guided tours and presentations are given to groups upon request. A picnic area, pit toilet and drinking water are available at the center.

Visitors are asked not to climb or sit on the fragile ruins' walls. Wheeled vehicles, metal detectors, digging tools and guns are prohibited. All historic and natural features, horseshoes, nails, and rocks, are strictly protected. A park ranger is usually on duty to assist with interpretation and to enforce regulations.

Chiricahua National Monument is best seen by hiking any of the moderately strenuous trails – more than 20 miles. They go past such unusual rock formations as **Duck on a Rock, Totem Pole** and **Big Balanced Rock**. Trails range from a quarter-mile to nine miles, round-trip. Pace yourself to allow for the altitude and the rough terrain.

Summer hikers should carry a canteen. Temperatures can climb above 100°. Sudden summer storms may briefly flood the washes. Wait out the high water and be alert for an occasional rattlesnake. Watch where you put your hands, where you sit, and where you walk) and look out for rocks. There is an easy half-mile self-guided trail at **Massai Point**, which describes the animals, plants and geology of the area. **Lookout Point** on the trail offers views of the monument's unusual rock formations.

Faraway Meadow Trail at Chiricahua National Monument, an easy 1½-mile walk between the visitor center and Faraway Ranch, is a good place for birdwatching.

A longer, three-mile walk, moderate to difficult, is the **Rhyolite Canyon Nature Trail**, a self-guided trail describing the plant life of the area.

Also moderate to difficult is **Echo Canyon Loop Trail**, a 3½-mile loop, one of the most scenic in the park, featuring a rock grotto carved by wind and water erosion.

Bonita Creek Trail is an easy mile walk along the creek, good for seeing birds – quail and migrating birds – and an occasional deer.

Inspiration Point Trail is another mile round-trip, moderate with elevation changes of 500 ft. through pine and juniper trees and spectacular views down the full length of Rhyolite Canyon.

The **Natural Bridge Trail**, a 2½-mile, one-way, moderate-to-difficult trail, leads to a small natural rock bridge in an Apache pine forest.

The **Sarah Demming Trail** is a strenuous three-mile round-trip with elevation changes of 500 to 1,000 ft.

Sugarloaf Mountain Trail, a moderate one-mile, one-way hike, leads to one of the highest elevations in the park, with wonderful views in every direction.

BISBEE

The **Bisbee Mining & Historical Museum** has maps of walking tours of Main Street, the Commercial District of Old Bisbee and Brewery Gulch, the Market District and Immigrant Neighborhood.

Mild temperatures and low humidity provide pleasant hiking in all seasons in the **Coronado National Memorial**.

Coronado Peak Trail, with elevations from 6,575 to 6,864 ft., is an easy half-mile, with benches provided along the way. At scenic overlooks along the trail, quotations from the journals of Coronado's captains bring to life the conquistadores pushing northward in their search for gold. Atop the peak, the panoramic view of the desert grasslands of San Rafael and San Pedro Valleys is spectacular.

The **Coronado Cave Trail**, three quarters of a mile each way with elevations from 5,230 to 5,700 ft., is moderate in length but is steep and rocky as you climb along the limestone ridge to the entrance of the cave. Wear appropriate clothing and sturdy hiking shoes. The cave, which is 600 ft. long, is entered by permit only. Free permits are available at the visitor center. You are required to take at least two sources of light – candles and flares are not permitted. The trail up to the cave is steep and the entrance is unimproved, so it can be difficult but negotiable. It's not a good idea to go it alone.

Joe's Canyon Trail, about three miles, is a moderate hike with elevations from 5,230 to 6,575 ft. The trailhead is 500 ft. west of the visitor center on Montezuma Canyon Road at the picnic area turnoff. You'll climb about 1,000 ft. the first mile, past scenic views of Montezuma Canyon and the San Pedro River Valley. When you reach the saddle at the top of Smuggler's Ridge, follow the trail west and look south over the grasslands of Sonora, Mexico. The trail joins the Coronado Peak Trail on the northeastern side of Colorado Peak, about 200 yds. from the Montezuma Pass parking area.

The **Crest Trail** is a 5¼-mile hike each way, and is strenuous – you are asked to check in at the visitor center prior to starting out. The goal is **Miller Peak**, the highest peak in the Huachuca Mountains, and the elevations range from 6,575 to 9,456 ft. The trailhead is across the cattle guard at the northeast end of the Montezuma Pass parking area. The trail climbs for two miles to the northwestern boundary of the Memorial and enters Coronado National Forest, continuing along the crest of the Huachuca Mountains to the turnoff for Miller Peak. (If you want more, the trail continues north through Miller Peak Wilderness Area for 24 miles along the southern section of the **Arizona Trail** to Parker Lake Canyon, 20 miles one-way.)

There are several major hiking trails in the Madera Canyon area of the Saint Rita Mountains in Coronado National Forest:

The **Super Trail**, well graded and maintained, is 3¼ miles to Josephine Saddle and about eight miles to Mt. Wrightson Peak, highest mountain point (9,453 ft.) in two counties and visible from Tucson.

Old Baldy Trail, shorter but steep, goes 2½ miles to Josephine Saddle and 5½ miles to Mt. Wrightson Peak.

Two paved loops, one from **Whitehouse** (elevation 4,500 ft.) and another from **Proctor Parking** (elevation 4,400 ft.) are good for birders and walkers.

TUMACACORI/TUBAC

Juan Bautista de Anza National Historic Trail between Tumacacori National Historical Park and Tubac Presidio State Historic Park is a hike of 4½ miles, crossing the Santa Cruz River several times. (If the hiker does not wish to cross the river, it's approximately 1¼ miles from either trailhead to the first river crossing.) Every October there is a reenactment of de Anza's famous trek.

TUCSON

The **Santa Rita Mountains**, approximately 40 miles south of Tucson, offer more than 70 miles of hiking trails.

Mount Wrightson rises to an altitude of 9,543 ft. in the **Mount Wrightson Wilderness**, and the trail is a challenging 13½-mile round-trip.

Another popular hike is **Bog Springs**, a 4½-mile loop from the Bog Springs Campground to Bog and Kent Springs.

In **Saguaro East** there are about 128 miles of trails winding through the desert and mountain country. The **Desert Ecology Trail** along Cactus Forest Drive is a quarter-mile self-guided walk with interpretive signs explaining the role of water in the desert.

The **Freeman Homestead Nature Trail** is a one-mile loop descending slowly from the desert landscape to a sandy wash and up again.

Douglas Spring Trail, 2½ miles, leads to Wild Horse Canyon in the Rincon Unit of the Saguaro National Monument and ends at several pools called Little Wild Horse Tank. Water is usually low in the pools except after a spring thaw or summer shower.

A hike in **Saguaro West** can be a short stroll on a nature trail or a day-long wilderness trek. Straying from trails can be dangerous; there are abandoned mine shafts off-trail.

The **Cactus Garden Walk** of 100 yds. begins in front of the parking lot at the visitor center. The interpretive signs describe the most common native vegetation in the Tucson Mountain District.

The **Desert Discovery Trail** is a self-guided half-mile walk to familiarize hikers with the native plants, animals and ecology of the Sonoran desert.

Valley View Overlook Trail, 1½ miles, passes through two washes and gradually ascends a ridge, with a view of Picacho Peak to the north.

Signal Hill Petroglyphs Trail is a short quarter-mile walk to dozens of ancient Indian art works.

King Canyon Trail, a 3½-mile hike, begins with a gradual climb to steeper switchbacks leading to the top of Wasson Peak, elevation 4,687 ft., the highest point in the Tucson Mountains.

Sendero Esperanza Trail, just over three miles, follows the sandy path of an old mine road, then climbs a series of switchbacks to the top of the ridge west of Amole Peak. After descending to King Canyon Trail it ends directly across from the Arizona-Sonora Desert Museum.

The **Hugh Norris Trail** – at five miles, the longest trail in the Tucson Mountain District – begins immediately with switchbacks to the top of a ridge overlooking a cactus forest. It continues through areas of splendid views and rock formations to Amole Peak, and it ends atop Wasson Peak.

Organ Pipe National Monument is desert, so be sure to take along one gallon of water per person per day and avoid overexertion and exposure to the sun. Watch out for desert plants with spines and thorns. At night carry a flashlight and watch for rattlesnakes, but do not harm them – they are protected.

The **Visitor Center Nature Trail** is a one-tenth-mile introduction to the desert and its plants. There's a guide pamphlet at the trailhead.

The **Campground Perimeter Trail** is a mile round-trip, ideal for a leisurely stroll.

The **Desert View Nature Trail** is a circular loop a little over a mile long, leading to vistas of Sonoyta Valley and the pink granite

Cubabi Mountains across the border in Mexico. There are trail signs describing the features along the way.

There are 12 hiking routes of varying degrees of difficulty. Here are several:

The **Palo Verde Trail** is a 2½-mile round-trip connecting the campground with the visitor center. Highlights of the trail are views of the rugged Ajo Mountains.

Estes Canyon-Bull Pasture Trail is a 4½-mile round-trip strenuous climb, with grand views of the surrounding terrain, to a high plateau once used by ranchers to winter their cattle.

The **Victoria Mine Trail**, 4½ miles round-trip, is a hike over rolling terrain to the monument's oldest and richest gold and silver mine.

The monument also has five backcountry routes, which can be used as starting points for a more intense nature experience. Cross-country hiking in the open desert can be enjoyable, but first check your route with a park ranger.

On Horseback

TUMACACORI/TUBAC

Juan Bautista de Anza National Historic Trail between Tumacacori National Monument and Tubac Presidio State Historic Park is a ride of 4½ miles, crossing the Santa Cruz River several times. If the equestrian does not wish to cross the river, it's approximately a mile and a quarter from either trailhead to the first river crossing. Every October there is a reenactment of de Anza's famous trek.

On Wheels

CHIRICAHUA NATIONAL MONUMENT

Bonita Canyon Drive is a scenic loop that climbs gradually through oak, juniper and pine forests, winding eight miles to the crest of the mountains, reaching Massai Point. The overlook presents a wonderful view of the park, the desert valleys beyond, and the landmark peaks of Sugarloaf Mountain and Cochise Head. Along the road are stops pointing out exhibits, rock formations, and other geologic features.

Chiricahua National Monument permits mountain bikes on the established paved roads of the site but prohibits them on monument trails.

SIERRA VISTA

Sierra Vista Tourist & Visitors Center in the heart of Cochise country offers a self-guided tour with audiotape narrated by cowboy Rex Allen, ☎ 800/288-3861.

AJO

The scenic loop road begins at the Plaza alongside the Catholic Church and winds between the "A" Mountain and the Growler Mountains. It runs past the Little Ajo Mountains (be on the watch for big horn sheep and rattlers!) on the left and Black Mountain on the right, then curves around the 1½-mile open pit mine that supported Ajo's citizens for so many years, before connecting with AZ 85 and returning to town.

ORGAN PIPE CACTUS NATIONAL MONUMENT

There are two scenic loop roads, both winding, graded dirt roads suitable for passenger vehicles but not for motorhomes, especially those more than 25 ft. long. Pick up a guidebook at the visitor center. Remember water and emergency tools.

The 21-mile **Ajo Mountain Drive** winds along the foothills of the Ajo Mountains, which are the highest range in the area. You'll see impressive stands of organ pipe cactus as well as outstanding desert landscape during the two-hour drive.

There are several unimproved dirt roads that go further into the backcountry than the graded dirt roads. Check at the visitor center for road conditions first. See historic sites such as abandoned gold and silver mines, windmills, ranchhouses and other reminders of the past.

The 53-mile **Puerto Blanco Drive** circles the Puerto Blanco Mountains, passing through a variety of scenery.

You'll go from the desert oasis of Quitobaquito to a true Sonoran Desert environment of saguaros, organ pipe cacti and elephant trees. This drive takes about half a day. Both have tables and pit toilets but only the visitor center has water.

CABEZA PRIETA WILDLIFE REFUGE

For the truly adventurous, this refuge just west of Organ Pipe Cactus National Monument offers 860,000 acres of real desert, wild with low rocky ranges sheltering endangered Sonoran pronghorn deer, desert bighorn sheep and desert mule deer. There are no paved roads. Only jeep tracks and remnants of an old road cross the refuge. There are no facilities and no water; take lots of water and other supplies for desert travel. Remember, too, that desert means hot, especially in the summer.

Because the refuge is located just south of the Barry M. Goldwater Air Force Range, the military sometimes use the skies overhead for missile and gunnery tests, so be sure to obtain permits and information from the Refuge Visitor Center in Ajo before entering the refuge.

On Water

NOGALES/TUBAC/TUMACACORI NATIONAL HISTORIC PARK

Patagonia Lake State Park, 12 miles east of Nogales on Hwy 82 northeast of Nogales, contains a 250-acre lake, the largest in the area. It has good fishing for bass, crappie, bluegill and catfish, with trout stocked in winter months, boat launching and boat rentals. ☎ 520/281-6965.

CORONADO NATIONAL MEMORIAL

Parker Canyon Lake, elevation 5,200 ft., is a 130-acre fishing lake approximately 18 miles west of the Coronado National Memorial Visitor Center. The lake is stocked with trout in the fall, and there are bass, bluegill, catfish and sunfish all year. There is a fishing pier, paved ramp, boat dock, general store and boat rental at the lake.

Pena Blanca Lake, 13 miles northwest of Nogales, is 52 acres, yielding bass, bluegill, catfish crappie and, in winter, rainbow trout. ☎ 520/281-2296.

Upper White Rock (Pena Blanca), 16 miles northwest of Nogales, has boat launching for single electric boats only. ☎ 520/281-2296.

On Snow

TUCSON

Mount Lemmon, just a few minutes north of Tucson, is 9,000 ft. high at the top of the ski runs and has a vertical drop of 870 ft. There is a chairlift and two bar lifts.

Other winter fun nearby includes cross-country skiing and tobogganing, ☎ 520/576-1400.

CHIRICAHUA

There is cross-country skiing in the Chiricahua Mountains.

Eco-travel & Cultural Excursions

WILLCOX

The **Chamber of Commerce** has a Walking Tour map of the historic downtown. If you're interested in wandering around a few ghost towns of the Old West, **Dos Cabezas** is 15 miles southeast of Willcox on AZ 186 (on the way to Fort Bowie) and Pearce is south of I-10 a few miles south of Sunsites on US 191.

DRAGOON

The **AMERIND Foundation Museum** is devoted to the study of the American Indian. Historic Indian cultures from across America are represented, from Cree snowshoe-making tools to fine Navajo weavings. Exhibits include ritual masks, tribal costumes, weapons, children's toys and art work. Dragoon is south of I-10 at Exit 318.

BISBEE

Don a hard hat complete with miner's lamp and a bright yellow slicker to ride deep into the earth for a tour of the **Queen Mine**. The guide, usually a miner himself, leads through the mine explaining how it's done: the drilling tools, the blasting methods, loading the ore, as well as the history of the mine. The mine's four levels consist of 147 miles of passageways, so you won't cover them all. The tour lasts about an hour.

SIERRA VISTA AREA

This self-styled "Hummingbird Capital of America" attracts bird watchers all year long. The following include habitats ranging from mesquite shrubland, grassland and desert riparian to high mountains with Douglas fir and aspen, all havens for rare and unusual bird species: **Garden Canyon** on the grounds of Fort Huachuca; **Empire-Cienega Ranch** off AZ 83 north of Sonorita; **Madera Canyon** in the Santa Rita Mountains off AZ 83 via Greaterville Road; **Patagonia-Sonorita Creek Sanctuary** off AZ 82; **Ramsey Canyon Preserve** near Hereford; and **Carr Canyon** in the Coronado National Forest. Contact the **Sierra Vista Chamber of Commerce, ☎** 520/458-6940 and 800/288-3861 for more information.

NOGALES

While in the vicinity, cross the border into Mexico for an international experience. No permit is needed to drive or walk across the border into Mexico, if you stay no longer than 72 hours. The simplest thing is to park your car on the Arizona side and walk across, saving the sometimes considerable delay if traffic is heavy, not to mention the difficulty in finding parking places in Mexico. You won't need pesos; most places accept dollars willingly (and credit cards in the major shops). Bargaining is expected, most salespeople speak English, and you should be able to find some bargains in excellent Mexican handicrafts.

TUMACACORI NATIONAL HISTORICAL PARK

Fiesta de Tumacacori celebrates the heritage of the upper Santa Cruz Valley with visitor participation in a variety of Apache, Yaqui, Pima and Tohona O'odham ceremonies, both regional and Mexican. There are historic demonstrations, foods and crafts from all of the cultures. (First weekend in December, no entrance fee.)

TUBAC

Each Sunday from October through March there are living history presentations of **Life at the Tubac Presidio** during the years 1752-1776.

TUCSON

For an easy look at the flora and fauna of the area, the **Arizona-Sonora Desert Museum** south of Saguaro West has a live collection of some 200 desert animals and 300 kinds of plants.

The **International Wildlife Museum** provides wildlife appreciation with hands-on experiences, interactive computer wizardry and wildlife films.

AJO

At the **Mine Lookout** there's a panoramic view of the 1½-mile **New Cornelia Open Pit Mine**. The various stages of mining operations diagrammed at the visitor's ramada or shelter are informative.

Ajo Stage Line offers tours to southern Arizona and Mexico, both historical and natural history tours – Rocky Point Kino Missions, Kitt Peak and others, ☎ 520/387-6559.

ORGAN PIPE CACTUS NATIONAL MONUMENT

For a little taste of Mexico across the border, stop at **Lukeville** on the southern border of the monument. You'll find an immigration and customs office as well as a small store, gas station and motel. Two miles beyond the border is **Sonorita**, a small Mexican town with an attractive plaza, several restaurants and shops. To go further into Mexico, both travel permit and Mexican auto insurance are required.

Where To Stay & Eat

WILLCOX

Accommodations

Best Western Plaza Inn, 1100 W. Rex Allen Dr., Willcox AZ 85358, ☎ 520/384-3556, fax 520/384-2679. Lounge and dining room, waterbeds and free breakfast, golf, beauty salon.

EconoLodge, 724 N. Bisbee Ave., Willcox AZ 85358, ☎ 520/384-4222 and 800/221-2222, fax 520/384-3785. Restaurant adjacent.

Motel 8, 331 N. Haskell Ave., Willcox AZ 85358, ☎ 520/384-3270.

Sands Motel, 400 S. Haskell, Willcox AZ 85358, ☎ 520/384-3501.

Desert Inn of Willcox, I-10, Exit 340., Willcox AZ 85358, ☎ 520/384-4222.

Muleshoe Ranch/The Nature Conservancy CMA, 30 miles NW of Willcox in foothills of Winchester & Galiuro Mountains, RR#1, Box 1542, Willcox AZ 85643, ☎ 520/586-7072.

Restaurants

Cactus Kitchen Restaurant, 706 S. Haskell, ☎ 520/384-3857. Breakfast, lunch and dinner, Mexican food, salad bar.

La Kachina Restaurant, 1005 Rex Allen Dr., ☎ 520/384-2175. Breakfast, lunch and dinner, Mexican food, salad bar.

Solarium Dining Room, 1100 Rex Allen Dr. (Best Western Plaza Inn), ☎ 520/384-3556. Breakfast, lunch and dinner, steaks and seafood.

Brown's Ice Cream Parlor, 135 E. Maley, ☎ 520/384-2057. Soup and sandwiches, home-made desserts and ice cream, 8 AM-4 PM.

Restaurant at LifeStyle, 622 N. Haskell Ave,. ☎ 520/384-3303. Lunch and dinner, American and Mexican food, salad bar and pizza.

Plaza Restaurant and Brass Rail Lounge, 1190 Rex Allen Dr., ☎ 520/384-3819. Lunch, dinner, Sunday buffet, steaks, Mexican food, salad bar.

TOMBSTONE

Best Western Lookout Lodge, Hwy 80 W., PO Box 787, Tombstone AZ 85638, ☎ 520/457-2223 and 800/652-6772. Pool, free continental breakfast.

Adobe Lodge, Fifth and Fremont in historic district, Tombstone AZ 85638, ☎ 520 /457-2241.

Tombstone Boarding House, Tombstone AZ 85638, ☎ 520/457-3478. With full breakfast.

BISBEE

Copper Queen Hotel, 11 Howell St., Bisbee AZ 85603, ☎ 520/432-2216. Restaurant, historic saloon.

Bisbee Inn, 45 OK Street, Bisbee AZ 85603, ☎ 520/432-5131.

The Clawson House, 116 Clawson Ave., Bisbee AZ 85603, ☎ 520/432-5237.

The Greenway House, 401 Cole Ave., Bisbee AZ 85603, ☎ 520/432-7170 and 800/253-3325.

Bisbee Grand Hotel, 61 Main St., Bisbee AZ 85603, ☎ 520/432-5900.

El Rancho Hometel, 1104 Hwy 92, Bisbee AZ 85603, ☎ 520/432-2293.

Jonquil Motel, 317 Tombstone Canyon, Bisbee AZ 85603, ☎ 520/432-7371.

Mile High Court, 901 Tombstone Canyon, Bisbee AZ 85603, ☎ 520/432-4636.

SIERRA VISTA

Thunder Mountain Inn, South Hwy 92, Sierra Vista AZ 85635, ☎ 520/458-0790 and 800/222-5811.

Sierra Suites, 391 E. Fry Blvd, Sierra Vista AZ 85635, ☎ 520/459-4221, fax 520/459-8449.

Carroll Drive Apartments, 250 Carroll Dr., Sierra Vista AZ 85635, ☎ 520/459-7110 and 800/833-3651.

Ramada Inn-Sierra Vista, 2047 S. Hwy 92, Sierra Vista AZ 85635, ☎ 520/459-5900 and 800/825-4656, fax 520/458-1347. Restaurant.

Sun Canyon Inn, 260 N. Garden Ave., ☎ 800/822-6966, fax ☎ 520/458-5178.

Vista Inn, 201 W. Fry Blvd., Sierra Vista AZ 85635, ☎ 520/458-6711. Coffee Shop.

NOGALES

Nogales has two **Best Western** motels, ☎ 800/528-1234, as well as other accommodations:

Super 8 Motel, I-19 and Mariposa Rd, Nogales AZ 85621, ☎ 520/281-2242.

Americana Hotel, 639 N. Grand Ave., Nogales AZ 85621, ☎ 520/287-7211 and 800/874-8079, fax 520/287-5188. Restaurant and cocktail lounge.

Best Western Time Motel, 921 N. Grand Ave., Nogales AZ 85621, ☎ 520/287-4627, fax 520/287-6949.

El Dorado Motel, 945 N. Grand Ave., Nogales AZ 85621, ☎ 520/287-4611.

Mission Motel, 820 N. Grand Ave., Nogales AZ 85621, ☎ 520/287-2472.

TUMACACORI

Rancho Santa Cruz Guest Ranch, Box 8, Tumacacori AZ 85640, ☎ 520/281-8383 and 800/221-5592.

Green Valley Quality Inn, 111 S. La Canada Dr., Green Valley AZ 85614, ☎ 520/625-2250.

TUBAC

Tubac Golf Resort, #1 Otero Rd, Tubac AZ 85646, ☎ 520/398-2211 and 800/848-7893, fax 520/398-9261. Coffee shop, restaurant, lounge.

Burro Inn, one mile west of I-19, exit 40, Tubac AZ 85646, ☎ 520/398-2281.

Tubac Country Inn, 409 Burruel St, Tubac AZ 85646, ☎ 520/398-3178.

Old Mission Store Bed and Breakfast, Frontage Road, Tubac AZ 85640, ☎ 520/398-9583.

TUCSON

Tucson has a large choice of chain motels and fast foods in addition to standard accommodations and restaurants.

There are three **Best Westerns,** ☎ 800/255-3371, two **Embassy Suites,** ☎ 800/262-8866, three **Ramada Inns,** ☎ 800/333-3333, and a **Comfort Inn,** ☎ 520/791-9282.

Others include:

Aztec Inn, 102 N. Alvernon, Tucson AZ 85748, ☎ 520/795-0330 and 800/227-6086.

Canyon Ranch Spa, 8600 E. Rockcliff Rd., Tucson AZ 85748, ☎ 520/749-9000 and 800/742-9000.

El Presidio Inn, 207 N. Main, Tucson AZ 85748, ☎ 520/623-6151.

Mariposa Inn, 940 N. Olsen, Tucson AZ 85748, ☎ 520/322-9157.

AJO

Marine Motel, 1966 N. 2nd Ave., Ajo AZ, 85321, ☎ 520/387-7626.
La Sierra Motel, 2561 N. Hwy 85, Ajo AZ, 85321, ☎ 520/387-6569.

The Guest House Inn, Guest House Rd., Ajo AZ, 85321, ☎ 520/387-6133.

Mine Manager's House Inn, 1 Greenway Dr., Ajo AZ 85321, ☎ 520/387-6505.

Dago Joe's Restaurant, 2055 AZ 85 N, ☎ 520/387-6904. Lasagna and steaks.

Camping

BOWIE/WILLCOX/CHIRICAHUA NATIONAL MONUMENT

Campgrounds are available at the nearby towns of Bowie and Willcox and at Chiricahua National Monument and Coronado National Forest, 25 miles south of the park. Stores and gas stations are available in Bowie and Willcox.

- ❏ **Bonita Canyon Campgrounds** in Chiricahua National Monument, alt. 5,400 ft., open all year, with 26 units and water available.
- ❏ About 35 miles north on US 191 just south of Safford are **Roper Lake Campgrounds**, elevation 3,100 ft., open all year with 22 units, water, waste disposal, boating and fishing.
- ❏ **Cochise Stronghold**, once the granite hideout from the US Cavalry of the famous Apache Indian chieftain, is now a site for camping, day-use and hiking. The chief was buried by his tribesmen somewhere within the granite fortress.

CORONADO NATIONAL MEMORIAL

Camping is available in the adjacent **Coronado National Forest** to the west and north.

- ❏ **Ramsey Vista Campground**, elevation 7,400 ft., open spring, summer and fall, has eight units with toilets, waste disposal and horse corral available.

- ☐ **Reef Townsite Campground**, elevation 7,200 ft., open spring, summer and fall, has 14 units with water, toilets and waste disposal.
- ☐ **Lakeview Compound**, elevation 5,400 ft., open year-round, has 65 units with water, toilets and waste disposal.

NOGALES/TUMACACORI/TUBAC

- ☐ **Patagonia Lake State Park**, 12 miles east of Nogales on Hwy 82 has 115 units, open all year water, waste disposal, restrooms, general store (☎ 520/281-6965).
- ☐ **Calabasas** (Pena Blanca), 13 miles northwest of Nogales, has six units, water and restrooms, RV and tents welcome. (☎ 520/281-2296).
- ☐ **Upper White Rock** (Pena Blanca), 16 miles northwest of Nogale, has 15 units, water, waste disposal, restrooms, RV and tents welcome (☎ 520/281-2296).
- ☐ **Mountain View Campground**, open all year, has 60 units, water, waste disposal, restrooms, full hookups, swimming pool, RV and tents welcome (☎ 520/398-9401).
- ☐ **Bog Springs**, 16 miles southeast of Green Valley in Madera Canyon, open all year, has 13 units, water, restrooms, back-packing area, RV and tents welcome (☎ 520/281-2296).

TUCSON

- ☐ **Catalina Campground**, elevation 2,650 ft., open all year, has 160 units, water comfort station and hot showers.
- ☐ **Gilbert Ray Campground**, elevation 2,600 ft., open all year, has 160 units and water and comfort station.
- ☐ **Colossal Cave Campground**, open all year, has water.

The **Santa Catalina District** of the Coronado National Forest has four public campgrounds:

- ☐ **Molina Basin**, elevation 4,500 ft., open October 15-April 15, no water or facilities.
- ☐ **Gen. Hitchcock**, elevation 5,800 ft., open all year, no water or facilities.

☐ **Rose Canyon**, elevation 7,000 ft., open April 15-October 15, water.

☐ **Spencer Canyon**, elevation 7,700 ft., open April 15-October 15, water and comfort station.

SAGUARO NATIONAL MONUMENT

Rincon Mountain District has the following six campgrounds, with water at Manning Camp only, seasonally at other campgrounds.

☐ **Manning Camp**, elevation 8,000 ft., six units.

☐ **Spud Rock Spring**, elevation 7,400 ft., three units.

☐ **Happy Valley**, elevation 6,200 ft., three units.

☐ **Juniper Basin**, elevation 6,000 ft., three units.

☐ **Grass Shack**, elevation 5,300 ft., three units.

☐ **Douglas Spring**, elevation 4,800 ft., three units.

ORGAN PIPE CACTUS NATIONAL MONUMENT

The campgrounds, elevation 1,700 ft., open all year, have 208 units, water, waste disposal, restrooms, grills (wood gathering prohibited), an amphitheater and evening programs during the winter.

The communities of Lukeville, five miles south of park headquarters, and Why, 27 miles north of the monument visitor center, maintain campgrounds.

INFORMATION

Ajo Chamber of Commerce, ☎ 520-387-7742.

Arizona State Parks, ☎ 520/542-4174.

Bisbee Chamber of Commerce, ☎ 520/432-2141.

Cabeza Prieta National Wildlife Refuge, ☎ 520/387-6483.

Chiricahua National Monument, ☎ 520/824-3560.

National Park Service, ☎ 520/826-3593, 520/640-5250.

Nogales-Santa Cruz County Chamber of Commerce, ☎520-287-3685.

Organ Pipe Cactus National Monument, ☎ 520/387-6849.

Sierra Vista Chamber of Commerce, ☎ 520/458-6940, 800/288-3861.

Superintendent Coronado National Memorial, ☎ 520/366-5515.
Tombstone Tourism Association, ☎ 520/457-2211.
Tucson Metropolitan Chamber of Commerce, ☎520/624-1817.
US Forest Service, ☎ 800/280-2276.
Willcox Chamber of Commerce and Museum of the Southwest, ☎ 520/384-2272, or 800/200-2272.

The West Coast

Introduction

Landlocked though it seems to be, Arizona surprisingly can boast more than 1,000 miles of shoreline – and all of it is in the west. From the Grand Canyon, the Colorado River turns directly west, flowing across to Nevada's Lake Mead and through Lake Havasu on Arizona's northwest border with California. It continues all the way down to Mexico, thus forming the western boundary of the state.

To get to this paradise for boaters, anglers and waterskiers, you must drive across more than one hundred miles of desert.

Geography & History

Before the arrival of the white man, Indian tribes such as the Maricopa inhabited the shores of the Colorado River. It wasn't the Spaniards who displaced them; they were routed by Quechan Cocopa and Mojave Indians and forced to migrate eastward up the Gila River.

The Spaniards attempted some excursions up the Colorado River in 1540 but didn't persevere. Spanish explorer Hernando de Alarcon was the first white man to set eyes on the shores of the Colorado River. He was looking for Coronado, but they never connected.

Suspicious of Russian expansion from northern California and what is now Alaska, the Spanish built two missions in 1780. This enraged the Quechan Indians and they attacked, killing the men and taking women and children captive. The captives were ransomed by Spanish troops. That ended Spanish attempts to dominate Yuma Crossing and to colonize along the Colorado River.

Trappers came in 1829, Kit Carson among them, and he returned in 1846 to aid soldiers trying to wrest some of the land from Mexico. Next came Colonel Philip Cooke and his Mormon Battalion, who opened the first transcontinental road across the Southwest. This was a green light for the 49ers seeking California gold.

Forts and mining camps sprang up along the Colorado River and steamboats plowed up and down the waters when gold was discovered in Gila City upstream from Yuma in 1858. The gold only lasted three years but other gold and silver deposits were found elsewhere in the area, as well as lead, copper and zinc. Today, the mines are abandoned.

Finally in 1851 the Army built Camp Yuma to protect Yuma Crossing from Indian attacks and the present city of Yuma evolved from the camp.

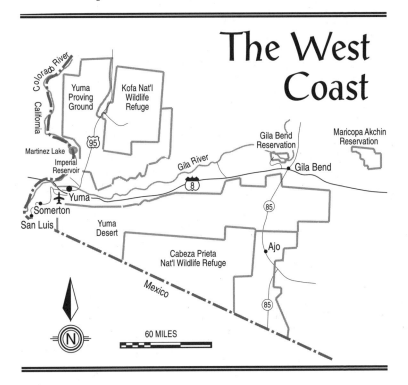

Getting Around

INFORMATION

Air
America West Express, ☎ 520/341-1276.
Delta Connection/Sky West, ☎ 800/453-9417.

Motor Coach
Greyhound Bus Lines, ☎ 520/783-4403 and 800/231-2222.

Train
Amtrak, ☎ 520/344-0300 and 800/872-7245.

Car Rental
Avis, ☎ 520/344-5772.
Budget, ☎ 520/344-1822.
Enterprise Rent-A-Car, ☎ 520/344-5444.
Hertz, ☎ 520/726-5160.

Practicalities
Arizona Office of Tourism, 1100 West Washington, Phoenix AZ 85007, ☎ 602/542-8687 or 800/842-8257.
Arizona Game and Fish Department, 2222 West Greenway Rapid, Phoenix AZ 85023, ☎ 602/942-3000, fax 602/789-3924.
Arizona State Parks, 800 West Washington, Phoenix AZ 85007, ☎ 602/542-4171 and 542-4174, fax 602/542-4180.
Bureau of Land Management, 3707 North 7th Street, Phoenix AZ 85011, ☎ 602/640-5501, fax 602/640-2398.
Arizona Republic Weatherline, ☎ 602/271-5656, Ext. 1010.

Touring

Heading north on AZ 85 from Ajo, our route picks up I-8 at **Gila Bend** past the small Gila Bend Indian Reservation.

Gila Bend

This small town of about 2,000 was a stop on the Butterfield Overland Stage in the 1850s, but before that Padre Kino came through in 1699. He found a prosperous village, with Maricopa Indians harvesting two crops every year. Just north of town is a small Tohono O'odham Indian village, San Lucy, but there's nothing adventurous there for visitors. The Gila Bend Museum and Tourist Center provides information on the history and the community of the area. Our route turns west on I-8 to Yuma past cotton fields and the Painted Mountains. About 14½ miles west of Gila Bend, the road north to Painted Rock Dam leads past a campground where rock petroglyphs are collected in heaps (access all the way to the dam is closed). I-8 continues on through the Barry M. Goldwater Air Force range. From this point to Yuma do not leave the right of way on main traveled roads; only use roads open to the public and observe all warning signs.

Yuma

From 1550 to 1854 Yuma was under the Spanish, then the Mexican flag until the Gadsden Purchase. In the 1850s, seekers of California gold crossed the river here at a city with changing names. From 1854 to 1858 Yuma was named Colorado City; from 1858 to 1873 it was called Arizona City.

Finally in 1873 it officially became Yuma, named for the chief inhabitants, a combination of Indian tribes – Quechan, Cocopahs and Mojave of the lower Colorado region. They shared a common language and collectively were known as Yuma.

Today Yuma is a rich agricultural center and one of Arizona's important cities. Exceptionally fine weather, several military installations, tourists, winter visitors from colder climates, and proximity to Mexico (San Luis is 23 miles south) all contribute to Yuma's importance. In Yuma, the **Century House Museum** presents exhibits relating to Yuma's colorful history, from Indians, missionaries, explorers, miners, soldiers, settlers, riverboat captains, all housed in one of Yuma's oldest and most historic buildings. The gardens and aviaries are maintained as they were at the turn of the century. **Yuma Crossing Quartermaster Depot Historic Site**, authorized by Congress in 1865, served the entire southwest as a distribution point for troops stationed at the military outposts of the Arizona Territory. Today it's a living history museum, bringing alive Arizona's most colorful eras, from Indians and Spanish explorers to the gold prospectors on their way to California.

If you'd like a look at a grim reminder of frontier justice, visit the **Yuma Territorial Prison** (once called "the Hellhole of Arizona,") now an Arizona State Park. The cells, main gate and guard tower are left from the years between 1876 and 1909 when the penitentiary incarcerated Arizona's most dangerous criminals. The rock walls and studded iron bars look positively medieval.

From Yuma our route turns north on US 95, past **Imperial** and **Cibola National Wildlife Refuges** on the west and **Kofa National Wildlife Refuge** on the east.

Imperial National Wildlife Refuge

A refuge for waterfowl, and particularly a winter sanctuary for Canadian geese, this wildlife refuge lies along both Arizona and California sides of the Colorado River, flanking much of Martinez Lake and incorporating both wetlands and desert. Besides the river and river-bottom lands, there are backwater lakes, ponds, and marshlands. This is a popular area for hikers and birders, especially in spring and fall.

Cibola National Wildlife Refuge

Located just north of the Imperial Refuge, Cibola shares the same characteristics as Imperial. For birders, this refuge is noted for the Canada geese and sandhill cranes that winter here; there's also some boating and fishing. Like Imperial, Cibola lies on both sides of the Colorado and consequently is partly in California.

Kofa National Wildlife Refuge

Located in the Kofa Mountains, which took their name from the King of Arizona Mine of goldrush days. Gold was discovered here in 1896 and the refuge still contains some mining claims to this day.

(Some may post No Trespassing Signs.) The refuge covers 665,400 acres of wilderness, totally without visitor facilities. There are several good hikes of assorted lengths among the desert critters – coyote, bobcat, mule deer, and desert bighorn sheep. Quail, falcons and eagles can be seen overhead.

Narrow Palm Canyon in the refuge shelters a rare stand of native Arizona palm trees, but a hike there is not recommended during the hot summer months.

The route continues north on US 95 to Quartzsite on I-10.

Quartzsite

Named for the rock found here, Quartzsite originally was known as **Tyson's Wells** after being settled in 1856 by Charles Tyson to fend off Indian attacks. In 1856-57, the US Army, looking for better desert transportation, imported both camels and camel drivers from the Middle East. The Civil War disrupted this enterprise, and the camels, turned loose, were a nuisance to both cattle and wild animals for years. All of the camel drivers, except one, Hadji Ali, returned home. With his name changed to "Hi Jolly" by the soldiers, he stayed on to take up prospecting. Buried in the local cemetery, his grave is marked by a sculpture of a pyramid topped by a camel.

True to its name, the town hosts one of the largest gem and mineral shows in the world, with more than 100,000 rock hounds attending the show every February.

At Quartzsite, we leave the West Coast and head east on I-10 to the Valley of the Sun.

Adventures

On Foot

While hiking, drink plenty of water, use sunscreen and wear a hat. Steep grades and uneven surfaces can create hazards. Rattlesnakes, honey bees and cactus spines can all be potentially dangerous; if rattlesnakes are sighted, retreat slowly and report the sighting.

YUMA

There are scores of places you can find garnet, tourmaline, pyrite, agate, jasper and cat's eye quartz treasures, among others within 80 miles of Yuma. Check the Chamber of Commerce or local rock shops for specific information.

Betty's Kitchen (not a restaurant) is a small area on the Colorado River where people come to enjoy the easy 15-minute half-mile loop interpretive nature walk. Years ago a woman named Betty had a cabin here; locals say she cooked and sold food. Now the "Kitchen" is in the state park system and there are picnic tables under a shelter, and restrooms.

Kofa National Wildlife Refuge, is a 660,000-acre wilderness that provides a desert habitat for bighorn sheep and mule deer, as well as a home for coyote, bobcat, fox, quail, doves and golden eagles.

California palms make the refuge beautiful. There is a trailhead off US 95 between Yuma and Quartzsite, but there are no visitor facilities, so be sure to carry plenty of water; visitors are warned that this refuge gets very hot in the summer.

On Wheels

KOFA NATIONAL WILDLIFE REFUGE

Most roads recommend four-wheel-drive only, but there are some for any high-clearance vehicles or mountain bikes. There are no visitors' facilities, so be sure to carry plenty of water.

Mountain bikes are considered vehicles on the refuge; roads off-limits to vehicles refer to mountain bikes, too.

YUMA

The **Yuma Valley Railroad,** Yuma County Live Steamers Assn., 8th St. West, ☎ 520/783-3456, is a ride on the historic Yuma Valley Railroad along the winding banks of the Colorado River.

Passengers ride in a 1922 Pullman Coach, pulled by a 1941 first generation diesel locomotive. The trip includes a visit to "The Spirit of Yuma," a KSC 1924 live steam engine presently being restored.

A four-wheel-drive vehicle is necessary to visit the ghost town of **Old Tumco**, 22 miles northwest of Yuma. Tumco originally was a roaring mining town called Hedges, with a population of about 3,000. The mines here poured out $11 million in gold between 1870 and 1909; be aware of open mine shafts. The town had several saloons, two churches, two cemeteries and a school, but little remains.

On Water

YUMA

Boating

Ride the Colorado River on the **Colorado King I Paddleboat** to relax and relive a colorful part of Yuma and western Arizona history. Departures are from Martinez Lake at Fisher's Landing, ☎ 520/782-2412.

Jetboat tours and Sunset Dinner Cruises are offered by the **Knowlton family**, ☎ 520/783-4400.

Martinez Lake Resort and **Fisher's Landing** at Martinez Lake, about 40 miles north of Yuma, offer camping, marinas, a motel and restaurant.

Mittrey Lake is a small lake off US 95 east of town; the road is paved as far as Laguna Dam, then graded but rough to the lake, where there are a couple of boat launches.

Fishing

Area fish include largemouth bass, striped bass, tilapia, channel catfish and bluegill.

Martinez Lake Resort and **Fisher's Landing** at Martinez Lake, about 40 miles north of Yuma, offer camping, marinas, a motel and restaurant.

Mittrey Lake Barrier offers free access to a fishing jetty on an unimproved road past the Laguna Dam.

IMPERIAL NATIONAL WILDLIFE REFUGE

The nearly 26,000 acres of this long narrow refuge along the Colorado River are home to desert mule deer, waterfowl and other wildlife, as well as a winter refuge for Canadian geese, falcons and golden eagles. Canoe rentals are available nearby.

The nearly 26,000 acres of this long narrow refuge along the Colorado River are home to desert mule deer, waterfowl and other wildlife, as well as a winter refuge for Canadian geese, falcons and golden eagles. Fishing is a popular activity.

Betty's Kitchen (not a restaurant) is a small area on the Colorado River where people come to fish. Years ago a woman named Betty had a cabin here, locals say; she cooked and sold food; now the "Kitchen" is in the state park system and there are picnic tables under a shelter, and restrooms.

CIBOLA NATIONAL WILDLIFE REFUGE

Consisting of 16,667 acres on the Colorado River between Yuma and Blythe, California, the waters of this wildlife refuge offer canoeing.

Eco-travel & Cultural Excursions

YUMA

Jeep tours through local desert canyons are offered by the **Knowlton family,** with more than 35 years' experience of the desert area, ☎ 520/783-4400.

Fort Yuma and the **Quechan Indian Museum** are located on a hill across the Colorado River from Yuma. The building itself was built in 1851 as an officers' mess, and is now utilized by the tribe to depict their history as well as that of the early Spanish explorers and the story of the military.

For an unusual adventure with animals of the Arabian Desert, the **Saihati Camel Farm**, northwest corner of Ave. 1E and County 16th St., has one of the largest camel herds in North America. On-site are Arabian camels, horses and oryx, as well as African pygmy goats, Asian water buffalo, Dama gazelle, scimitar-horned oryx and Watusi cattle. Call for information and reservations, ☎ 520/627-2553.

QUARTZSITE

Two miles south of town in Tyson Wash, **Tyson Tank** is a prehistory site with shelter caves, petroglyphs and mortar and pestle grinding stones.

Where To Stay & Eat

GILA BEND

Best Western Space Age Lodge & Restaurant, 401 E. Pima, Gila Bend AZ 85337, ☎ 520/683-2273 and 800/528-1234, fax 520/683-2273, 41 units. An adventure – there's a spaceship on the roof – plus a restaurant with good American and Mexican food, pool, heated spa, and some rooms with a refrigerator.

YUMA

Accommodations

Best Western Chilton Inn & Conference Center, 300 E. 32nd St., Yuma AZ 85364, ☎ 520/344-1050 and 800/528-1234, fax 520/344-4877. 123 units in a pleasant resort atmosphere, pool, free breakfast, 24-hour restaurant, fitness center.

Caravan Oasis Motel, 10574 Fortuna Rd., Yuma AZ 85364, ☎ 520/342-1292.

Corcovado Motel, 2607 S. 4th Ave., Yuma AZ 85364, ☎ 520/344-2988.

Desert Grove Resort Motel, 3500 S. 4th Ave., Yuma AZ 85364, ☎ 520/344-1921.

El Rancho Motel, 2201 S. 4th Ave., Yuma AZ 85364, ☎ 520/783-4481.

Travelodge, 2050 S. 4th Ave., Yuma AZ 85364, ☎ 520/782-3831.

Holiday Inn, 3181 S. 4th Ave., Yuma AZ 85364, ☎ 520/344-1402.

Interstate 8 Inn, 2730 S. 4th Ave, Yuma AZ 85364, ☎ 520/726-6110 and 800/821-7465, fax 520/726-7711.

La Fuente Inn, 1513 E. 16th St., Yuma AZ 85364, ☎ 520/329-1814 and 800/841-1814, fax 520/343-2671.

Palms Inn, 2655 S. 4th Ave., Yuma AZ 85364, ☎ 520/344-4570.

Park Inn, 2600 S. 4th Ave., Yuma AZ 85364, ☎ 520/726-4830.

Regalodge, 344 S. 4th Ave., Yuma AZ 85364, ☎ 520/782-4571.

Torch Lite Lodge, 2501 S. 4th Ave., Yuma AZ 85364, ☎ 520/344-1600.

Restaurants

Yuma has the usual large-city assortment of pizza parlors, fried chicken, hamburger and other fast foods, as well as a varied assortment of other restaurants.

Beto's Mexican Food, 812 E. 21st St., Yuma AZ 85364, ☎ 520/782-6551. All-you-can-eat Mexican buffet.

Brownie's Restaurant, 1145 S. 4th Ave., Yuma AZ 85364, ☎ 520/783-7911. Good home cooking.

Chretin's Mexican Food, 485 S. 15th Ave., Yuma AZ 85364, ☎ 520/782-1291. Good nachos and margaritas.

The Crossing, 2690 S. 4th Ave., Yuma AZ 85364, ☎ 520/726-5551. Tasty seafood and prime rib.

Golden Corral Family Steakhouse, 2401 S. 4th St., Yuma AZ 85364, ☎ 520/726-4428. Specializes in a potato and salad bar.

Hensley's Steak House, 2855 S. 4th Ave., Yuma AZ 85364. ☎ 520/344-1345. Specializes in beef.

Hungry Hunter, 2355 S. 4th Ave., Yuma AZ 85364, ☎ 520/782-3637. Fine prime rib.

Mandarin Palace, 250 E. 32nd St., Yuma AZ 85364, ☎ 520/344-2805. Good place for Oriental food.

The Panda, 711 E. 32nd St., Yuma AZ 85364, ☎ 520/341-0323. Good Oriental food.

Sky Chief, 1530 E. 32nd St., Yuma AZ 85364. ☎ 520/726-0847. Specializing in shrimp dishes.

Camping

GILA BEND

Painted Rock Petroglyph Camgrounds, 14½ miles west of Gila Bend off AZ 85; 10.8 miles of paved road from highway, half a mile farther to campground.

YUMA

Martinez Lake Resort and Fisher's Landing at Martinez Lake, about 40 miles north of Yuma, offer camping, marinas, a motel and restaurant, ☎ 520/783-9589. Crappie, bass, bluegill, stripers and catfish are the catch. Fuel for both boats and cars is at Fisher's Landing.

There is public camping at Kofa National Wildlife Refuge. Visitors may select their own campsites but by state law may not camp within a quarter-mile of a waterhole and must remain within 100 ft. of designated roads. For more information contact the refuge at PO Box 6590, Yuma AZ 85364, ☎ 520/783-7861.

INFORMATION

Gila Bend Chamber of Commerce, ☎ 520/683-2002.
Yuma Convention & Visitors Bureau, ☎ 520/783-0071.
Betty's Kitchen Protective Society, ☎ 520/627-2773.
Quartzsite Chamber of Commerce, ☎ 520/927-5600,
or 800/815-2694.
Kofa National Wildlife Refuge, ☎ 520/783-7861.
Imperial National Wildlife Refuge, ☎ 520/783-3371.
Cibola National Wildlife Refuge, ☎ 520/857-3253.

Valley Of The Sun

Introduction

Our route travels east on I-10, approximately 180 miles to Phoenix, which lies directly south of the Colorado Plateau. This is Arizona's golden heart. Phoenix, the center, is surrounded by the prestigious Sun Valley communities of Scottsdale, Paradise Valley, Sun City and Tempe. Surrounded by mountains, lush orchards and desert cactus, huge shopping centers and Indian trading posts, fine art museums and prehistoric ruins, Phoenix is known worldwide as a vacation destination.

This is predominantly desert country, with summer temperatures often exceeding 100°. In July and August there often are thunderstorms. Winter temperatures average 60 to 80°. While touring, take precautions against summer heat and sudden rain or dust storms; watch out for poisonous snakes; do not feed wild animals or pick wild plants; all ruins, artifacts, and natural features are protected by law and must be left undisturbed.

In the Phoenix area there are **Casa Grande Ruins National Monument, Picacho Peak State Park, The Apache Trail, Lost Dutchman State Park, Tonto National Monument** and **Tonto National Forest** to explore.

Geography & History

The Salt River, running through the southern edge of the city, was home to Hohokam Indians as early as 300 BC. They used its waters to irrigate their fields of corn, beans, cotton, and squash. Disappearing mysteriously around the mid-1400s AD, they were replaced by the Gila Indians who had been driven from the Colorado River by the Yumas.

The Spanish were too busy south of here, looking for the cities of gold, to pay much attention to this central area. So were American explorers until after the Civil War, when tales of gold attracted them. Apaches did their best to discourage the invaders, but in 1865 the Army built Camp McDowell, assuring safety for prospectors, ranchers and farmers alike. A former Confederate soldier named Jack Swilling turned farmer and hired miners to excavate the Hohokam canals in order to plant the first American crops – wheat and barley.

So, in effect, the city arose from the ashes of the Hohokam civilization. Just as the famous bird of mythology rose from its ashes, the city was named Phoenix. In 1889 it became the state capital, winning the title from Prescott on the west.

Phoenix, with an elevation 1,100 ft. of desert land, enjoys an inordinate amount of sun, but with that comes high daytime temperatures often reaching more than 100° in the summer. But thanks to the altitude temperatures can drop to the 80s and 70s at night. Winter temperatures average in the high 60s and low 70s, there is very little rainfall, and snow is almost unheard of.

Getting Around

West of Ajo and the Monument, beyond the Growler Mountains, lies the **Cabeza Prieta Wildlife Refuge**. From Ajo continue north on AZ 85 to Interstate 10 and the **Gila Bend Indian Reservation** before turning west on the interstate to **Yuma** and the **Fort Yuma Indian Reservation** on the Colorado River boundary of the state. From Yuma you will pass **Imperial, Cibola,** and **Koba National Wildlife Refuges,** then east to **Phoenix.**

From Phoenix the route goes south to Coolidge and follows signs to Casa Grande Ruins National Monument, then to Picacho State Park. Next, the route leads to Florence and the Apache Trail. Along the way are several exciting places: **Lost Dutchman State Park, Tortilla Flat, Goldfield Ghost Town, Saguaro, Canyon** and **Apache Lake,** all leading to Roosevelt Dam and Lake, **Tonto National Monument,** and Tonto National Forest. From here either follow the loop to Phoenix, or travel north through the Tonto National Forest back to Strawberry, and you will have made a complete circle of southern Arizona's adventurous lands.

The Valley of the Sun

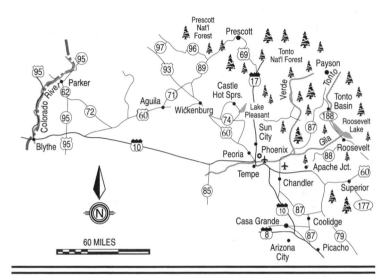

60 MILES

INFORMATION

Car Rentals
All major rental car companies have offices in Phoenix.

Public Transportation
Valley Metro has scheduled public bus service throughout the Valley Monday through Saturday, ☎ 602/253-5000.

Air
America West Airlines, ☎ 800/235-9292.
American Airlines, ☎ 800/433-7300.
Continental Airlines, ☎ 800/525-0280.
Delta Airlines, ☎ 800/221-1212.

Southwest Airlines, ☎ 800/435-9792.
Trans World Airlines, Inc., ☎ 602/252-7711.

Motor Coach
Greyhound Bus lines, ☎ 520/882-4386 and 800/231-2222.

Train
Amtrak has several departures weekly, ☎ 800/872-7245.

Phoenix & Valley of the Sun Convention & Visitors Bureau,
☎ 602/252-5588.

Practicalities
Arizona Office of Tourism, 1100 West Washington, Phoenix AZ
85007, ☎ 602/542-8687 or 800/842-8257.
Arizona Game and Fish Department, 2222 West Greenway
Rapid, Phoenix AZ 85023, ☎ 602/942-3000, fax 602/789-3924.
Arizona State Parks, 800 West Washington, Phoenix AZ 85007,
☎ 602/542-4171 and 542-4174, fax 602/542-4180.
Bureau of Land Management, 3707 North 7th Street, Phoenix AZ
85011, ☎ 602/640-5501, fax 602/640-2398.
Arizona Republic Weatherline, ☎ 602/271-5656 Ext. 1010.

Touring

Phoenix/Scottsdale/Tempe/Mesa

Phoenix is a large city with a great many things to see and do.
Here are several unusual or exceptional attractions that the
adventurous traveller ought not miss. **Pueblo Grande Museum
and Cultural Park** is the only national landmark inside the city.
On-site are an actual Hohokam ruin and a museum.

The **Desert Botanical Garden,** founded in 1937, displays one of
the most extensive collections of desert plants in the world.

The **Heard Museum** focuses on cultures and arts of Native
Americans and the Southwest. The 125-acre **Phoenix Zoo** features
five trails of naturalistic settings for 1,300 animals and 320 species

– 200 of them endangered. There are four monkey islands, an African savanna, a tropical rain forest, and a children's petting zoo.

Phoenix Museum of History is a repository of prehistoric and modern Indian crafts and historic pioneer artifacts. The **Arizona Mining and Mineral Museum** exhibits some of the gold, silver and copper that brought prospectors – and pioneers – to the state. Also on display are the tools of the miners' trade, and beautiful specimens of semi-precious gems. In Scottsdale, the **Scottsdale Historical Museum** in The Little Red Schoolhouse is a reminder of the town's past. The large 5/12 scale trains at the **McCormick Railroad Park** are a must-ride for train buffs. On Sunday afternoons local model-railroad clubs run their model trains. **Taliesin West** is famous as a center for architecture students.

Tempe has a **Historical Museum** as well, with a model of an archaeological dig on the Salt River among other exhibits.

In Mesa, the **Mesa Southwest Museum** also shows how prehistoric Indians lived, as well as displaying examples of early pioneer life.

For information on the above as well as the many other Valley of the Sun attractions contact the **Phoenix Convention & Visitors Bureau, ☎** 602/254-6500.

From Phoenix the route goes south on I-10 to the small town of Coolidge, Exit 185, and follows signs to Casa Grande Ruins National Monument, about an hour's drive southeast of Phoenix.

Casa Grande Ruins

Located in the city of Coolidge (not in the city of Casa Grande), the monument contains a mystery the Spaniards called Casa Grande, the Great House. How did they manage to build a house four stories high and 60 ft. long? It's the largest structure known to exist from the Hohokam era. Like Mexican and Mesoamerican ruins and Stonehenge in England, it seems to have astrological significance; the walls face the four cardinal points of the compass, a circular hole in the upper west wall aligns with the setting sun during the summer solstice, and other openings align with the sun and moon at specific times.

The visitor center has a museum displaying a collection of Hohokam artifacts, along with interpretive material on known facts of the culture. There is a 400-yd, self-guided tour through the ruins, as well as ranger-guided tours during the winter months. The picnic area has shade and water. From Casa Grande return to I-10 and continue south to Picacho State Park at Exit 219.

Picacho Peak State Park

Monuments in the park commemorate the westernmost battle of the Civil War, the **Battle of Picacho Pass**, which took place on April 15, 1862. This was the only Civil War battle to occur in Arizona. Confederate forces killed the Union detachment leader and two privates but, aware that Union reinforcements were on the way, they retreated to Tucson.

Picacho Peak has served as a landmark for Indians, Spanish explorers, and frontiersmen, as well as tourists. From the park, retrace your route back north on I-10 and turn east on AZ 287 to Florence, the fourth oldest town in Arizona.

Florence

The town's first settlers in the mid 1860s were farmers who quietly tended their crops, irrigating them with the waters of the Gila River. Some of their buildings can be seen on the **Historic Florence Walking Tour;** one of the most intriguing homes is the **Pauline Cushman House**. According to the story, she was a Southern belle who became a Union spy during the Civil War. Captured near New Orleans, she was sentenced to be hanged, but was rescued by Union forces. She married a sheriff in Florence and helped him resist a lynch mob of some 40 vigilantes.

When rich silver deposits were discovered near Florence, the town became a typical mining boom town, with 28 saloons where gambling and brawls flourished and liquor flowed. The citizens of the town had hopes of it becoming the state capital but had to settle for being the county seat of Pinal County. The **Pinal County Historical Society Museum** contains quite a collection, from prehistoric Indian artifacts to hangman's nooses from the days of prisoner executions. The Arizona State Prison is still standing on the edge of town. Built in 1909, it replaced the territorial prison in Yuma.

The route heads north on AZ 79 to meet with US 60 at Florence Junction, taking the highway west to Apache Junction and Loop 88, past the ghost town of Goldfield to Lost Dutchman State Park.

Lost Dutchman State Park

This 300-acre desert park is sheltered under the sheer-walled escarpment of the Superstition Mountains, whose name was inspired by legends of the Pima Indians. In the rocky mountains lives the legend of the fabulous **Lost Dutchman Mine**. A greedy old German immigrant, Jacob Walz, claimed to have found untold riches in gold. He did away with everyone who tried to follow him to the site. On his deathbed he said "the key is in a striped palo verde tree with one arm pointing away from Weaver's Needle and the mine is halfway in between." Needless to say, that's why it's called the Lost Dutchman Mine, and cynics in the area believe it's all a tall tale.

Ocotillo, palo verde, cholla and saguaro thrive with other desert plants in this unspoiled desert setting. **Superstition Wilderness** of **Tonto National Forest** on the north border of the park makes a good base for both hikers and horseback riders.

The park offers nature trails, campsites, restrooms and picnic facilities. The road goes on through Tortilla Flat past Canyon, Saguaro and Apache Lakes to Lake Theodore Roosevelt, Tonto National Monument and into Tonto National Forest. The road is unpaved and mountainous from beyond Tortilla Flat to the lake; an alternate way is to return to US 60 and head east to just beyond Claypool, turning north on the far end of Loop 88 and through the Queen Creek Tunnel to reach the monument, the forest and the lake.

Tonto National Monument

The monument is located near Roosevelt Lake, 3½ miles east of the dam. The Tonto Basin was home to the prehistoric nomadic peoples as early as 5000 BC. The first permanent settlements date from the last half of the eighth century AD when the Hohokam people established themselves in pit house villages. By 1150 AD the inhabitants of the basin no longer followed Hohokam traditions, and a new culture emerged – the Salado, (named in the 20th century after the Salt River, in Spanish the Rio Salado). For three centuries they made their living in the river valley, surrounded by steep slopes rising some 2,000 ft. Some time around 1400-1450 AD they left – no one knows why – and their cliff dwellings were abandoned.

During the construction of the Roosevelt Dam on the northern boundary of the monument, the ruins were to be protected from vandals by being declared a national monument. Inside the visitors center there are exhibits on the culture and crafts of the Salado people, as well as an audiovisual program. There are guided and self-guided walks to the cliff dwellings, and there is a picnic area but no camping.

Summers are 100° and higher. Winters are mild, with periods of rain.

Tonto National Forest

The forest contains 2,969,602 acres of different recreational opportunities year-round, from the cool pine forest north along the Mogollon Rim to desert lands in the south. This chapter deals with areas accessible from Phoenix and Sun Valley. Road conditions vary so inquire locally for information.

Return either to US 60 and back to Phoenix or head north on AZ 188 to AZ 87 and Payson, Pine and Strawberry, where this section of the guide began.

Adventures

On Foot

While hiking, drink plenty of water, use sunscreen and wear a hat. Steep grades and uneven surfaces can create hazards. Rattlesnakes, honey bees and cactus spines are all potentially dangerous.

PHOENIX

Squaw Peak in Squaw Peak Recreation Area in the Phoenix Mountain Preserve is one of the city's best-known landmarks. A trail of just over a mile leads to the peak's summit and a panoramic view of the Valley of the Sun.

PICACHO PEAK STATE PARK

There are hiking trails on the rocky hillsides, picnicking and camping areas in the park amid saguaro cactus and other Sonoran Desert plants. **Sunset Trail**, a moderate to difficult three-mile hike, leads up a mildly hilly area and then drops down through the Sonoran Desert. The last mile is considered difficult; the trail climbs up to the junction of Hunter Trail on the way to the top of the peak.

Hunter Trail is a difficult two miles long and climbs from 2,000 to 3,374 ft. at the top of the peak. There are 12 sets of cables to assist hikers in maneuvering the more difficult portions of the trail.

Neither trail is recommended for inexperienced hikers or children under 10 years of age.

LOST DUTCHMAN STATE PARK

There are several trails here, of varying difficulty:

Treasure Loop Trail, a 2½-mile round-trip, is about a two-hour hike with an elevation change of 480 ft.

Prospector's View is less than a mile long. It connects Treasure Loop Trail with Siphon Draw Trail and with Jacob's Crosscut Trail.

Jacob's Crosscut Trail, moderately easy, runs less than a mile along the base of the mountain connecting Treasure Loop Trail with Prospector's View Trail.

Siphon Draw Trail winds into the Siphon Draw Canyon past the old 1886 Palmer Mine, a scenic hike. It's possible to hike to the top, Flatiron, on a non-maintained trail, but only for experienced hikers in good shape – the trail is steep and difficult to follow.

Discovery Trail connects the campground and the day-use areas. There are interpretive signs, a wildlife pond, bird feeder and viewing bench.

TONTO NATIONAL MONUMENT

The quarter-mile **Cactus Patch Trail** leads past several varieties of cacti and other plants native to the Sonoran Desert, and takes about 20 minutes to complete.

The **Lower Ruin Trail** leads to a 19-room cliff dwelling. Trailside signs provide information about the Salado, the ruins and the surrounding area. With a vertical ascent of 350 ft., this trail is considered to be moderately strenuous.

Visitors with respiratory or heart conditions should use caution, especially during hot weather. Allow about an hour for the round-trip walk.

The 40-room **Upper Ruin** is open only to those on guided tours, November through April, depending upon the weather. The three-mile trip includes a 600 ft. ascent, particularly strenuous in warm weather. The three- to four-hour tours are limited to 15 people.

TONTO NATIONAL FOREST

Forest Service employees lead a variety of walks in the Tonto Basin District, related to area history, natural history, wildflower and wildlife viewing.

Cottonwood Trail meanders for 1¼ miles, over low ridges and dropping into Cottonwood Canyon, ending at Thompson Springs.

Thompson Trail follows a level contour for about 2½ miles until it descends toward the junction of Cemetery Trail.

Cemetery Trail, two-tenths of a mile, visits the cemetery and returns hikers to Highway 88. The three-trail complex offers spectacular views of Roosevelt Lake and interesting of native plants and animals. This is a segment of the proposed Arizona Trail, which eventually will stretch from Coronado National Forest north through Tonto National Forest and Coconino National Forest to Kaibab National Forest. There are four wilderness areas in this part of Tonto National Forest: **Superstition Wilderness, Four Peaks Wilderness, Mazatzal Wilderness** and **Sierra Wilderness**. All offer hiking, camping, horse/pack saddle, and photography opportunities. For more information contact **Forest Supervisor's Office**, Tonto National Forest, 2324 E. McDowell Rd., Phoenix AZ 85006, ☎ 602/225-5200.

On Horseback

APACHE JUNCTION

Don Donelly Stables are open seven days a week for short rides or multiple day pack trips in the Superstition Mountains, 6010 S. Kings Ranch Rd., Gold Canyon AZ 85219, ☎ 602/982-7822.

OK Corral Stables offer guided and unguided horseback rides in the Superstition and Goldfield Mountains, ☎ 602/982-4040.

Superstition Stables offer all sorts of Old West adventures, 2151 North Warner, ☎ 520/982-6353 and 800/984-5488.

On Wheels

PHOENIX

Camelback Mountain, with its hump-like silhouette, is the city's most prominent landmark. To see it, Echo Canyon, with sheer red cliffs, and the Praying Monk rock formation, take East McDonald Drive to Tatum Blvd.

Follow in the footsteps of the Apaches along Apache Trail (Loop 88), a six-hour round-trip the Indians used as a shortcut through the Superstition Mountains to reach early Salt River settlers. Uninhabited, the mountains reveal volcanic debris, deep canyons, sparkling lakes, towering saguaro cactus and, in the spring, wildflowers. Be sure to carry plenty of water. Take US 60 and 89 east to Loop 88 and the trail. After passing Roosevelt Dam and Tonto National Monument, return to Phoenix on US 60.

Phoenix area tour operators offer a multitude of jeep and desert tours. Below are several. For Apache Trail Tours, with jeep and hiking tours of the Apache Trail and mountains, canyons, lakes, Lost Dutchman Mine and Apache Indian campfires, ☎ 602/982-7661.

Old West Jeep Adventures, has all day tours from Phoenix of Tombstone, ghost towns and the desert, ☎ 602/945-5253.

Wild West Jeep Tours, Inc. specializes in Indian ruins and petroglyphs, ☎ 602/941-8355.

For more information contact the Phoenix Convention & Visitors Bureau, ☎ 602/254-6500.

APACHE JUNCTION

Goldfield Ghost Town offers **Superstition Scenic Narrow Gauge Railroad**, Arizona's only narrow gauge railroad in operation, ☎ 520/983-0333.

TONTO NATIONAL FOREST

Particularly suited to all-terrain biking is the **White Hills Route** in Tonto National Forest, approximately 10 routes at elevations of 3,400 to 5,320 ft. Others are:

- ☐ **New River** and **New River Mesa** routes, **Cave Creek Ranger District**, approximately 12 miles each; difficult.
- ☐ **Icehouse CCC Loop**, Globe Ranger District, approximately 5½ miles; difficult.
- ☐ **Slate Creek Divide Loop**, Mesa Ranger District, 10-16 miles; very difficult.
- ☐ **White Hills Route**, Payson District, approximately 10-11 miles; difficult.
- ☐ **Buzzard Roost Canyon Route**, Pleasant Valley Ranger District, about 15 miles; difficult.
- ☐ **Three Bar Route**, Tonto Basin District, approximately 6½ miles; difficult.

On Water

APACHE TRAIL

Canyon Lake, **Saguaro Lake** and **Apache Lake**, part of the series of lakes along Loop 88 formed by damming the Salt River, offer fishing and boating. Boat rentals are available at Canyon Lake Marina, ☎ 602/986-5546.

Precision Marine offers boat rental and complete marine service on Saguaro and Canyon lakes, ☎ 520/986-0969.

Arizona Steamboat Cruises runs a relaxing cruise on Dolly's Steamboat, exploring portions of Canyon Lake that are accessible only by boat. There are also twilight dinner cruises, ☎ 602/827-9144.

Roosevelt Lake, at 17,315 acres with 88 miles of shoreline, is the largest of the lakes fed by the Salt River, and is popular for boating and water-skiing. Roosevelt Marina features boat rentals, a paved boat ramp and boat storage. Cholla Boating Site and Point Windy Hill are boat launching sites with paved boat ramps.

Others are Cholla Bay, Bermuda Flat, Orange Peel, Bachelors Cove and Schoolhouse Point.

TONTO NATIONAL MONUMENT

Roosevelt Lake, the largest of the lakes fed by the Salt River, is popular with anglers for bass, crappie, sunfish and catfish. Roosevelt Marina has boat rentals, fishing supplies, ☎ 520/467-2245.

Precision Marine offers fishing and boating supplies on Saguaro and Canyon lakes, ☎ 520/986-0969.

In Air

PHOENIX

Apache Trail Tours, helicopter view of the Superstition wilderness, ☎ 602/982-7661.

Southwest Jet, Aviation Ltd., scenic tours of the Valley of the Sun, rivers and lakes, ☎ 602/991-7076.

Superstition Mountain Helicopter Tours ghost towns, Salt River lakes, ☎ 602/396-9202.

American Balloon Adventures promises gentle and silent floats in the air over the Sonoran Desert, ☎ 800/999-2474.

A Balloon Experience also offers hot air ballooning, ☎ 800/866-3866.

Unicorn Balloon Company offers sunrise flights daily and sunset flights November-March from Scottsdale, ☎ 602/991-3666 and 800/468-2478.

Eco-travel & Cultural Excursions

PHOENIX

Phoenix area tour operators operates a multitude of tours. Here are several; for more information contact the **Phoenix Convention & Visitors Bureau.**

Accent Arizona Advisors, Inc. offers agricultural farms, artists studios, archaeological Indian-heritage tours, ☎ 602/943-3694.

Canyon Trail Motorcycle Tours offer half- to multi-day on/off-road adventure motorcycle tours, camping, fishing, Western cookouts, etc. ☎ 602/519-1936.

The **Dons of Arizona** travel the lands of the Conquistadores presenting scenery, history and folklore, ☎ 602/893-0154.

Moccasin Tracks Tour, visit the Apache reservation; you learn Apache culture, legends, arts and crafts, ☎ 602/254-6978.

Wilderness Adventures, has hiking, backpacking, rock climbing, rappelling, canyon adventures, ☎ 602/708-6786 and 800/462-5788.

On the Gila River Indian Reservation at Exit 175 off I-10, the **Gila River Arts and Crafts Center** exhibits artifacts and interprets the history of the Pima and Maricopa Indians. Occasionally Indians present craft demonstrations and performances.

APACHE TRAIL

Goldfield Ghost Town and Mine Tours offer a chance to try your luck at goldpanning, in addition to tours of a recreated underground mine, ☎ 602/983-0333.

Gold mining supplies are for sale at **Pro-Mack South**, 940 West Apache Trail, Apache Junction AZ, ☎ 602/983-3484. They offer free gold panning lessons and a video on how the experts do it.

APACHE JUNCTION

High Chaparral Off-Road & Sightseeing Tours offer Apache Trail tours, desert tours, canyon tours and an open pit copper mine tour among others, ☎ 520/671-3009.

TONTO NATIONAL FOREST

Sears-Kay Ruin is one of a series of prehistoric hilltop villages occupied by the Hohokam people approximately a thousand years ago. The ruin contains remains of about 40 rooms and is listed in the National Register of Historic Places.

Where To Stay & Eat

PHOENIX

Phoenix has five **Best Western** motels, ☎ 800/528-1234, two **Comfort Inns,** ☎ 800/228-5150, two **Embassy Suites,** 800-EMBASSY, three **Pointe Hiltons,** ☎ 800/528-0428, three **Quality Inns,** ☎ 800-4-CHOICE, and two **Ramadas,** ☎ 800/527-3467, in addition to a large variety of other accommodations. Contact the Phoenix & Valley of the Sun Convention & Visitors Bureau for a complete list.

There is a huge variety of restaurants in Phoenix, Scottsdale, Tempe and Mesa, including all the usual fast food places. Also:

Waterfront Restaurant, 5350 S. Lakeshore Dr., Tempe AZ, ☎ 602/756-0508. Prime rib, hand cut steaks, seafood, all with a terrific view.

CASA GRANDE

Best Western Casa Grande Suites, 665 Via Del Cielo, Casa Grande AZ 85222, ☎ 520/836-1600 and 800/528-1234, fax 520/836-7242.

Francisco Grande Resort & Golf Club, 26000 Gila Bend Hwy, Casa Grande AZ 85222, ☎ 520/836-6444 and 800/237-4238, fax 520/836-6444. Dining room and restaurant.

Holiday Inn Casa Grande, 777 Pinal Ave., Casa Grande AZ 85222, ☎ 520/426-3500 and 800/858-4499, fax 520/836-4728. Restaurant, lounge.

APACHE JUNCTION

Mining Camp Restaurant & Trading Post, ☎ 602/982-3181, all-you-can-eat family-style mining camp dinners of barbecue beef, chicken and roast beef coleslaw and beans, sourdough rolls and homemade raisin bread, prospector cookies.

Gila River Indian Reservation, **Gila River Arts & Crafts Center Restaurant**, ☎ 602/963-3981. Serves Indian cuisine as well as American and Mexican food and is famous for fry bread.

Camping

PHOENIX

White Mountain Tanks Campground, elevation 1,500 ft., open all year, has 40 units and water.

CASA GRANDE

Picacho Peak Campground, elevation 2,000 ft., is open all year, with 31 available units and water.

APACHE TRAIL

Lost Dutchman Campground, elevation 1,700 ft., stays open all year, with 35 units, water and waste disposal.

McDowell Mountain Campground, elevation 2,000 ft., is open all year, with 40 units, water and waste disposal.

Usery Mountain Campground, elevation 2,000 ft., remains open all year, with 75 units, water and waste disposal.

There are also campgrounds at Canyon and Apache Lakes.

TONTO NATIONAL FOREST

Windy Hill Campgrounds, with an elevation 2,100 ft., stays open all year, 347 units, water, toilets and waste disposal.

Cholla Campgrounds, 2,200 ft. elevation, is open all year, and has 206 units, water, toilets.

Burnt Corral Campgrounds, elevation 1,900 ft., has 79 units always open, water and toilets.

INFORMATION

Arizona State Parks, ☎ 602/542-4174.
Arizona Republic Weatherline, ☎ 602/271-5656, Ext. 1010.
Casa Grande Chamber of Commerce, ☎ 520/836-2125, 800/916-1515.
Florence Chamber of Commerce, ☎ 520/868-9433.
Pinal County Visitor Bureau, ☎ 602/868-4331.
Lost Dutchman State Park, ☎ 602/982-4485.
Apache Junction Chamber of Commerce, ☎ 602/982-3141.
Tonto National Monument, ☎ 520/467-2241.
Tonto National Forest, ☎ 602/225-5200.
Phoenix & Valley of the Sun Convention & Visitors Bureau, ☎ 602/252-5588.

Index